The New CAMBRIDGE English Course

PRACTICE

UPPER-INTERMEDIATE

**DESMOND O'SULLIVAN
MICHAEL SWAN
CATHERINE WALTER**

Published by the Press Syndicate of the University of Cambridge
The Pitt Building, Trumpington Street, Cambridge CB2 1RP
40 West 20th Street, New York, NY 10011–4211, USA
10 Stamford Road, Oakleigh, Melbourne 3166, Australia

© Desmond O'Sullivan, Michael Swan and Catherine Walter 1993

First published 1993

Cover design by Michael Peters & Partners Limited, London
Typeset by The University Press, Cambridge
Printed in Great Britain by the Bath Press, Avon

ISBN 0 521 37652 1 Practice Book 4
ISBN 0 521 37664 5 Practice Book 4 with Key
ISBN 0 521 37640 8 Student's Book 4
ISBN 0 521 37668 8 Teacher's Book 4
ISBN 0 521 37672 6 Test Book 4
ISBN 0 521 37505 3 Class Cassette Set 4
ISBN 0 521 37509 6 Student's Cassette 4

Copyright
This book is in copyright. No photocopying may take place without the written permission of the publisher, except where an institution within the United Kingdom holds a licence from the Copyright Licensing Agency.

Contents

Block A
- A1 Art, bird-watching, cars, dancing … — 4
- A2 Focus on systems — 6
- A3 Situations — 8
- A4 The sun was in the north — 10
- A5 Secret thoughts — 13
- A6 Focus on systems — 15
- A7 Cruelty to cars — 17
- A8 Here is the news — 20

Block B
- B1 Learning a language — 23
- B2 Focus on systems — 26
- B3 I'll give you £25 for it — 28
- B4 It must be true: it's in the papers — 30
- B5 Work — 33
- B6 Focus on systems — 35
- B7 The Lonely One — 37
- B8 My heart is too full for words — 40

Block C
- C1 It makes me want to scream — 45
- C2 Focus on systems — 48
- C3 I'm a bit short of time — 51
- C4 We regret … — 54
- C5 The voice of democracy — 57
- C6 Focus on systems — 59
- C7 People going hungry — 61
- C8 A lot needs doing to it — 65

Block D
- D1 What do they look like? — 69
- D2 Focus on systems — 72
- D3 I don't like playtime — 75
- D4 I knew everyone — 79
- D5 A beautiful place — 80
- D6 Focus on systems — 84
- D7 Boy meets girl — 86
- D8 Different kinds — 89

Block E
- E1 They saw wonderful things — 93
- E2 Focus on systems — 96
- E3 Looking forward — 100
- E4 Coincidences — 102
- E5 I don't know much about art, … — 105
- E6 Focus on systems — 107
- E7 You can say that again — 110
- E8 Who invented writing? — 112

Basic grammar revision exercises — 115
Language summary — 134
Solutions to crosswords and problems — 144
Key to Basic grammar revision exercises — 146
Acknowledgements — 152

A1 Art, bird-watching, cars, dancing ...

1 Vocabulary revision and extension. Can you match words from the two boxes? Example:

<u>cooking – saucepan</u>

| art   bird-watching   cooking |
| the countryside   dancing   drawing |
| driving   gardening   history   jazz   opera |
| reading   shooting   sport   swimming |
| theatre   travel |

| aria   canvas   crawl   cup final   eagle |
| footpath   lawnmower   Middle Ages |
| novel   partner   pencil |
| petrol consumption   saucepan   saxophone |
| shotgun   stage   suitcase |

2 Vocabulary and grammar revision. Decide on the correct word.

1. I'm not very *interested/interesting* in poetry.
2. There's a really *interested/interesting* film on TV tonight.
3. Do you find bullfighting *excited/exciting*?
4. I went to a bullfight once, and I was *disgusted/disgusting*.
5. Penny and I went to the opera last night. I'm afraid I was very *bored/boring*.
6. Psychology is a *fascinated/fascinating* subject.
7. I'm *delighted/delighting* to see you again.

3 Grammar revision. Look at the examples, and then complete the sentences with *as, than, then* or *that*. Examples:

It's about **the same** size **as** a telephone.
It's not quite **as** heavy **as** a TV.
It's a bit **bigger than** a camera.
I started to say something and **then** I stopped.
Do you think **that** she'll be all right?

1. I'm a bit older .... I look.
2. But I'm not nearly as old .... I feel.
3. She's got the same sense of humour .... her mother.
4. You paid him far more .... the car was worth.
5. Go straight on for 300 metres and .... turn right.
6. Could we have the bill as soon .... possible, please?
7. I'm quite sure .... he's gone home.
8. Nobody's funnier .... my uncle Harry.
9. Do you think we should have the curtains exactly the same colour .... the carpet?
10. This year things have been better .... ever.

4 Grammar revision. Write true answers to each sentence, as in the example. Use *So am I, So do I, So can I*, etc., and *I'm not, I don't*, etc.

1. I'm tired.
   <u>So am I. OR I'm not.</u>
2. I was in France last summer.
3. I used to get more exercise than I do now.
4. I've got a colour television.
5. I believe that you can sometimes communicate your thoughts to another person.
6. When I was a child, I thought people on television could see me.
7. I can play the violin.
8. I'll speak English much better by this time next year.

Now write answers about your family and friends, as in the examples.

9. My mother was very politically active when she was younger.
   <u>So was my mother. OR So was mine.</u>
   <u>OR So was my aunt. OR My mother wasn't.</u>
10. My mother was always very tired in the evenings.
11. My father used to tell us bedtime stories almost every night.
12. My husband has got a good sense of humour.
13. My little nephew believes in ghosts.
14. My family lived in a very small village when I was a child.
15. My sister can play the piano beautifully.
16. My brother will be a terrific father.

5 Grammar revision. Write five or more things that you used to do when you were a child. Example:

<u>I used to go skating in winter.</u>

6 Write 150 words or more about your past and present interests. What were you interested in when you were a child? What did you want to do in life? How much have your interests changed? What are your present ambitions? Try to include some words and expressions from the Student's Book lesson.

7 Look quickly at the three texts. Choose the one that looks most interesting and read it (using a dictionary if you wish). Then write two or three sentences, explaining why you chose the text, whether you found it interesting or not, and why.

First US city to be bombed from the air

In 1921, during one of the worst race riots in American history, Tulsa, Okla., became the first US city to be bombed from the air. More than 75 persons – mostly blacks – were killed.

Before the riot, Tulsa blacks were so successful that their business district was called 'The Negro's Wall Street'. Envy bred hatred of the blacks, who accounted for a tenth of the segregated city's population of 100,000.

Then on May 30, 1921, a white female elevator operator accused Dick Rowland, a 19-year-old black who worked at a shoeshine stand, of attacking her. Though he denied the charge, Rowland was jailed. *The Tulsa Tribune* ran a sensational account of the incident the next day, and a white lynch mob soon gathered at the jail. Armed blacks, seeking to protect Rowland, also showed up. Someone fired a gun, and the riot was on.

Whites invaded the black district, burning, looting and killing. To break up the riot, the police commandeered private planes and dropped dynamite. Eventually, the National Guard was called in and martial law declared.

The police arrested more than 4,000 blacks and interned them in three camps. All blacks were forced to carry green ID cards. And when Tulsa was zoned for a new railroad station, the tracks were routed through the black business district, thus destroying it.

(from *Parade Magazine*)

shoeshine stand: a place in a city street where you can get your shoes polished
lynch mob: a crowd of people who attack and try to kill someone they think is guilty of a crime, without a lawful trial
ID cards: identification cards
zoned: divided into different areas

Commuter who talks to strangers!

Peter Lloyd does something extraordinary on the Underground each day – he talks to total strangers.

He struck up his first conversation four weeks ago and found that people actually enjoyed talking.

Peter is now London's leading Tube talker, dedicated to converting a silent public to the joys of a nice chat.

He followed up the first experimental chat with a letter published in *The Evening Standard*, announcing the Tube Talker project.

The project is still in the discussion stage, but Peter is considering membership cards on which people would pledge their support for Tube talking and even a newsletter with accounts of interesting chats.

Most of all he wants London Transport to designate some Tube carriages as compartments where talking is encouraged.

Peter, a 24-year-old personnel consultant, is quite serious about his plans and has won some converts.

"People often look so sad and lonely on the Tube," he said. "They're usually pleased when I break the ice."

(from *The Evening Standard*)

break the ice: get friendly with someone you don't know

What are his intentions?

DEAR ABBY: My daughter met a smooth-talking fellow nine months ago and really fell for him. She's 22 and he's 21. He isn't working now and he's not even looking. He keeps saying that the jobs he wants don't pay enough. In the meantime he borrows from my daughter, drives her car, eats every meal at my table, and his clothes are washed in my machine! He never mentions marriage, but my daughter looks at him like he's a god, and she calls this "love".

Would I be wrong to ask this guy what his intentions are?
– FED UP

DEAR FED UP: You can ask him, but I think I can tell you. His intentions are to eat at your table, drive your daughter's car, get his clothes washed in your machine, and freeload off you and your daughter as long as you let him.

(from *The Houston Post*)

freeload off: exploit

"Don't worry, the wife won't be back from her macramé, or origami, or whatever the hell she's studying these days."

"It's good for a man to have a hobby."

A2 Focus on systems

1 Grammar. Put in the *-ing* form or the infinitive.

1. I hate .... on my own. (*be*)
2. What I like about my job is .... my own decisions. (*make*)
3. By the time I have had my shower my wife is just about .... into her car and leave for work. (*get*)
4. I usually put off .... work until about 9.30. (*start*)
5. Most doctors agree that .... is very bad for your health. (*smoke*)
6. What do you hope .... after you leave school? (*do*)

2 Grammar. Find one or more ways to complete each of the following sentences. Use an *-ing* form in each sentence as in the examples. Examples:

When I was a child, what I liked most about summer was …
  going barefoot.
  visiting my grandmother's farm.
… always reminds me of when we rode old Mr Fistner's horse, without a saddle.
  Seeing a white horse
  Talking about childhood summers

1. I was always a little afraid of …
2. It was … that my sister was afraid of.
3. But … made me feel brave and adventurous.
4. What my sister really loved was …
5. We were never satisfied with …
6. I always insisted on …
7. … was against my parents' rules, but we did it anyway when we thought they wouldn't find out.

3 Write down four things you like doing and four things you don't like doing. Then write a sentence about each one, using the forms shown in the examples. Examples:

Like: being outdoors
Don't like: having too much work

What I like is being outdoors.
It's having too much work that I don't like.

4 Find Lesson A2, Exercise 6 on the Student's Cassette. Repeat each sentence on the recording, paying particular attention to the correct pronunciation of the contractions and unstressed syllables.

5 Vocabulary. Which is the odd word out in each of the following lists? Give your reasons. Sometimes more than one answer is possible.

1. Ukraine, Italian, Singapore, Israel, New Zealand
2. Chile, Canada, Colombia, Peru, Argentina
3. the Scots, the Swiss, the Welsh, the English, the Chinese
4. Egypt, Malawi, Arabic, Nicaragua, Kenya
5. Australia, Indonesia, Ireland, Cuba, Austria
6. Portugal, Hungary, Brazil, Romania, the Netherlands
7. Danish, Turkish, Germany, Japanese, Greek

6 Write at least 150 words. Try to include at least one sentence using the structure shown in the examples.

EITHER: Describe the character of a typical person from your country. Example:

What the typical Frenchman/Frenchwoman really enjoys/hates/loves doing is …

OR: Write about what you really like/dislike about living in your country. Example:

What I really like/hate about living in Japan is …

7 Read the text, using a dictionary if you wish.

DREAMING IN A FOREIGN LANGUAGE

What is it to love someone if you don't share the same mother-tongue? My companion's English is reasonably good; infinitely better than my Russian. But many of the fine shades of meaning that would normally be possible in a conversation between two intimately connected people are out of reach. Do our nerve endings converse more intelligently by way of compensation; do we know by instinct most of the things that must be unsaid or imperfectly understood? In a sentimental mood, I'd say yes. But at the back of my mind is always the notion that you can only understand someone when you understand how, on the deepest level, they make use of language.

Sometimes I gaze at the optimistic row of Russian primers, readers and dictionaries on my bookshelf and think: but it will never be the language of my infancy, my school-days, my first loves, it will never truly be mine – just as English will never be truly his. And so there will always be something about each other we don't know. My mother and he agree on one thing – that my poems are incomprehensible. So the best of me is closed to him. But the best isn't good enough. If he could read me so well he'd know all my faults, human as well as literary. It would pin me down. I write more freely, knowing that I can never either fulfil or disappoint the expectations of those who truly love me.

Sometimes I feel as if I have no language at all, that my country is called Nowhere. For example – we're listening to Radio Svoboda, and I must either interrupt every few seconds to ask the meaning of this and that, or understand practically nothing. I sit silently, knowing that it's a programme about dissident writers which I would lap up greedily if only I could ... I concentrate on my food or my thoughts or read an English newspaper in which the words are somehow like dead insects. I am a foreigner. I am a little island of Englishness in this Russian kitchen. It is the same when he entertains friends or talks to them on the phone – I think: they make him laugh in a way I never can, and a cold ugly jealousy comes down on me like fog. And yet my own culture is all around me in the world outside, and his is not: how dare I begrudge him a few moments when a warm voice holds exile at bay? Perhaps it's because I don't feel I belong in the world outside either. This Russian kitchen in an English flat, this nowhere language made of English-Russian and Russian-English and silence, these stories we tell one another about our unimaginable pasts – these are home.

Just before the O-level exam which I took recently, I began to dream in Russian. I don't know how ungrammatical or even nonsensical it was, but in the dream at least, it looked or sounded OK. One night I found myself reading through an O-level translation text. It was about an old man who lived in a big house that had once been a hotel: he grew strawberries in the garden, as I distinctly remember. Public-spiritedly, I divulged my dream in advance to my fellow candidates, but, to our chagrin, the passage the universities' board came up with was about a young doctor called Vera who hated flying. At any rate, I consoled myself, something of the language must have filtered through to my subconscious mind if I can dream in it ... there is hope for me yet ...

(from *Dreaming in a Foreign Language* by Carol Rumens)

A3 Situations

1 Grammar and vocabulary. Put in suitable prepositions. Some can be used more than once; more than one answer is possible in some cases.

across	along	by	down	for	into
outside	over	past	round	through
to	towards	under	until

Let me tell you how to get ......1...... our place. Are you coming ......2...... car? OK. You drive ......3...... the A1734 ......4...... Blackstone ......5...... about twelve miles; go ......6...... the first turn to Stroop, take the second turn, and then go straight on ......7...... you come to a crossroads. Go straight ......8...... the crossroads, ...9...... a petrol station, take the next right and drive ......10...... the park. On the other side of the park, go ......11...... the canal bridge, ...12...... the hill, turn left ......13...... the Market Square, keep straight on ......14...... the railway bridge and you'll come ......15...... Miller Street. It's probably best to park there, because there isn't usually a space ......16...... our house. We're just ......17...... the corner from the post office – 37 Jackdaw Lane.

2 What would you say in the following situations?

1. Someone says, 'Oh, thank you very much!'
2. Someone phones for a chat just as you are about to leave to catch a train.
3. A good friend wants to borrow your car, but you are not insured for other people to drive it.
4. You and your partner want to borrow a good friend's road map of England for a few days (you know he or she will not be needing it).
5. A friend asks to borrow your cassette recorder for the evening. You are happy to lend it to her.

3 What situations would the following expressions be used in? Choose one of the situations and see how many more typical English expressions you can write down.

Boarding at 3.15, Gate 6.
What size are you?
Could you pass the salt?
How many miles does it do to the gallon?
Double, with bath, please.

4 Write the other side of this telephone conversation. You can change some of the answers if you want to.

Hello, Carlingford 71661.
...
Speaking.
...
I'm not sure. Let me just look in my diary. Yes, I think so.
...
Well, I don't know.
...
Are you sure?
...
Why?
...
I don't think I'd like that.
...
No. Anyway, I really ought to wash my hair.
...
No, I'm going to the theatre.
...
I'm not sure.
...
She's not in.
...
I don't know.
...
No.
...
Goodbye.

"I'm afraid you've got the wrong number. This is Louis XV."

5 Find Lesson A3, Exercise 2 on the Student's Cassette. Listen to the recording while looking at the map in the Student's Book lesson, and write directions from Lacy's to the bus stop in front of the cathedral.

6 The sentences in this letter are out of order. Rewrite the letter, putting the sentences into a logical order.

```
                                              28 March

Dear Marilyn,

I think you mentioned that you had someone to
look after your kids, and I thought she might
include Helen. Please don't hesitate to say no if
this presents any sort of problem. I won't
actually be working most of the time — just
giving one talk on each of the first three days,
and a half-day session on the last morning. Love
to Jerome and the kids — even if you can't fit
Helen in, I hope we can see something of one
another when I'm in Nice. I'm writing to ask you
a favour. Would there be any possibility of her
fitting in with your child-care arrangements? I
have to come to Nice from the 7th to the 10th of
May for my work. Of course I would pay her extra
for this. I thought it would be nice to bring
little Helen along with me; but of course I have
to make some arrangement for her to be looked
after while I'm working.

Love,

Alex.
```

7 Do one of these writing tasks. Write at least 150 words and try to include some words and expressions from the Student's Book lesson.

1. Imagine the letter in Exercise 6 was written to you instead of Marilyn. The woman who looks after your children has made it clear that she doesn't want to look after any others. Suggest another solution, or say you'll try to find someone and write again soon.
2. Write about a time when you got lost.
3. Write about a day when things kept going wrong.

9

A4 The sun was in the north

1 Grammar revision. Simple Past or Past Progressive?

1. I (*mend*) my sails one day when a man I had worked with before (*walk*) up and (*ask*) me if I'd like to have a drink.
2. I (*think*) he probably had more than just a friendly drink in mind, so I (*stop*) what I (*do*), (*wipe*) off my hands, and (*follow*) him to the local drink shop.
3. It (*be*) there that I (*find*) out that he (*recruit*) people to work on Necho's project.
4. Nowadays, everybody knows about our journey, but then, it (*sound*) a bit strange.
5. At first I thought the man (*try*) to play a trick on me.
6. But the more he (*talk*), the better it (*sound*) – a real adventure.
7. I (*get*) tired of the same old sea routes year after year.
8. Besides, I (*think*) it would be a great trading opportunity; the route to Carthage, across Greek waters, (*get*) more and more dangerous.
9. You may not believe this, but it (*only take*) me a few minutes to decide; I (*sit*) there in that shop with a cup in my hand, and I (*make*) a decision that would change my life – and lots of other people's lives as well.
10. There were times on the journey when I (*have*) doubts about my decision.
11. Once while we (*be*) pushed south-west by the monsoon winds, I (*nearly be*) washed off the deck by a big wave.
12. And one day during the long sail south, one of the men (*try*) to convince the rest of us that we were under a magic spell when a dead blackbird (*fall*) on the deck; believe me, we (*be*) scared.
13. But there were some good times, too: we (*have*) to stop and collect supplies on the west coast, and we (*stay*) there for a long time, in one of the most beautiful places I've seen.
14. One evening while I (*sit*) under a tree with the wind in my face and a luscious big mango to eat, I almost (*decide*) to stay there for the rest of my life.
15. But of course I (*not stay*); I (*know*) that I would get tired of it soon enough, and besides, my wife and children (*wait*) for me back in Tyre.
16. We (*see*) thousands of birds at Gibraltar: they (*fly*) over, on their way south for the winter.
17. In December, when I (*get*) home, I (*make*) sure that no one told my family before I (*arrive*).
18. When I (*walk*) in the door, my wife (*put*) supper on the table, and my son and daughter – whom I (*hardly recognise*) – (*play*) by the fireplace.
19. I (*know*) when I (*see*) them that I had done the right thing not to stay under that tree.
20. I still think of that big tree in the jungle sometimes, though; and I'll bet there's not a man who (*go*) on that journey who wouldn't like to go back.

2 Grammar revision. Use an infinitive to answer these questions.

1. Why do tourists go to France?
   To see Paris.
   To visit Provence.
2. Why do tourists go to Italy / Spain / Greece / the USA / Egypt?
3. Why do people go to banks?
4. Why do people go to post offices?
5. Why do people go to airports?
6. Why do children go to school?
7. Why are you learning English?

3 Underline the stressed syllable in each word. Use your dictionary if necessary. Practise saying the words with the correct stress.

amaze   arrive   avoid   become   begin
believe   businessman   civilised   control
delay   difficult   discover   enormous
eventually   experience   fantastic
interested   journey   Portuguese   publish
report   steadily   supplies   travel
unknown   welcome   wonderful

4 Vocabulary revision. Can you match the words and the pictures?

| catch | climb | dance | drop | fall | hit | jump | kick | lift | pull |
| push | roll | run | slip | swing | throw | trip | turn | walk | |

5 Do one of these writing tasks. Write at least 150 words and try to include some words and expressions from the Student's Book lesson.

1. Write about a journey you (or someone you know) made when something went wrong, or when you had a lot of problems.
2. Read the poem (using a dictionary if you wish) and write a story (or a poem) about a chance meeting on a journey.

The woman from Carrick

Travelling homeward, westward
Across Ireland on a bus
We shared a laugh
At Longford.
Not much, I know,
(Not even a name)
With which to build a bridge
Across the aisle
Between us.
Your stop approached,
And at the lights
I scribbled a note –
Shaky with the motion
(And emotion).
You said you'd call,
But that was then.

(Nicholas Denis)

6 Read these texts, using a dictionary if you wish.

The least successful explorer

Thomas Nuttall (1786–1859) was a pioneer botanist whose main field of study was the flora of remote parts of North-west America. As an explorer, however, his work was characterised by the fact that he was almost permanently lost. During his expedition of 1812 his colleagues frequently had to light beacons in the evening to help him find his way back to camp.

One night he completely failed to return and a search party was sent out. As it approached him in the darkness Nuttall assumed they were Indians and tried to escape. The annoyed rescuers pursued him for three days through bush and river until he accidentally wandered back into the camp. On another occasion Nuttall was lost again and lay down exhausted. He looked so pathetic that a passing Indian, instead of scalping him, picked him up, carried him three miles to the river and paddled him home in a canoe.

(from *The Book of Heroic Failures* by Stephen Pile)

scalping: cutting off the skin on the top of the head of a dead enemy

Summer in Antarctica

Antarctica is the highest, coldest, and most desolate place on earth, a continent twice the size of Western Europe, capped by ice over two miles thick. In 1987 glaciologist Dr Liz Morris became the first British woman to undertake remote field work with the British Antarctic Survey. Here she describes daily life during her second five-month summer stint in the frozen wastes.

NOVEMBER 'Summer starts in Antarctica, and then I fly to the Falklands. Then, weather permitting, I travel by ship and then by plane to the glaciology base at Rothera, 900 miles south of Cape Horn. Here I put together my equipment for going into the field – sledges, food and a tent. Martin, my general assistant, travels with me, using his two-year experience of weather and travel for our safety.

'There are at most 50 people here. Rothera is quite luxurious, with heating, a doctor and a cook. We sleep in tiny rooms with four bunks, like a ship's cabin. There's no privacy. There are separate stalls in the loos and I can wash separately, but it's a community life.

'I tell my problems to the dogs. Only twenty huskies, born and bred in Antarctica, are left at Rothera. These days Skidoos – motorbikes with tank tracks – avoid the environmental problem of killing seals for dog food and are considered more practical. But the dogs are more reliable, intelligent and loving. They are very important to me.

'It was tough being the first woman. All the men were very courteous, but some of them, particularly the new guys, felt strongly that to have women there was wrong. Perhaps they thought that if a middle-aged woman with no particular physical skill could do it, how could they be heroes?'

DECEMBER 'I'm set down by plane on the Ronne Ice Shelf. It is awe-inspiring. There you are in a white expanse of nothingness, a thousand miles from base. There are just two of us and for the next few months we would be utterly dependent on ourselves and each other. This gives you an amazing commitment, both to each other and the job.

'In December it's daylight all the time, and the sun goes round in circles overhead. I wake up at about 6 a.m. Martin and I share a small two-man tent. I've been on so many expeditions that I'm used to the lack of privacy, and as for any relationships with my colleagues, my boyfriend knows that I would never get involved with anyone else. Anyway, you can't get romantic when you're worried about frost-bite.

'The cold is a nightmare. I sleep and work in most of my clothes. All the gear makes peeing difficult for women. What's so terrible is baring your bottom to the icy blast. I never wash and rarely change my clothes because it's too cold, and at that temperature no bacteria work so you don't smell. Last time we changed only three times in 73 days. I clean my teeth with snow on the toothbrush, but that's all.

'We never go more than a couple of hundred yards from the tent, and we carry another small tent and radio with us, so if our big tent gets blown away we can at least survive a couple of days.

'We take turns to cook supper. Everything's rationed and there's very little choice – no fresh food, all dried. The bonus is one tin of sardines and one tin of sausages each, every twenty days.'

JANUARY 'We travel every few days from site to site on Skidoos. This is the best bit, travelling through the open landscape. There's such a sense of freedom: all my belongings are on the sledge behind me. I am self-sufficient and enjoying the adventure and the romance.

'I've only had one frightening moment, when we were flying in a blizzard. We had to land blind and were then stranded for three days in the storm. I was pleased I didn't panic.

'There are problems with people not getting on. I know of people who have become irrational because of the isolation and the stress, even threatening to kill each other. It's rare, but it does happen – more so in the winter. But everyone's very carefully selected over a week's residential course. I'm on the selection panel; we look for a happy, calm, mature temperament and have to reject anybody who appears to be trying to escape from something or who doesn't mix well with others.'

FEBRUARY 'It's getting really cold now, with winter coming on. There are even a few sunsets, although it's never actually dark. Night temperatures go down as low as -30°F (a domestic freezer is -20°F). When it's cold I can't sleep. We've read the three or four books we could bring, so we're reliant on each other for amusement. I feel it will be nice when this is over, but I'm not bored because I am fascinated by every aspect of the Antarctic experience.'

MARCH 'The pack ice takes all summer to melt and then quickly starts freezing again, but with luck we've got two weeks when a ship can get in.

'Leaving is terribly emotional, the people who are staying behind for the winter lining up to watch the boat go, the ship hooting mournfully. Those who are leaving after two years – the non-scientists such as doctors and cooks – weep because they know they're unlikely to go back to Antarctica. In fact, the whole thing is an incredibly emotional experience.'

(from *Marie Claire* – adapted)

A5 Secret thoughts

1 Vocabulary revision. Can you match the words and the shapes in each group?

circle   cube   curve   dotted line   oval   pyramid   rectangle   sphere
square   straight line   triangle

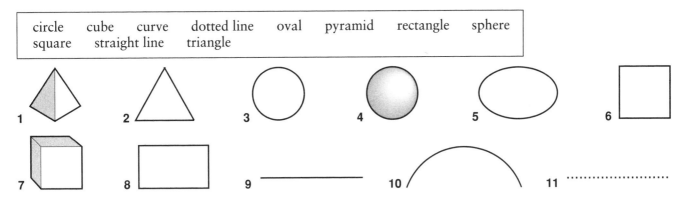

2 Look at the pictures. How could you warn the people? Examples:

'Don't open the door, or you'll get wet.'   'Look out! If you open the door, you'll get wet.'

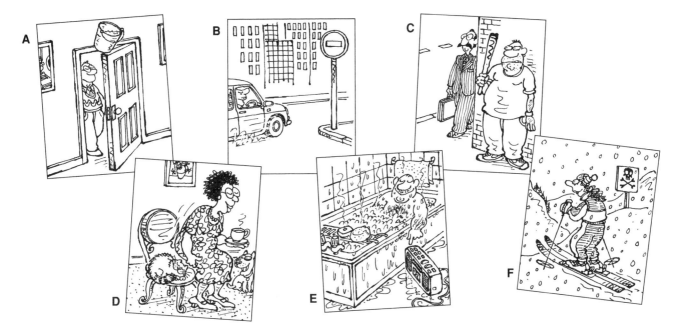

3 Grammar. Some verbs are not often used in progressive forms. Examples are *believe*, *feel* and *think* (used to talk about people's opinions); *hope*; *know*; *like*; *look* (meaning *appear*, *seem*); *love*; *need*; *remember*; *seem*; *understand*. Can you put in the correct verb forms?

1. 'Would you like to come out for a drink?' 'Sorry, I (*work*).'
2. 'How do you like my hair?' 'I (*think*) it (*look*) great.'
3. 'Where's Deborah?' 'I (*believe*) she (*play*) tennis.'
4. 'George (*come*) next weekend, isn't he?' 'I'm not sure, but I (*hope*) so.'
5. 'There's somebody on the phone. He says he (*want*) to talk to you.' 'Who is it?' 'I (*not know*).'
6. 'Hello. What (*you do*) these days?' 'Sorry – I (*remember*) your face, but I'm afraid I've forgotten your name.'

4 Grammar. Decide on the correct tenses.

I (1. *had / was having*) lunch in a small restaurant near the office. She (2. *sat / was sitting*) at a table near the window. I (3. *wondered / was wondering*) why she (4. *looked / was looking*) at me so intently. (5. *Did she know / Was she knowing*) me? I (6. *didn't think / wasn't thinking*) I (7. *ever saw / had ever seen*) her before. Suddenly she (8. *stood up / was standing up*) and (9. *walked / was walking*) slowly towards me. I (10. *still remember / am still remembering*) my feelings exactly. I (11. *wanted / was wanting*) to run away, but I (12. *knew / was knowing*) I couldn't. She (13. *stopped / was stopping*) by my table and (14. *smiled / was smiling*) down at me. She had on a purple dress – I (15. *think / 'm thinking*) it had a flower pattern – and she was amazingly beautiful. 'Excuse me,' she said. 'Have you got a light?'

13

5 🔊 Find Lesson A5, Exercise 3 on the Student's Cassette and write down all the shop assistant's secret thoughts.

6 Here is part of a political speech. Write the speaker's secret thoughts. (The first two are done for you.) Or if you prefer, write a new political speech with secret thoughts included.

My fellow Fantasians! (1. *You poor fools!*) This is a serious crisis in our country's affairs. (2. *In my affairs – if I don't get elected I'll have to find an honest job.*) If we are to come safely through the next five years, we must choose wisely. (3.) The Fantasian National Democratic Liberal Party is not interested in power for its own sake. (4.) It is interested in the welfare of the people. (5.) It is the party of the common man – and the common woman too. (6.) If you elect me, I will work day and night on your behalf. (7.) I will fight for better conditions for the workers. (8.) I will fight for higher wages. (9.) I will fight for better housing. (10.) Together, we will march towards a bright and glorious future. (11.) A future in which the citizens of this great country can join hands in peace and love. (12.) A future in which our children, and their children, will be proud to be Fantasians. (13.) Vote for me – for the FNDLP – for peace, democracy and freedom. (14.)

Sempé

7 How imaginative are you? Answer the questions and check your score.

How imaginative are you?

1. If you were expecting a friend to come round to your place and he/she was late, would you:
   a) assume something ordinary had happened to delay him/her, and not worry?
   b) feel slightly worried?
   c) think he/she must have been in an accident?
2. When other people tell you about their troubles, do you:
   a) feel very upset?
   b) feel bored?
   c) feel some sympathy?
3. When you look at clouds, do you:
   a) see pictures in them?
   b) feel thoughtful?
   c) think about the weather?
4. When you first meet somebody who attracts you, do you:
   a) think sensibly about your chances?
   b) think he/she is the most wonderful person in the world, and imagine yourselves living together?
   c) tell yourself not to lose your head?
5. While staying in an old house, you are woken up by strange noises. Do you think of:
   a) water pipes?
   b) burglars?
   c) ghosts?
6. Do you get an idea that you think would make a good book, film, poem or song:
   a) never?
   b) often?
   c) sometimes?
7. Do you daydream:
   a) often when you should be thinking about other things?
   b) sometimes?
   c) hardly ever?
8. Can you imagine yourself doing something that would cause you to go to prison?
   a) not at all
   b) with difficulty
   c) easily
9. When you talk about something that has happened to you, do you:
   a) give all the details?
   b) change things to make it more interesting?
   c) just give the main points?
10. Which of these kinds of book or magazine article do you like most?
    a) biography/history
    b) fiction (novels, stories, etc.)
    c) practical (information about how to do things)

(*See score table at the top of the next page.*)

How imaginative are you?

Total 10–16: You are a practical, down-to-earth person. You don't usually let your imagination run away with you, and you are not afraid of very much. But you may sometimes have trouble understanding other people's feelings.

Total 17–23: You have an average amount of imagination, and you are quite good at understanding how other people feel. Sometimes you live too much inside your own head, but your common sense usually keeps you in touch with reality.

Total 24–30: Your imagination is your greatest strength and your greatest weakness. On the one hand, you live a rich interior life, and you experience the pleasures and excitement of the true creative artist. However, you often suffer from irrational fears and superstitious beliefs. And you must be careful not to spend so much time watching the 'cinema' inside your own head that you completely lose touch with the real world.

Your score:
1. a–1 b–2 c–3
2. a–3 b–1 c–2
3. a–3 b–2 c–1
4. a–2 b–3 c–1
5. a–1 b–2 c–3
6. a–1 b–3 c–2
7. a–3 b–2 c–1
8. a–1 b–2 c–3
9. a–2 b–3 c–1
10. a–2 b–3 c–1

A6 Focus on systems

1 Grammar. Rewrite these sentences, adding the phrases below. (More than one answer may be possible in some cases.)

1. The man is actually a liar and a thief.
   The man you think is so wonderful is actually a liar and a thief.
2. The music makes me feel like crying.
3. That house is where my mother was born.
4. The woman used to be married to my brother.
5. The day was the loneliest day of my life.
6. The reason is that he is very disorganised.
7. The best thing to do is to count to ten very slowly.
8. People should think about what they are doing to the environment.
9. That book was still in my suitcase!
10. The week always seems to be incredibly busy.

---

you lent me when we went to Greece together last year
before I go away on holiday
you think is so wonderful
being played on the radio at the moment
after he went back home to Australia
with big cars who always drive too fast
why he never knows where anything is
on the corner on the right opposite the school
you were talking to in the bank yesterday
when you are very angry and feel like killing someone

---

2 Grammar. Complete these sentences.

1. The town where I come from …
2. The best idea of all …
3. The company he has been working for since February …
4. The moment they first saw each other …
5. The car parked next to the lorry in front of the post office …
6. That house you were telling me about on the phone yesterday …
7. The woman who reads the seven o'clock news on the TV …
8. The day after Richard left school …

3 Contrastive stress. Which of the words in italics has the strongest stress? Can you say the sentences?

1. 'It's ten past two.' 'Your watch is wrong. It's *ten past three*.'
2. I said I wanted a *glass of milk*, not a glass of water.
3. She asked for hot milk, but the waiter brought her *cold milk*.
4. 'Who's the girl in red?' 'You mean the one in the red skirt or the one in the *red sweater*?'
5. Some people think that *brown sugar* is better for you than white.
6. 'When are we seeing Peter – is it Thursday?' 'No, Tuesday – we're seeing *Jim and Elsa on Thursday*.'
7. 'Shall we look at the plans before dinner?' 'I'd prefer *after dinner*, if you don't mind.'

4 Vocabulary. Match the words and the numbers.

| back | bottom | button | corner | edge | end | front | handle | knob |
| point | side | switch | top | | | | | |

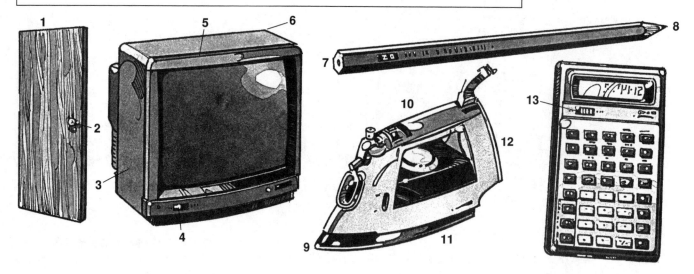

5 Translate these into your language.

1. What he's really interested in is making lots of money.
2. When I work in the garden, it's the fresh air that I enjoy the most.
3. It isn't English that's boring, it's the way it's taught.
4. Olivia arrived home eventually, but Tom didn't.
5. Actually, I think the jacket suits you very well, sir.
6. But the trousers don't fit you: they're too long.
7. According to this newspaper article, the government is going to lose the election.
8. Trying to connect you. Her line's busy. Can you hold?
9. Go straight ahead for 100 metres and take the second road on the left. You can't miss it.
10. The best holiday I ever had was when I visited Yemen.
11. The house she lived in before she got married didn't have any heating.
12. The man sitting in front of Julia and opposite Frank is Angela's husband, Bill.

6 Fast reading test. First have a quick look again at Exercise 1 in Lesson A5 and check that you remember the meanings of *circle, cube, curve, pyramid, rectangle, sphere, square, straight line* and *triangle*. Then, using a watch, see how many answers you can write in three minutes.

1. If the pyramid is on the cube, write the opposite of *black*; otherwise write your name.

2. If the cube is higher than the sphere, write the letter that comes after S in the alphabet; otherwise write the letter that comes before S.

3. If a square has got fewer corners than a triangle, write the name of the day after Tuesday. Otherwise write the name of the month before October.

4. Write the name of the shape that is between the square and the circle.

5. Write the name of the shape that is between the cube and the triangle.

6. Write the name of the day before the day after the day before yesterday.
7. If a cube has not got more corners than a sphere, draw a straight line. Otherwise draw a curve.
8. If two pyramids have more corners than a cube, draw a square. Otherwise draw a circle.
9. Write the name of the day before the day after the day after tomorrow.
10. Write your name backwards or draw a pyramid upside down.
11. What time will it be this time tomorrow?
12. Draw a circle inside a rectangle inside a triangle inside a square.

7 Write an exact description of where some of the students usually sit in your classroom. Try to include some words and expressions from the Student's Book lesson. Example:

Jean-Pierre sits at the front on the right; Tomoko sits at the back between ...

A7 Cruelty to cars

1 Vocabulary revision. Do you know the names of the main parts of a car? Match the words and the letters.

| dashboard   seat belt   wiper   engine   brake (pedal)   headlight
speedometer   petrol tank (*American* gas tank)   roof rack (*American* luggage rack)
bonnet (*American* hood)   clutch (pedal)   windscreen (*American* windshield)
boot (*American* trunk)   accelerator (pedal)   wing mirror (*American* side mirror)
radiator   indicator light   steering wheel   handbrake (*American* emergency brake)
seat   gear lever (*American* gear shift)   bumper |
|---|

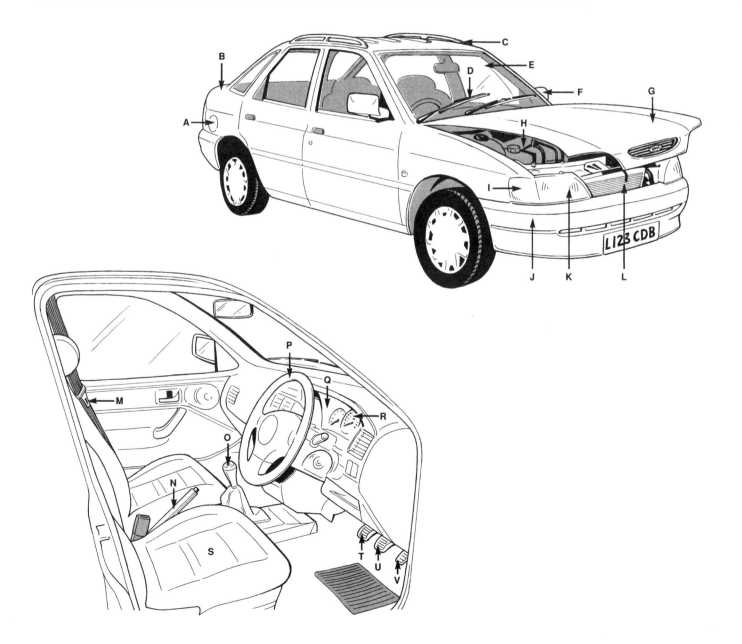

2 This car hasn't been looked after. What's the matter with it? Write five sentences, using the words in the box if you wish.

| bent | body | rusty | worn |

3 Grammar. Use verbs in the passive to complete these sentences.

1. One of our windows (*break*) by the wind last night.
2. This camera (*make*) in Germany.
3. 'What does Joan think about the changes?' 'She (*not tell*) yet.'
4. This (*write*) by a child. Look at the handwriting.
5. Alice thinks her firm is in trouble. She (*not pay*) this month.
6. 'How's your new house?' 'It (*still, build*). We think it'll be finished in August.'
7. 'That's a lovely necklace.' 'Yes, it (*give*) to me by my grandmother when I was eight.'
8. English (*speak*) here.
9. 'I heard you had an accident.' 'Yes, but nobody (*hurt*).'

"Careful, Wally, there's a drunk driver ahead."

4 Grammar revision. Here are some ways of comparing things. Study the examples.

MORE/LESS

| Car A uses | much / far | more/less petrol than car B. |
| Car B is | a lot / rather / slightly | faster/slower than car A. |

THE SAME
Car A uses the same amount of petrol as car B.
Car B uses as much petrol as car A.
Both car A and car B do 18 miles to the gallon.
Car A and car B both do 18 miles to the gallon.
Neither car A nor car B is very economical.

SIMILAR
Car A's design is similar to car B's.
Car A's bonnet looks very like car B's.
Car A and car B have similar styling at the back.

DIFFERENT
Car A's headlights are not at all like car B's.
Car B's engine design is different from car A's.
Car A doesn't use as/so much petrol as car B.
Car A is very/rather/quite different from car B.

Use some of the structures to compare one or more of the following pairs of things.

two different cars, motorbikes, bicycles or aeroplanes
two different means of transport (e.g. bus and train)
two different buildings that you know
two makes of CD player, cassette player, TV or computer

5 Read these texts, using a dictionary if you wish. (The first text is taken from a book published nearly 60 years ago.)

EXAMINATION

Parking Limit – Two Hours.
Write on one side of the road only.

(a) *Mechanics*
Your car, except for a tendency to slow down on hills, runs perfectly all day.
On starting it up next morning, however, you find that it will only move a few inches. What would you do?
Answer: Open the garage door.

(b) *History*
Describe the difference between roads made by the Romans and those constructed nowadays.
Answer: The roads made by the Romans have lasted until the present time.

(c) *English grammar*
What is wrong with the following: 'When I got to the crossroads I hooted and slowed down and looked to see if it was safe to cross'?
Answer: It isn't true.

(d) *General knowledge*
1. Why is a red light used for danger?
Answer: Because a bright colour that cannot be confused with anything else is essential.
2. Why is a red light used for advertising restaurants, cinemas, drink, shops, pills and everything else?
Answer: See above.

(e) *Legal*
A motorist comes suddenly out of a small side road, dashes straight across a main line of traffic against the lights, mounts the pavement, runs right up the steps of a public house, crashes through the door and finally comes to rest hard up against the bar. Is he breaking the law?
Answer: No, not unless he has his car with him.

(from *You Have Been Warned* by Fougasse and McCullough)

Car Correspondence

Sir, – The warning to all motorists – around the corner you are going to meet another damn fool – is particularly true for my uncle, who took a corner at fifty miles an hour on the wrong side of the road and was passed by another car doing exactly the same thing in the other direction. Without speaking a word the men got out of their cars, shook hands, and drove away.

John Rae, Hallam St, W1

(from *The Times*)

LAST MONDAY a garage fitted a new radio aerial to my car. I have now discovered that I have five different ways of turning off my radio. They are: (1) by operating the foot brake; (2) by changing gear; (3) by touching the loudspeaker cover; (4) by tapping the speedometer glass; and (5) the on-off switch.
I also find that I can increase the volume by operating the heater control. I doubt if any of the expensive cars at this year's Motor Show have such an elaborate radio system incorporated!

(from *The Sunday Mirror*)

The least successful car

Ford produced the car of the decade in 1957 – the Edsel. Half of the models sold proved spectacularly defective. If lucky, you could have got a car with any or all of the following features: doors that wouldn't close, bonnets and boots that wouldn't open, batteries that went flat, hooters that stuck, hubcaps that dropped off, paint that peeled, transmissions that seized up, brakes that failed and push buttons that couldn't be pushed even with three of you trying.

In a stroke of marketing genius, the Edsel, one of the biggest and most lavish cars ever built, coincided with a phase when people increasingly wanted economy cars. As *Time* magazine said: 'It was a classic case of the wrong car for the wrong market at the wrong time.'

Unpopular to begin with, the car's popularity declined. One business writer at the time likened the Edsel's sales graph to an extremely dangerous ski-slope. He added that, so far as he knew, there was only one case of an Edsel ever being stolen.

(from *The Book of Heroic Failures* by Stephen Pile)

6 Read the letter, and rewrite it putting in commas, full stops, question marks, apostrophes and capital letters where necessary.

```
                                    14 hillside road
                                    dover
                                    12 december 1992
dear sir

i am writing to complain about the car that i bought
from you yesterday it is just a heap of scrap when i
tried to start it this morning the key wouldnt turn in
the lock the battery was flat and two of the plugs
needed changing then when i finally got it going the
bonnet wouldnt stay closed and the drivers side door
fell off and when i tried to stop to pick up the door
the brakes didnt work so i crashed into a tree and
smashed the radiator also one of the wheels came off

do you really think this car is worth £250 well if you
do i dont what are you going to do about it

yours faithfully

eric smith
```

7 Do one of these writing tasks. Try to include some words and expressions from the Student's Book lesson.

1. Write an advertisement for something you want to sell.
2. Write a letter of complaint (better expressed than the one in Exercise 6) about something you have bought that doesn't work.

A8 Here is the news

1 Vocabulary. Put in words from the box.

available	average	demonstration	details
efficient	figures	inflation	opposition
policies	prompt	reported	violence

1. According to government ...., unemployment is down by 13%, and .... has fallen to 3%.
2. The .... weekly wage has gone up by 80% since 1980.
3. The government say that this is due to their economic ....
4. Mr Gresk, leader of the Trade Union Confederation, has criticised Fantasian management for not being .... enough.
5. There was a large .... against educational reforms yesterday. It was mainly peaceful, but there were a few outbreaks of .... at the end, following speeches by .... leaders. However, ... action by police stopped the fighting and restored order. Several people are .... to have been hurt, but no further .... are .... for the moment.

2 Vocabulary revision. Match the adjectives and the nouns. (Some adjectives can go with more than one noun.) Can you add some more words and expressions to do with the weather?

heavy	sunshine
thick	temperatures
deep	wind
loud	hailstones
brilliant	snow
enormous	rain
strong	fog
high	thunder

3 🎧 Find Lesson A8, Exercise 2 on the Student's Cassette. Listen again to the news items and spot the twelve differences in the transcript.

It's one o'clock. I'm Linda Cooch.

Gunmen have opened fire on a busload of women and children in Ulster, wounding four people. The bus was ambushed near Market Hill in County Armagh. David Stokes reporting:

'The minibus was taking mothers and their children on a hospitals visit to Belfast when it was wrecked by gunfire. Two women are among those hurt. They're suffering wounds to their arms and body. It's believed the gunmen's target may have been the bus driver, normally top Sinn Féin man Tommy Carroll from Armagh, but he apparently had taken the day off. David Stokes, IRN, Belfast.'

Figures on the economy just out offer little hope of an early recovery from recession. Despite apparent euphoria on the stock market this afternoon, the jobless total is up, and there's little sign of an economic recovery this month. Meanwhile unemployment in Wiltshire has risen by 0.3%. The number of people out of work is now just over fifteen and a half thousand; that's an increase of just under 800 on the previous month.

Finally, a woman who lost half her weight says the answer to fat was to stick a 'before' picture on her kitchen door. Amanda Brimble, from Bromley, turned her 18 stone 5 into 9 stone 5 to take the *Slimming Magazine* title of 'Slimmer of the Month'.

The weather check from the Bristol Met Office: dry, warm, spells of sunshine, temperatures up to 22, dry and clear at first this evening, but clouding over later with a little drizzle on the coast.

Linda Cooch for GWR; your next news at one.

4 Read these extracts from a radio commentary on a football match and see how quickly you can answer the questions.

Merton City v New Park Rangers

... and so it's Merton City in the dark blue stripes who kick off ... that's Harris ... that's Carrick ... Keith Dawson wearing number 6 ... Littlecote in there challenging ...

... throw again for New Park ...

... goal kick ... that's Barrow ... good ball, a good chance – it's a goal! A beautiful ball through by Peter Carrick and then Saunders number 10, makes it one goal to nil for Merton.

... and Dawson trying to find ... and almost got through ... Steve Rukin with the interception ... away by Delaney ...

... now it's Keith Dawson – and Rangers are really keeping up the pressure in these last ten minutes of the first half ... neat, very neat – Carrick got the return ball ... and Carrick still going ... and Carrick with a shot! ...

Tring with a cross ... Hutchins coming in ... away by Delaney ... that's Rukin, to Barrow ... corner ...

... and that's the whistle for half-time with Merton City leading by one goal to nil.

... Tring ... free kick – two Park players and another ... and it almost went in – it must have hit the post and rebounded – what a remarkable piece of luck for City!

... one minute to go of playing time ... throw in to Merton City ... it's a corner – could this be the last corner of the match? ... the whistle has blown – and Merton City has knocked New Park Rangers out of the FA Cup – a great, great victory by Merton City.

1. Which team won the match?
2. What colour were they wearing?
3. What team were Harris and Carrick playing for?
4. Were Carrick and Saunders on the same side?
5. Who scored Merton's goal?
6. Did Carrick score?

5 Write one or more items for an imaginary radio or TV news programme. Include some of the words in the box.

ambush	armed	bank	bomb	concert
crash	crowd	demonstration	drizzle	
dry	economy	escape	hospital	
inflation	nearby	pop star	recession	
raid	recovery	seriously	temperature	
tiger	unemployment	violence	vote	
wreck	zoo			

"Just once, Alfred, I wish you'd get on the news."

6 Try the crossword.

ACROSS

1. The noun from *responsible*.
9. The past participle of *win*.
10. Take the first road .... the left.
12. The .... of a pencil is usually quite sharp.
13. Made of rubber, filled with air, and goes round the wheel on a car.
14. 'Are you the .... of this vehicle?' 'Yes, it's mine.'
16. Do you know the .... about when to use the *-ing* form?
18. This looks like a full stop.
20. Another word for *neither*.
21. Thanks very much ....
24. Try them on again just to make ....
25. The past participle of *lead*.
26. The opposite of *higher*.
28. I can't stop – I'm on my .... to work!
30. The opposite of *4 down*.
32. My grandmother used to like jazz, and .... did my grandfather.
33. If you can drive, you probably have one of these.
34. Don't go – please .... !
35. United States.
36. A dog might chase this.
37. I think that painting is a real work of ....
39. London, New York, Tokyo and Hongkong all have important .... markets.
41. Not *come*.
42. Carrying weapons.
44. This sounds like *9 across*.
45. The Simple Past of *eat*.
46. We all live on this.
49. The part along the outside of something.
51. I'll call again .... a minute.
53. '............... be or not .... be, that is the question.'
54. Something you try to hit.
55. You've probably got five of these on each foot.

DOWN

1. Come back.
2. Food, drink, and other things you need for a long journey.
3. If something is yours, then you .... it.
4. 'Did you enjoy the film?' '..............., I didn't.'
5. White stuff which falls out of the sky in cold countries.
6. The opposite of *interested*.
7. *Actually* means .... *fact*.
8. Not *out of*.
11. Not far away.
14. I lent you £50. You gave me £40 back. So you now .... me £10.
15. Increased.
17. Not the beginning.
19. .... right at the T-junction.
20. This sounds like the Simple Past of *know*.
22. The verb from *election*.
23. 'I hate traffic wardens.' 'So .... I.'
25. The opposite of *most*.
27. A lot of people get killed in this.
29. Stronger than *surprise*.
31. Usually made of wool, cotton or nylon and worn on the foot.
34. Towns and cities are full of these.
35. Not unusual.
38. The Simple Past of *run*.
40. A kind of musical entertainment.
41. Sorry, we .... cut off.
43. The Simple Past of *draw*.
46. A round thing which you can eat.
47. A small, furry animal with a long tail.
48. The past participle of *hit*.
50. 'I love pop music.' '............... you?'
52. The opposite of *30 across*.

(*Solution on page 144.*)

"*Do you mind if I interrupt your programme to make a special announcement?*"

B1 Learning a language

1 Here is the beginning of a vocabulary network. Put the words and expressions from the box in suitable places. Can you add some more?

| adjectives | cloud | consonants | Greek | intonation | Japanese |
| languages | prepositions | Present Perfect | Simple Past | stress |
| think |

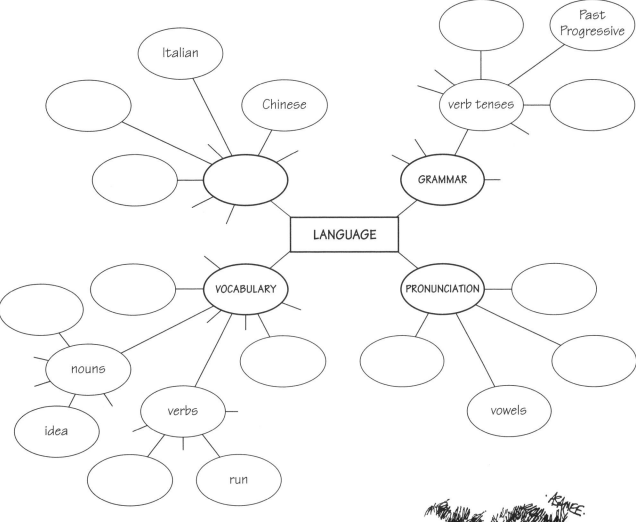

2 Can you add five words to each of these groups? Do you know what the different kinds of words are called? The names are in the box.

1. sit, get, write, belong, ...
2. hotel, film, idea, cow, ...
3. green, heavy, wrong, late, ...
4. on, by, with, ...
5. quickly, easily, now, there, ...
6. although, after, when, ...

| adjective | adverb | conjunction | noun |
| preposition | verb |

"You no believe no believe no believe I learn English from old from old from old gramophone."

3 Vocabulary. Can you match the countries and the languages? Can you add the names of any more countries with their languages?

Algeria	Australia	Austria	Brazil
Holland	Mexico	Norway	Pakistan
Uganda	Wales		

Arabic	English	Dutch	German
Norwegian	Portuguese	Swahili	Spanish
Urdu	Welsh		

4 Vocabulary. Can you match the British words and their American equivalents? Do you know any other words which are different in British and American English?

British

angry   autumn   film   first floor   flat
ground floor   holiday   ill   lift   mad
maths   motorway   pavement   petrol
post   purse   reverse-charge call
road surface   shop   sweets   taxi   toilet
trousers

US

apartment   cab   candy   coin purse
collect call   crazy   elevator   fall
first floor   freeway   gas   mad   mail
math   movie   pants   pavement
restroom   sick   second floor   sidewalk
store   vacation

5 Word stress. Where do you think the main stress comes in each of the following words? Use a dictionary to check your answers.

ability   consonant   conversation
expression   important   intonation
language   pronunciation   translation
understand   vocabulary

Where does the main stress come in words that end in *-ation*?

"I don't know anybody who says 'It is I'."

6 Read both of these texts.

German-French-Japanese night song

There is a famous poem by the German writer Goethe, entitled *Nachtgedicht* ('Night Poem'). Roughly translated into English, it goes:

> Above all the mountain peaks
> Is peace.
> In all the treetops
> You can hear
> Hardly a breath of wind.
> The small birds are silent in the forest.
> Just wait, and soon
> You too will be at peace.

In 1902 a Japanese translation of Goethe's poem was published. Nine years later a French writer translated this into his own language, believing it to be an original Japanese poem. And finally, a German editor translated the French version back into German and published it in a magazine under the title *Japanisches Nachtlied* ('Japanese Night Song'). It now went roughly as follows:

> There is silence in the jade pavilion.
> Crows fly noiselessly
> to snow-covered cherry trees in the moonlight.
> I sit
> and weep.

> Dear sir,
>
> I'm writing this letter in a no good english, I cant this no perfect. I must say you very, very thank you very match for the sleeping in your Rooms. We was in the Houst with Mihail in St Germain and have visit Paris by Day and Night. Its was very nice and we have saved us Monay for this reason. Your ought to coming Germany, my house is open for you.

(Thank-you letter from a foreign friend)

7 Do one of these writing tasks. Write at least 150 words.

1. Write a few paragraphs about your experience of learning English (and other languages, if you have learnt any others). Use words and expressions from the Student's Book lesson.
2. Look at Exercise 2 in the Student's Book lesson. Choose one or more of the questions and write a few lines giving your opinion.

B2 Focus on systems

1 Grammar: passives. Complete the sentences using words from the box in the correct forms. You will not need all the words.

| build | completely destroy | construct | convert | enlarge | knock down |
| paint | rebuild | redecorate | sell | turn | visit |

1. The palace .... by Sir Robert Fleming.
2. It .... by fire in 1745.
3. Seven years later, it .... as an exact copy of the original.
4. In the 18th century it had 48 rooms, but it .... in the late 19th century, and now has 112 rooms.
5. In 1976 it .... to Leisuredesign Enterprises Ltd.
6. The house .... into a fun palace, and the gardens .... into a safari park.
7. Leisuredesign Enterprises Ltd. forecast that the palace and gardens .... by over a million people in the year to come.
8. Because of huge numbers of people expected, extra facilities .... at the moment in preparation for the new season.

2 Grammar: passives (continued). Here are some of the notices in the fun palace and safari park. Complete the sentences by putting the verbs in brackets into the passive.

1. Visitors (*allow*) into the house and grounds between 9.00 a.m. and 5.30 p.m.
2. A bell (*ring*) fifteen minutes before closing time.
3. Visitors (*request*) not to feed the animals.
4. People (*advise*) not to leave their cars while touring the safari park.
5. Dogs (*not allow*) in the safari park.
6. You (*ask*) not to touch the furniture.
7. Members of staff (*not permit*) to accept tips.
8. Lunch (*serve*) in the cafeteria from 11.00 to 2.30.

3 Grammar: passives (continued). Use passives to complete the text about a real accident which happened in 1986.

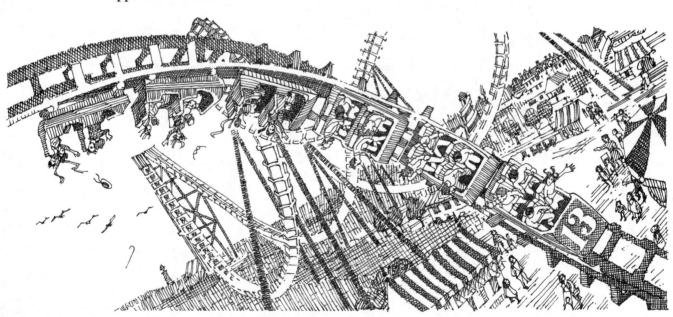

In Denmark, 24 people (1. *leave*) hanging upside down when a roller-coaster car made an unscheduled stop. The passengers (2. *trap*) 60 feet in the air for twenty minutes before they (3. *rescue*) by firemen with ladders. Nobody (4. *seriously hurt*) although five people (5. *take*) to hospital where they (6. *treat*) for shock. An official for the fairground, at Aalborg in western Denmark, said the riders (7. *firmly strap*) in and had not been in danger. 'They (8. *give*) their money back,' the official said. He also promised that the roller coaster (9. *thoroughly check*) in order to find the source of the problem.

4 Grammar: *can* + passive infinitive. How many ways can you find of using the following things? Examples:

A coin can be used as a screwdriver.
A bath can be used to hold drink for a party.

| a bicycle   a bra   a car   a chair |
| an English textbook   a fridge   a glass |
| a lampshade   a sheet   an umbrella |

5 Pronunciation. How many different ways are there to pronounce *-ed* at the end of a verb? Say the following words and try to work out the rules.

| added   boiled   collected   compressed |
| dried   glued   inserted   mixed   packed |
| passed   poured   pumped   pushed |
| removed   roasted   shaped   squeezed |
| striped |

6 Spelling revision: double or single letters? Write the past participles. Examples:

forget – forgotten
trap – **trapped**
wait – waited

| aid   beg   chat   clean   end   help |
| slam   start   stop   tin |

Check the rule on page 144.

7 Read the texts. In each text, two sentences have been added which should not be there. How quickly can you find them?

Instant coffee

When coffee arrives at an instant coffee factory, it has already been roasted and ground. In the factory, water is slowly passed through the coffee. The resulting liquid is then repeatedly pumped through tubes at a very high temperature (671°C) and speed (239 mph). The liquid is boiled, and sugar, salt and a variety of chemicals are carefully added. This makes some of the water evaporate, leaving very strong 'coffee liquor'.

To make instant coffee powder, the coffee liquor is poured through large cylindrical driers at a temperature of 250°C. The heat evaporates the liquid, leaving instant coffee powder which is collected and put into jars.

Granulated coffee is made by freeze-drying. The process is a secret one and is passed from one family of manufacturers to the next. The coffee liquor is rapidly frozen into blocks. After these have been broken up into very small pieces, they are dried in a vacuum. This removes the water without heat, leaving instant coffee granules.

Striped toothpaste

How are the stripes put into striped toothpaste? The toothpaste is not striped when it is put into the tube, as some people imagine. At the factory, red paste and white paste are put into the tube separately, with the red paste completely filling the part near the cap. This has several different effects. A short hollow pipe is also put into the toothpaste tube. When the toothpaste tube is squeezed the white paste is pushed down the inside of the small pipe, while the red paste is pushed into five grooves on the outside. Compressed air is then pumped between the two 'skins' forcing the water out and making it lighter. In this way, strips of red paste are mixed into the white paste as it comes out of the tube.

MARCIE GLICKMAN
85% PIZZA
15% PEPSI

"I'm ten per cent lover, eight per cent poet and two per cent librarian. The rest, I'm afraid, is water."

B3 I'll give you £25 for it

1 Look at the table of statistics about the average Fantasian household and answer the questions as quickly as you can.

Average Fantasian household expenditure 1992		
(Fantasian Grotniks per week)		
Housing	FGr	246.24
Fuel, electricity	FGr	72.48
Food	FGr	217.22
Alcoholic drink	FGr	101.40
Tobacco	FGr	57.93
Recreation, entertainment, education	FGr	130.30
Clothing, footwear	FGr	86.93
Household goods and services	FGr	101.41
Other goods and services	FGr	173.80
Transport and communication	FGr	231.71

1. What did the average Fantasian family spend most on in 1992?
2. Which of the things in the table did they spend least on?
3. True or false? They spent more on alcohol than on heating and electricity.
4. Did they spend more on food than on housing?
5. Did they spend less on clothing than on transport and communication?
6. True or false? They spent nearly twice as much on alcohol as on tobacco.
7. True or false? Alcohol and tobacco together cost more than half as much as housing.

2 EITHER: Comment on the figures in Exercise 1. Does the average Fantasian family spend too much on some things and not enough on others, in your opinion?
OR: Make some sentences about your own expenditure this year, last year and next year. Examples:

This year I've spent a lot of money on ...
    I've spent too much on ...
    I haven't spent much on ...

Last year I spent a lot on ...
    I spent too much on ...
    I didn't spend much on ...

This year I've spent less/more on ... than last year.

Last year I spent less/more on ... than this year.

I must spend less on ... next year.
I can spend more on ... next year.

3 Grammar revision. Put in *too much, too many* or *(not) enough*.

1. We've spent .... on alcohol this month. We *must* drink less whisky.
2. It's not really worth keeping the shop open – we aren't doing .... business.
3. You've really got .... cats – you should give some of them away.
4. I don't even want to read the newspaper any more. It's too depressing: there's .... bad news.
5. I've had .... bad luck in my life; I think it's time for some good luck.
6. I've done .... favours for her; she thinks I should do everything for her now.
7. He tells .... jokes; he should be more serious.
8. Don't worry – there are .... jobs to keep everybody busy.
9. We haven't had .... news about the accident to know whether it's really serious or not.
10. His books are far too serious for me; there's .... humour in them.

"When Daddy tells you how much he's worth, it means that's how much he has. Daddy as such has practically no market value."

4 Grammar revision. Complete the sentences with *too ... to* or *(not) ... enough to*. You can use the words in the box if you like.

calm	depressed	intelligent	old	strong
tall	tired	worried	young	

1. <u>I thought she was too intelligent to</u> make a stupid mistake like that.
2. .... be President / Prime Minister.
3. .... drive a big lorry.
4. .... play football.
5. .... have a lot of children.
6. .... have grandchildren.
7. .... go to a party.
8. .... carry that box.
9. .... be a police officer.
10. .... have a driving licence.
11. .... continue working now.

5 Find Lesson B3, Exercise 1 on the Student's Cassette. Listen to the recording and find twelve things which are different in the dialogue below.

A: How much did you want for it?
B: Forty.
A: Forty pounds?
B: Yeah. It's worth fifty, but I'm in a hurry.
A: I don't know. It isn't in very good condition. Look. It's broken. And look at this. It isn't worth forty. I'll give you twenty-five pounds.
B: Twenty-five? Come on. I tell you what – I'll take thirty-five. Since you're a friend of mine. You can have it for thirty-five.
A: No, that's too much. To tell the truth, I can't afford thirty-five.
B: Sorry. Thirty-five. That's my last word.
A: Come on, split the difference. Thirty pounds.
B: Thirty. OK. All right, thirty.
A: Can I give you a cheque?
B: Well, I prefer cash, if you don't mind.

6 Read the text, using a dictionary if you wish. Then write a few lines saying which suggestion you think is most useful, and why. Do you think any of the suggestions are useless? If so, why? Can you add any suggestions of your own?

Twenty ways of saving money!

1. Save money on holidays by exchanging homes with a foreign family.
2. Learn to do your own simple plumbing and electrical repairs.
3. Knit your own sweaters.
4. Drive smoothly, without sudden stops and starts – it uses less petrol.
5. Don't drive when you can walk.
6. Telephone people at times when you know they're busy – your conversations will be shorter.
7. Put your telephone in an uncomfortable noisy place.
8. Form a group with other people to share the shopping – you won't have to drive to the shops so often, and you'll save money by buying in bulk.
9. Invite people to tea or coffee instead of dinner.
10. Borrow books from the public library instead of buying them.
11. Buy fewer newspapers and magazines – you probably don't read them all anyway.
12. Don't use a dishwasher or washing machine without a full load.
13. Take showers instead of baths.
14. Buy cheap throwaway shoes for rough wear (expensive shoes need expensive mending).
15. Don't send sheets to the laundry – use non-iron sheets and wash them yourself.
16. Be very careful about turning lights off when they are not needed.
17. Eat less meat and more vegetables (cheaper *and* healthier).
18. If you have a garden, grow your own vegetables.
19. Make your own jam and marmalade.
20. Learn to do your own hair.

7 Do one of these writing tasks. Write at least 150 words and try to include some words and expressions from the Student's Book lesson.

1. Why do we have money? What are the advantages and disadvantages of the 'money system'. Can you think of a better system?
2. Think of a time in your life when you had too much, too many, or not enough of something. Write about what happened.
3. Write as many suggestions as possible for either saving water or saving electricity.

"Offer you £50,000 for him ... £60,000 ... £70,000 ... £5,000."

B4 It must be true: it's in the papers

1 Grammar revision. Put in *can, can't, will, would, should, may* or *must*.

1. He .... be drunk – I .... understand a word he's saying.
2. What .... you do if you lose your job?
3. What .... you do if you had to sell your house?
4. We haven't decided where to go on holiday. We .... go to Wales again, but I'm not sure if we .... afford it.
5. I .... write to Dick – I've owed him a letter for months.
6. Excuse me – .... you lend me your pen for a moment?
7. Everybody .... know how to do simple first aid.
8. 'There's somebody at the door. Who .... it be?' 'It .... be Barbara – she's in Scotland.' 'Of course, it .... be Mike. He said he'd call in to collect his shopping.'

2 Complex sentences. Use the structure *Are you sure that it's / it was ...?* to write answers to the sentences, as in the examples.

1. They speak French in Burkina Faso. (*French*)
   <u>Are you sure it's French that they speak in Burkina Faso?</u>
2. He broke into the Queen's bedroom. (*the Queen*)
   <u>Are you sure it was the Queen's bedroom that he broke into?</u>
3. The telephone's ringing. (*the telephone*)
4. Her brother writes for *The Independent*. (*The Independent*)
5. I need another drink. (*another drink*)
6. We decided on Tuesday for the meeting. (*Tuesday*)
7. My husband sent me these flowers for my birthday. (*your husband*)
8. I'm feeling ill – those shrimps have upset me. (*the shrimps*)
9. That girl keeps looking at me. (*you*)
10. Carol's madly in love with Simon. (*Simon*)

30

3 Vocabulary revision and extension. Can you put some or all of the words into groups? Some words will go in more than one group. Can you add any other words to the groups?

armed	back	bend	coast	connect
corner	die	economy	edge	engaged
extension	fight	fork	inflation	
journey	point	recession	recovery	
ring	roundabout	route	sail	set off
ship	side	soldier	stock market	
T-junction	transfer	war	wind	wound

4 Pronunciation. Say all the words in the box and pick out the words where the main stress is on the second syllable. Find one word where the main stress is on the third syllable and one where the main stress is on the fourth.

accent	accuse	apologise	arrest
certain	concrete	considerably	
consonant	culture	currency	difference
disaster	disturbance	domestic	electricity
enable	foreigner	frighten	imitate
insist	interview	manager	opinion
popular	previous	pronunciation	vowel

5 Read the story carefully and decide where the numbered phrases should be added. The first one has been done for you.

Julie is the kind of person who believes in anything.⁷⋀ She believes in reincarnation, telepathy, witches, black magic, white magic, and all of the world's religions. She doesn't need evidence for her beliefs. I sometimes have the impression that Julie still believes in Father Christmas. For some reason or other, she just has to believe in the supernatural.

Julie lives in an old house in the country. I go and stay with her sometimes, and I must say I have trouble getting to sleep. It sounds to me as if there's something wrong with the central heating. She's sure that it's ghosts that make the noises, and she walks round the house for hours at night.

Julie is saving up money to go to Egypt. According to her, it's obvious that they were built by refugees from the moon, and she's planning to write a book. Either that, or she's going to organise an expedition to Central Africa to prove that dinosaurs are still alive. She hasn't quite decided which yet, but she has an astrologer friend who is making a detailed horoscope for her.

1. – it's just obvious to her that they're true
2. because of all the noises that you get in an old house
3. , but that doesn't satisfy Julie
4. , and that should help her to make up her mind
5. at the same time
6. hoping to see one
7. Anything at all.
8. and study the pyramids
9. – and she's 34 years old
10. to prove it

6 Do one of these writing tasks. Write at least 150 words and try to include some words and expressions from the Student's Book lesson.

1. Write about the things you believe in (or don't believe in), giving your reasons. (Look again at Exercise 5 for ideas, if you wish.)
2. Do you believe what you read in the newspapers / hear on the radio / see on the television? Give your reasons.

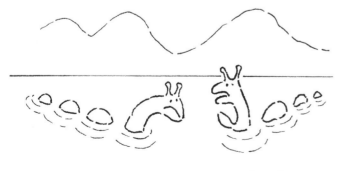

"Look, you've got to believe in yourself."

7 Read at least six of the following newspaper articles, using a dictionary if you wish. Write down how you feel about each one (e.g. *amazed, amused, disgusted, shocked, surprised.*)

A man, alleged to have been caught stealing six chickens from a butcher's shop, was said to have told the police: 'I was taking them home to throw at the wife. We've had a row.'

(from *The News of the World*)

I'll never forget my first kiss. I was 65 at the time and was having a snooze on the Fish Hoek beach when I got kissed. I looked up and saw a large dog running away.

(from *Cape Times Weekend Magazine*)

'Nothing annoys me more than finding a few stray maggots under the grill when I am about to do the toast for breakfast,' says Mrs V.M. Hart of West Drayton, whose husband is a keen fisherman.

Mr Hart, according to his wife, likes to keep a tin of maggots handy in the refrigerator. This, she says, is bad enough, but sometimes when the cold has made them lethargic, he warms them up under the grill.

(from *The Daily Telegraph*)

BEFORE going to sleep at night I read in bed for twenty minutes. During that time I warm my feet by breathing *in* through my nose and *out* through a length of rubber tubing reaching from my mouth to my feet. Within five minutes I am glowing with heat.

(from *The Daily Mail*)

A man I know locks up his alarm clock in a tin medicine chest (for extra noise) every night before retiring. To reach the key to open the chest to turn off the alarm he has to plunge his arm into a deep jug full of icy water where he dropped the key the night before. This is the only way he knows to be certain of waking up.

(from *The Sunday Graphic*)

In Oklahoma, 54-year-old Charlie Smith was driving steadily enough and at a moderate pace when police stopped him – because there was a horse sitting in the back seat of his car.

He explained: 'The poor old thing was looking so bored out there in the country I thought I'd bring him to town.' He was charged with being drunk while in control of a car and with stealing a horse.

(from *Weekend*)

A woman who had a passport picture taken in a 'While-you-wait' photographer's in the West End was told to call back next day for the print.

She said she wanted to wait for it. The reply was: 'We only take the photograph while you wait.'

(from *The Evening Standard*)

AN ELDERLY German decided to commit suicide, took a lot of sleeping pills, tied a briefcase full of stones around his neck, rowed out to the middle of the Rhine – and was found sound asleep in his boat.

(from *The Buffalo News*)

U.S. AIR FORCE General Don Flickinger said last night that all chimpanzees used in space flights would be volunteers. He was asked how chimpanzees could volunteer. He replied: 'We hold an apple in one hand and a banana in the other. If they choose the banana, they are judged to have volunteered. They almost always choose the banana.'

(from *The Daily Express*)

Bologna, December 13. Umberto Montanari was unable to get rid of a mouse which chewed holes in his car's carpet, so he put a pot of water inside the vehicle and dropped a block of carbide into it. The method succeeded. An explosion destroyed the mouse – and the car.

(from Reuter)

Moinesti, Romania, Wednesday. Mourners of the burial of Ann Bochinsky were astonished to see the 'dead' woman jump out of her coffin while it was being carried with the lid open – as is the custom in Romania – from the cemetery to the grave.

She ran into the road and was run over and killed by a motor-car.

(from *The Daily Express*)

The other morning you reported that a small quantity of washing powder put in a duckpond would make all the ducks sink to the bottom.

My neighbour's little boy put a whole packet in, but the ducks still went on swimming. It makes you wonder if you can believe everything you read in the newspapers.

(Letter in *The Birmingham Gazette*)

B5 Work

1 Vocabulary revision. Write descriptions for these jobs.

1. a pianist
   a person who plays the piano
2. a barmaid or barman
   a person who works in a bar
3. a violinist
4. a bus driver
5. a forester
6. a broadcaster
7. an actor or actress
8. a journalist
9. an (air) steward or stewardess
10. a housewife
11. a policeman or policewoman
12. an electrician
13. a carpenter
14. a writer
15. a gardener

2 Grammar revision. Make follow-up questions.

1. Alison's two sisters work for a bank. (*Which?*)
   Which bank do they work for?
2. Jill couldn't come to the party. (*Why?*)
3. Angela looks like her mother's father. (*Who, brother?*)
4. Tony does the ironing before breakfast. (*When, cleaning?*)
5. They usually have their lunch in the kitchen. (*Where, dinner?*)
6. The director of the car factory goes to work in a Rolls-Royce. (*How, employees?*)
7. My mother enjoys working outdoors. (*What, do?*)
8. Mrs Jackson teaches my son French. (*Who, German?*)

3 Grammar revision. Disagree.

1. Our cat likes meat. (*fish*)
   No, it doesn't. It likes fish.
2. People here usually finish work at 5 o'clock. (*5.30*)
3. It rains a lot in northern Sudan. (*hardly ever*)
4. There was a phone call for you. (*Sarah*)
5. Alice looks like her mother. (*father*)
6. You need to rest. (*feel fine*)
7. Deborah's a housewife. (*dentist*)
8. Eric can speak Spanish. (*Italian*)
9. Fiona's got light brown hair. (*dark brown*)
10. Most people of 60 look really old. (*My father*)

4 Translate these into your language.

1. A school in Chester has been destroyed by fire. The fire started in the school's kitchen.
2. Although Niamh has lived in England for 30 years, she's still got a strong Irish accent.
3. According to the weather forecast it's going to snow tomorrow. I hate snow.
4. This picture was painted by a friend of mine.
5. Bread is made with flour which is made from wheat.
6. Angela was given a sports car by her parents for her 21st birthday.
7. The result of the election is being announced at this moment.
8. I've never been asked to do anything like this before.
9. 'How much do you want for it?' 'I'll take £30.'
10. What do you call a person who designs homes?
11. Would you rather work indoors or outdoors?
12. When he's drunk, he does things which he would never do when he is sober.

5 Mark the main stresses. Then find Lesson B5, Exercise 1 on the Student's Cassette and check your answers with the recording. Say the sentences with the correct stresses.

KEITH: I would like to work in a museum.
JOHN: I think I'd love to own me own gardening centre. I'd love that. Yeah. I'd really like that.
SUE: I'd like to be a really good potter. Be on my own.
JANE: I'd like to be really good at something – anything!
ALEX: Actually with the job I've chosen, the police force, I'd like to go into dog handling in that. That's what I *would* like.
KATY: I think I'd just like to teach again.
MIKE: What I'd really like to spend my time doing isn't really classed as jobs.

"I warn you, Smedley, these blasted daydreams have to stop!"

6 Read at least two of these texts, using a dictionary if you wish.

WHAT IS HE?

What is he?
— A man, of course.
Yes, but what does he do?
— He lives and is a man.
Oh quite! but he must work. He must have a job of some sort.
— Why?
Because obviously he's not one of the leisured classes.
— I don't know. He has lots of leisure. And he makes quite beautiful chairs.
There you are then! He's a cabinet maker.
— No, no!
Anyhow a carpenter and joiner.
— Not at all.
But you said so.
— What did I say?
That he made chairs, and was a joiner and carpenter.
— I said he made chairs, but I did not say he was a carpenter.
All right then, he's just an amateur.
— Perhaps! Would you say a thrush was a professional flautist, or just an amateur?
I'd say it was just a bird.
— And I say he is just a man.
All right! You always did quibble.

(D.H. Lawrence)

Letter to the Editor

MADAM, – You have had a lot of letters about working people being unco-operative. You have not had any that I have seen about why people like me are unco-operative.

I read your paper in the public library – I can't afford to purchase it every day. It is the same for a lot of ordinary working people like me. So you don't get much of what we think.

I am 50 years of age. I started work at 15 years of age. I will work, if I am lucky, until I am 65 years of age. I might live to 70, but I will be lucky if I can work to 70 because, even if I am able and willing, the bosses don't want us. So I shall have the old-age pension. I have not been able to save. In all my working life the money I have got will amount to about £160,000. That is the highest it could be.

I saw in your paper that the Chairman of Bowring's Insurance gets £157,000 a year. And of course he gets a free car, free drinks, trips abroad with his wife, etc. He gets in a year as much as I get in all my working life. The differential is a bit wrong somewhere. Or what about your reports about wills? Often you see someone, a stockbroker, for example, leaving £500,000. That is his savings, not what he lived on. It would take me 500 years to earn that little lot. Something wrong with the differential there too.

I am not a communist or an anarchist. I believe there must be differentials. But the trouble is the differentials are all wrong, and there's too much fiddling at the top.

We know the papers and the telly and radio give one side of the story. We know the other. You don't. Or you don't want to. So there will be a fight. We might lose a round or two. But we will win in the end. And if we have to fight to win instead of being sensible on both sides, the losers are going to suffer a lot.

You can call this unco-operative. Try bringing up three kids on my pay and see how you like it. There's plenty for everybody if it's shared reasonably. And if, as my mate says, we want to try and have the bridge and beaujolais as well as beer and bingo, what's wrong with that?

Yours faithfully,
JAMES THOMSON

telly: TV   *kids*: children   *beaujolais*: a kind of (expensive) wine

Are you a work addict?

If you're addicted to alcohol or other drugs, it's bad for you: we know that. But what about being addicted to your job?

Being a workaholic can lead to mental and physical health problems and wreck marriages, families and friendships. Anyone can be a workaholic: lawyer, librarian, lorry driver ... it doesn't matter what your job is. These are the tell-tale signs that show you may be overdoing it:

• Do you wake up thinking about work?
• Do you find it hard to relax and switch off from the job?
• Have you given up other hobbies and pastimes because of work demands?
• Do you resent taking holidays and consider leisure time wasteful?
• Do you refuse to turn down work even when you're already busy?
• Do you regularly take work home with you after office hours?
• Are you constantly edgy and irritable, even when at home?
• Does work take up so much time that you rarely see your friends and family?

According to Cary Cooper, Professor of Organisational Psychology at the University of Manchester Institute of Science and Technology, if you answer yes to up to three of these questions, it shows you have a normal healthy enthusiasm for work; four to six indicates that you are a moderate workaholic, on the road to becoming an addict. 'Anybody who ticked seven or eight,' says Professor Cooper, 'needs to re-examine their lifestyle: he or she is an extreme workaholic – and probably doesn't realise it.'

(from *The Radio Times*)

7 Write two or three paragraphs about how you spend your day. Try to include some words and expressions from the Student's Book lesson.

B6 Focus on systems

1 Grammar. At the moment you are probably spending a lot of your time studying English. What could you have decided to do with the same time instead? Write at least five sentences, using the structure *I could have ...* + past participle. Examples:

I could have studied mathematics.
I could have built a boat.

2 Grammar. You probably didn't do everything that you should have done last weekend, last week, last year or at some time in your past life. There are probably also things you shouldn't have done, but did. Write at least five sentences about things that you should or shouldn't have done, using the structure *I should(n't) have ...* + past participle. Examples:

I should have cleaned the car on Sunday.
I shouldn't have started smoking when I was a teenager.

3 Vocabulary. Match the words and the facial expressions.

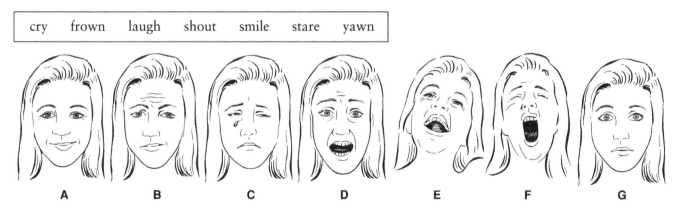

4 Vocabulary. Match the words and the faces.

5 Pronunciation: stress. Look again at the adjectives in Exercise 8 in the Student's Book. *Affectionate* is stressed on the second syllable. Find other words in the list which are stressed on the second syllable. Can you find any that have the main stress on the third syllable? Practise saying the words.

6 Read both of these texts, using a dictionary if you wish.

REVEALING FACES

The shape of your face can give a clue to your personality. What does yours say about you?

HEART-SHAPED
Practical rather than a thinker, you have a degree of charm that can be devastating. Your romantic judgement can sometimes let you down, though. You appear placid and cool in most situations, but this hides a quick temper when crossed. Relationships may suffer if your partner can't live up to your high expectations.

SMALL FACE
You don't enjoy people intruding into your personal life and invading your privacy and can be rather secretive. Reflective and intelligent, yours is a passionate but firm personality, although you find these two traits in conflict at times. A tendency to be cautious means you don't trust too easily, but you do value a circle of close friends and family members.

SQUARE FACE
You expect a lot from other people, but give as much in return. You're stubborn, strong-willed and quick to learn, but your staying power runs out when you lose interest. Highly sensitive to criticism, you're aggressive under pressure.

BROAD FACE
A strong sense of your own importance means you like to be taken seriously by friends. You can be kind and sympathetic, but won't waste it on those you feel don't deserve it. Affectionate and loving rather than passionate, yours is an energetic and intelligent nature with optimism high on your list of the important things in life.

OVAL FACE
A good decision-maker, you have strength of character, lots of energy, and usually finish what you start. Affectionate and outgoing by nature, you can be a bit gullible.

THIN FACE
You don't suffer fools gladly and have an offbeat sense of humour. Energetic but able to balance action with thought, you're not one who follows the crowd. You enjoy competition in the love stakes and opt for a partner who's companionable as well as attractive.

staying power: ability to keep going at something

ROUND FACE
Short and round shows you're slightly erratic and romantic. You're positive about your own aims, generous and an excellent host with close friends. You prefer mental activity to physical and there's a lazy streak that comes out now and then if you don't check yourself.

(Patricia Marne, *Bella* – adapted)

Reflecting upon love

ZACH turned to face the person he knew was there, waiting for him. Slowly, he stood and walked towards the beautiful face, smiling. Their lips brushed, he delighted in the smooth, cold response from those familiar lips, which he knew and loved so well.

Eventually Zach drew away, sighing ... It was always the same. This silent but beautiful, responding figure, whom he loved so much, could never be with him for long, their relationship could never go any further, it was impossible, people would not accept them ...

Zach turned reluctantly away from the mirror and went back to his desk.

(Charity Spain, aged 18, *The Guardian*)

7 Do one of these writing tasks. Write at least 150 words.

1. Write a careful description of yourself or somebody you know well. Describe both appearance and personality. Before you start writing, look back at the Student's Book lesson.

2. Make up a story which includes the structure *If ... had(n't) ..., ... would(n't) have ...* at least three times. Use two of the pictures in each of the *If* sentences.

B7 The Lonely One

1 Grammar and vocabulary. Put a word from the box into each blank. You may have to change verb tenses or make plurals; some words may be used more than once.

| around | dangerous | drugstore | lean | lonely | maybe | promise |
| purse | single | strange | stranger | terrify | waste | |

I had a really ...1... experience the other night. It was about 10.30, ...2... 11 o'clock; I had a headache, and there were no aspirins in the house, so I decided to walk down to Abel's, the all-night ...3... on Montrose Boulevard. My brother says I shouldn't walk by myself after dark, that it's ...4..., but I'm careful and don't take any unnecessary chances. I keep my money in a pocket, not in a ...5...; I carry my keys in such a way as to be able to hurt somebody with them if necessary; I walk briskly and confidently. Anyway, Abel's is only ...6... the corner from my apartment. I refuse to let myself be ...7... into staying inside the house after dark just because I'm a ...8... woman.

Well, anyway, when I walked out of the apartment building I noticed a ...9... ...10... against a parked car about 30 feet down the street, in the opposite direction from where I was going – kind of odd, but I didn't ...11... any time worrying about it. I went to the ...12... and got the aspirins, and spent a little time talking to Juanita behind the counter. She gets pretty ...13... here so far from her family; and working the night shift doesn't help, as far as meeting people socially goes.

After I made Juanita ...14... to come by for lunch whenever she felt like it, I headed for home and a good book. Little did I suspect that I wasn't going to get much reading done that night.

As I turned to go up the steps to my apartment house, I noticed something moving on the ground where the ...15... had been standing before. I carefully went a little closer, and realised that it was the ...16... – minus quite a bit of blood. I tore his shirt for bandages to stop the worst of the bleeding, ran home to call an ambulance and the police, and then came back outside to keep him company. He said something about Milton or Melton, and something else that I didn't understand, again and again until the ambulance came.

37

2 Grammar revision. Put one of the prepositions from the box into each blank. (You will not need to use all the prepositions.)

around	down	into	off	onto
out of	over	through	towards	up

1. Drive .... Cirencester, but turn off before you get there: watch for the sign that says 'Upton' and 'The Lamberts', to the left.
2. Let's just climb .... the wall – otherwise we'll have to walk miles.
3. I'm always a bit afraid of falling .... these stairs – they're really not very safe.
4. You can see .... the hedge now, but in the summer it makes a solid green wall.
5. Everyone else in the compartment got .... the train at Dundee, so I was alone for the last part of the journey.
6. We carried our cameras and binoculars all the way .... the mountain, and then it was so misty we couldn't see a thing.
7. You remember I was telling you about my old school friend Chris last week? Well, I saw him walk .... one of the buildings across the street from my office today! He noticed me at the same time and crossed the street to say hello.
8. It will be easier to sweep and mop in here if we put the chairs .... the tables first.
9. I didn't know which door she would be coming out of, so I walked .... the building several times.

3 Grammar revision. Here are some sentences from the story in the Student's Book. Can you choose the correct verb form in each sentence? Give a grammar rule for each sentence or group of sentences.

1. Maybe we shouldn't *go / to go* to the show tonight.
2. The Lonely One might *follow / to follow* us and *kill / to kill* us.
3. Logically, the Lonely One can't *be / to be* around.
4. *To think / Thinking* about the Lonely One terrified Francine.
5. Francine wanted Lavinia *spend / to spend* the night with her.
6. Lavinia told Francine not *be / to be* silly.
7. The police asked the cinema manager *close / to close* early that night.
8. Lavinia laughed at Francine for *to be / being* so afraid.
9. Lavinia couldn't get home from Main Street without *to cross / crossing* the ravine.
10. Before they went to the cinema, the three women stopped at the drugstore to get something *eat / to eat / eating*.
11. Helen didn't have anything *drink / to drink / drinking* at the drugstore.
12. There was no one *walk / to walk* Lavinia home.

4 Where are the stresses? Underline the stressed syllables. Sometimes more than one answer may be correct.

The first time it ever happened to me was in Borneo, when I was diving off a reef for shells. I was working up there for an oil company for six weeks once, and I used to dive off a reef from a shallow boat. And once I went so far from the boat – I was enjoying myself so much I wasn't looking where I was going, and I suddenly looked down. The reef that I'd been diving on just dropped away completely, and I couldn't see the bottom, and I panicked.

5 📼 Find Lesson B7, Exercise 2 on the Student's Cassette. Listen and answer the questions (one question about each section of the recording).

1. How did the Lonely One's victims die?
2. Why did Francine call the druggist a fool?
3. Why wasn't Lavinia worried about the Lonely One?
4. What did Francine suggest to Lavinia and Helen?
5. What was Helen's theory about Lavinia?

"Not to worry, Sir, most people get a little nervous the first time they crash."

6 Read the quotations and at least one of the other two texts, using a dictionary if you wish.

> To fear love is to fear life, and those who fear life are already three parts dead. (Bertrand Russell)

> And I will show you something different from either
> Your shadow at morning striding behind you,
> Or your shadow at evening rising to meet you
> I will show you fear in a handful of dust. (T.S. Eliot)

> Let us begin anew – remembering on both sides that civility is not a sign of weakness, and sincerity is always subject to proof. Let us never negotiate out of fear. But let us never fear to negotiate. (John F. Kennedy)

> Men fear death as children fear to go in the dark; and as that natural fear in children is increased with tales, so is the other. (Francis Bacon)

> Alas! the love of women! it is known
> To be a lovely and a fearful thing! (Lord Byron)

> Fear is the main source of superstition, and one of the main sources of cruelty. To conquer fear is the beginning of wisdom, in the pursuit of truth as in the endeavour after a worthy manner of life. (Bertrand Russell)

> You may take the most gallant sailor, the most intrepid airman, or the most audacious soldier, put them at a table together – what do you get? The sum of their fears. (Winston Churchill)

> The only thing we have to fear is fear itself. (Franklin D. Roosevelt)

> In the future days, which we seek to make secure, we look forward to a world founded upon four essential human freedoms.
> The first is freedom of speech and expression – everywhere in the world.
> The second is freedom of every person to worship God in his own way – everywhere in the world.
> The third is freedom from want.
> And the fourth is freedom from fear. (Franklin D. Roosevelt)

> Cowards die many times before their deaths;
> The valiant never taste of death but once.
> Of all the wonders that I yet have heard
> It seems to me most strange that men should fear;
> Seeing that death, a necessary end,
> Will come when it will come. (from *Julius Caesar* by Shakespeare)

> Through the Jungle very softly flits a shadow and a sigh –
> He is Fear, O Little Hunter, he is Fear! (Rudyard Kipling)

> It is a miserable state of mind to have few things to desire and many things to fear. (Francis Bacon)

> As for me, I see no such great cause why I should either be fond to live or fear to die. I have had good experience of this world, and I know what it is to be a subject and what to be a sovereign. Good neighbours I have had, and I have met with bad: and in trust I have found treason. (Queen Elizabeth I)

The Mystery Phobia

Jane Bruff was a 37-year-old married English woman who kept a fruitshop. Quite out of the blue she began to suffer 'attacks' of very rapid heartbeat which made her feel alarmed and panicky. She was able to put up with these funny turns at home, but when she began to get them in the street, she really began to worry. Eventually the fear of having an attack in public forced her to take a taxi even for the two-hundred-yard trip down the street to her fruitshop. If possible she preferred to stay indoors, and she became very anxious at the thought of having to step too far outside the familiar safety of her home.

Jane had not kept her suffering to herself; she had consulted her GP and a heart specialist. She was prescribed Sotalol, a drug used to correct abnormalities of the heart, but it did her no good.

Her persistent distress, combined with the fact that she showed no sign of having an identifiable organic problem, only succeeded in getting her labelled as a 'problem patient'. Her specialist eventually told her there was nothing wrong with her heart and took her off the Sotalol.

Fortunately for Jane, a hospital consultant in her area had recently taken an interest in food allergy and had decided to test whether or not it was a genuine disease. He had talked about it to his colleagues, and Jane was referred to his clinic. He found out that Jane was a 'tea fiend', drinking a dozen or more cups of tea a day. He tested her on several different occasions by putting a plastic tube down her throat (so she could not taste what was going into her stomach), and poured either coffee, tea, or water down it from an opaque syringe (so Jane could not see what was going into the tube). Every time tea or coffee was tested, after two and a half hours, Jane's heartbeat suddenly shot up from the regular normal 70 beats a minute to 250 beats, an alarming rate, which brought back her old feeling of panic.

Jane was asked to give up coffee and tea. It worked; within a very short time she had lost all her symptoms, was happy to walk down the street, and had returned to her job and a normal social life.

out of the blue: unexpectedly
funny turns: unexpected, mysterious, short attacks of illness
GP: (general practitioner) a doctor who treats all types of illness

(from *Eating and Allergy* by Robert Eagle – adapted)

FEAR IS NECESSARY

Not only is fear a very normal emotion, but it is also an essential emotion. To be totally without fear is to be in serious danger. Fear is an essential defence mechanism.

Fear is made up of an emotional feeling and a number of bodily changes. If we come face to face with a man wildly waving a hatchet we are likely to experience the emotion we describe as fear, and at the same time our hearts will start to race, our breathing will accelerate, and we may turn pale and sweat. We may experience an unpleasant sinking sensation in the stomach, weakness of the muscles, and trembling of the limbs. We may have a desire to micturate, defecate, or vomit, and may in fact carry out some of these functions. These physical changes have been described as the 'fight or flight phenomenon', and they are the body's preparation for either of these actions. An increased heart rate pumps more blood to the muscles, so they are ready for action. An increase in breathing ensures that more oxygen is available for the same use. Sweating makes it more difficult for us to be grabbed, while making our hair stand up would be protective if we were still well covered with hair. For human beings getting our hair erect is rather a waste of time, as unfortunately are other body changes that have been described. Weakness of the muscles and shaking is not much use for either fight or flight and neither are vomiting, defecating, or micturating. It appears that for one reason or another the body's mechanism to deal with emergencies sometimes goes wrong; and this is not confined to human beings. Other animals also become paralysed with fear and actually die from it.

(from *Fears and Phobias* by Dr Tony Whitehead – adapted)

7 Write at least 150 words about one of the following subjects. Use some words and expressions from the Student's Book lesson as well as material from the texts in Exercise 6.

1. Write about a time in your life when you were very frightened – either as a child or as an adult.
2. Do you know anyone who is very afraid of something, like spiders or heights? Describe the fear, how it makes the person feel and act, and what he or she has tried to do about it.
3. Write some advice for a person who is afraid of small closed spaces, or speaking in public, or aeroplanes.

B8 My heart is too full for words

1 Grammar revision: reported speech. What did they say?

SHE: Have you seen the new film at the Odeon?
She asked him if he'd seen the new film at the Odeon.
HE: It's terrible.
He said it was terrible.
SHE: What's so bad about it?
HE: My five-year-old daughter can write better dialogue.
SHE: Is there anything else on that you're interested in?
HE: There's the new Greenaway film at the Regent.
SHE: What time is it on?
HE: 7.15; do you want to go?
SHE: How long does it last?
HE: It's over at half past nine. We'll make it if we hurry.
SHE: Have we got to take a bus?
HE: No, we can walk.
SHE: OK, I've heard it's good. I can't stay out too late though.
HE: You're walking a bit fast for me.
SHE: Sorry. It's my job that makes me do that.
HE: Are you going to get that promotion you put in for?
SHE: I don't know yet.

2 Grammar and vocabulary. Put in *say, says, said, saying, tell, tells, told* or *telling*. (You may not need to use all of them.) If you have trouble, you can consult the rule on page 144.

1. 'Where's Alan? He .... he'd be here at six.'
2. 'Did he? He .... me he'd be here at half past.'
3. 'Typical. He never .... the same thing twice.'
4. 'The other day he .... Debbie that he was moving to London.'
5. 'And then he .... John he'd got a job in New York.'
6. 'Working in a news agency, he .... me.'
7. 'Jane .... he .... her he was going to Australia.'
8. 'Do you know what he .... to me last week?'
9. 'No, I can't imagine. Do .... me.'
10. 'He only .... me his uncle had died and left him three million dollars.'
11. 'That would be nice. He .... he was going to marry me.'
12. 'Well, I'll .... one thing for him – he keeps you interested. So where is he?'
13. 'I'd .... he's either in Australia, or on a plane to New York, or still in bed, or .... somebody else he's going to marry her.'

3 Grammar revision. In this dialogue, B is a rich banker who has been kidnapped by T, a mad terrorist. B is afraid of being killed, and agrees with everything T says. Write B's answers.

T: I don't like spinach.
B: Nor/Neither do I.
T: I like cauliflower, though.
B: So do I.
T: I can't stand people who wear rings on their little fingers.
B: ......1......
T: I had a cousin who wore a ring on her little finger.
B: ......2......
T: I've got a lot of admiration for rattlesnakes.
B: ......3......
T: I haven't got any idea why people think rattlesnakes are ugly.
B: ......4......
T: I can understand being a little scared of them, though.
B: ......5......
T: I'm not scared of them, though.
B: ......6......
T: When I was younger I didn't like school.
B: ......7......
T: I'm not in favour of making kids go to school.
B: ......8......
T: I wouldn't make one of my kids go to school.
B: ......9......
T: I think schools are at the bottom of everything that's wrong with our society.
B: ......10......

"It was a dark and stormy night..."

"I would be happy to marry you for money," she sighed...

4 Read the text and answer the questions.

THE PRISON CELL

The cell door slammed behind Rubashov.

He remained leaning against the door for a few seconds, and lit a cigarette. On the bed to his right lay two fairly clean blankets, and the straw mattress looked newly filled. The washbasin to his left had no plug, but the tap functioned. The pail next to it had been freshly disinfected, it did not smell. The walls on both sides were of solid brick, which would stifle the sound of tapping, but where the heating and drain pipe penetrated it, it had been plastered and resounded quite well; besides, the heating pipe itself seemed to be noise-conducting. The window started at eye-level; one could see down into the courtyard without having to pull oneself up by the bars. So far everything was in order.

He yawned, took his coat off, rolled it up and put it on the mattress as a pillow. He looked out into the yard. The snow shimmered yellow in the double light of the moon and the electric lanterns. All round the yard, along the walls, a narrow track had been cleared for the daily exercise. Dawn had not yet appeared; the stars still shone clear and frostily, in spite of the lamps. On the rampart of the outside wall, which lay opposite Rubashov's cell, a soldier with slanted rifle was marching the hundred steps up and down; he stamped at every step as if on parade. From time to time the yellow light of the lamps flashed on his bayonet.

Rubashov took his shoes off, still standing at the window. He put out his cigarette, laid the stub on the floor at the end of his bedstead, and remained sitting on the mattress for a few minutes. He went back to the window once more. The courtyard was still; the sentry was just turning; above the machine-gun tower he saw a streak of the Milky Way.

Rubashov stretched himself on the bunk and wrapped himself in the top blanket. It was five o'clock and it was unlikely that one had to get up here before seven in winter. He was very sleepy and, thinking it over, decided that he would hardly be brought up for examination for another three or four days. He took his pince-nez off, laid it on the stone-paved floor next to the cigarette stub, smiled and shut his eyes. He was warmly wrapped up in the blanket, and felt protected; for the first time in months he was not afraid of his dreams.

When a few minutes later the warder turned the light off from outside, and looked through the spy-hole into his cell, Rubashov, ex-Commissar of the People, slept, his back turned to the wall, with his head on his outstretched left arm, which stuck stiffly out of the bed; only the hand on the end of it hung loosely and twitched in his sleep.

(from *Darkness at Noon* by Arthur Koestler – adapted)

1. Do you think Rubashov has been in prison before? Give reasons for your answer.
2. Why do you think the 'sound of tapping' is mentioned?
3. What do you think the 'daily exercise' consists of?
4. What do you think Rubashov has been dreaming about for the past few months?
5. What country do you think the story takes place in?

5 Read the letter, using a dictionary if necessary.

17 Harlow Road
East Muirhead
Edinburgh EH6 7BK

18 January, 1993

Dear Alice,

Thanks a lot for your letter. It was good to hear from you and to get all your news. I was sorry to hear about Jeremy, but in any case I'm glad the kids are doing so well.

I was interested to hear about your plan for a book about people's earliest memories. You're certainly welcome to mine — I hope you can use it.

I must have been two at the time — certainly no older than two and a half, because we still lived by the sea. I was playing by the big window in our front room, where I used to sit on wet days looking at the rain on the window and listening to the sea crashing on the beach. That window was very important to me — I can remember not only the way it looked, but also the feel of the window-pane against my face, and even the taste of the glass — you know how children like to touch everything with their mouths. Well, while I was playing I heard a noise outside in the street — people shouting, something like that. So I ran over to the window and looked out. And there was a fight going on in the street. Two men were hitting each other, and a lot of women and children were watching them and shouting. Then one of the men fell over and the other man ran away. It looked a bit like my Daddy, but I wasn't sure. I don't know whether I asked him afterwards or not. I felt strange about it. I was neither frightened nor excited, but it must have affected me quite deeply, because I still remember it very vividly, as if it had happened yesterday. And I have very few other memories from that time. Even now, if I see the sea through a window it reminds me of that strange fight.

Love to Andy and Phil. And good luck with the book.

Love,

Eve

6 Write a letter, using the following 'skeleton' as a basis. Imagine an English-speaking friend to write to if you don't have a real one. You can change the order of words, and make any other changes you need to, but you must use plenty of the words and expressions in the skeleton.

ADDRESS
DATE

Dear ....,

Thanks a lot for your letter. It was good to hear from you and to get all your news. I was sorry to hear about ...., but in any case I'm glad ....

I was interested to hear about your plan for a book about people's earliest memories. You're certainly welcome to mine – I hope you can use it.

I must have been .... at the time – certainly no older than ...., because ....
I was ....ing ...., where .... That .... was very important to me – I can remember not only ...., but also ....
Well, while I was ....ing, I .... a ....
So I .... and ....
And there was a ....
Then .... and ....
I was neither .... nor ...., but it must have affected me quite deeply, because I still remember it very vividly, as if it had happened yesterday. Even now, if I see ...., it reminds me of ....

Love to .... and .... And good luck with the book.

Love,

YOUR NAME

7 Try the crossword.

ACROSS

1. Not a vowel.
6. The centre of your feelings?
10. Do you get .... well with your parents?
11. .... to date.
12. My garage is .... the side of my house.
13. Not calm.
14. .... quickly .... possible.
15. Not dishonest.
17. .... soon .... I saw her, I knew she was the one for me.
18. I've .... out of milk. Would you like lemon in your tea?
21. This sounds like the letter 'o'.
22. You do this with a knife.
23. 'Shall I get your coat?' is an example of an ....
25. The opposite of *generous*.
27. .... tell you the truth, I just don't know.
28. Is her baby a girl .... a boy?
29. This is usually full of teeth.
30. In a town or in the country – where would you .... live?
32. The short form for *Street*.
34. Not polite.
36. The Simple Present of *was*.
38. £45. That's my last ....
39. Give money to someone for doing a job.
40. Vegetarians don't eat this.
41. A piece of paper which helps you find a place you want to get to.
43. Turn this on and water comes out.
44. It's not .... very good condition.
45. Let's .... the difference.
46. He looks very similar .... his brother.
48. She's so ....-going – she doesn't worry about anything.
51. Not 19 *down*.
53. 'Who's that?' 'Don't worry – it's only ....'
54. This person works with doctors in looking after sick people in a hospital.
55. Finished.

DOWN

1. A kind of building material.
2. Half of two.
3. You can do this with money and time.
4. Someone who has written a book.
5. I can't hear very well – could you .... the TV up, please?
7. The sun rises here.
8. He's not very good .... organising himself.
9. Belief in someone's honesty and goodness.
14. Not proud of something.
16. ...., very well.
17. A German-speaking country in the centre of Europe.
19. What you say when you don't want something.
20. I'm .... she's busy at the moment.
24. She's been learning Turkish .... five years.
25. You might do this if you really loved someone.
26. This sounds like *know*.
31. The very top of your leg.
32. A kind of bird, usually white, with large, powerful wings and a long neck.
33. Your keys are on .... of the fridge.
35. Take everything out of.
37. Another word for *hit*.
41. Yes, I know Tom – he's a good friend of ....
42. Not healthy.
43. According .... the government, unemployment is going down.
45. Not very self-confident.
47. This sounds like the letter 'i'.
49. I'll be back in half .... hour.
50. Is it the first .... the second road on the left?
52. She was tired .... she went to bed early.
53. ...., Mrs, Ms or Miss?

(*Solution on page 144.*)

C1 It makes me want to scream

1 Grammar. Look at the examples to check how *let* and *make* are used. Examples:

She lets us do anything we like.
My parents never made me help with the housework.

Now write:

a. what your parents let you do when you were small.
b. what your parents made you do when you were small.
c. what you will let (would let / let) your children do.
d. what you will make (made / make / would make) your children do.

2 Make sentences with *let*.

1. I felt like crying. I didn't stop myself.
   I let myself cry.
2. Liz wants to go on the school skiing holiday, but her parents say it's too expensive.
   Liz's parents aren't going to let her go on the school skiing holiday.
3. Janet wanted to leave work early. Her boss said it was OK.
4. John asked his dad if he could go to the disco, and his dad agreed.
5. Julie's hair is growing long, and she's not going to cut it.
6. My brother makes his children go to bed at eight o'clock except on Friday and Saturday. Then they stay up late.
7. No one ever knows how Dunstan is feeling; he would rather keep his emotions to himself.
8. Ruth wanted to borrow Kate's car, and Kate said she could.
9. The fire went out because we didn't put any more wood on it.
10. Joan says to her children: 'You can wear anything you want as long as it's clean and comfortable.'

3 Vocabulary revision. Put one of the words from the box in each blank.

calm	changes	cried	cross	different
easy-going		ourselves	sad	shouted
talked	upset	usual	went	worried

My mother and my father are very ....1.... people. Mum is always very ....2....; not exactly ....3.... because she does take things very seriously sometimes, but she doesn't get excited. When we were small she almost never ....4.... at us. When we did something wrong she ....5.... to us about it very firmly, but in a calm tone of voice. If we shouted and ....6.... she made us go and sit by ....7.... in her sewing room until we calmed down. So when the news came she reacted in her ....8.... way, quietly seeing what she could do to prepare for the ....9.... that were coming.

Dad, on the other hand, shouted, kicked a chair, and ....10.... for a long walk to try and cool off. During the next few days he was ....11.... with us a lot of the time, which ....12.... us, as nothing was our fault. All of us kids were ....13.... about what was going to happen, and a bit afraid, but we didn't talk to our parents much. Most of all we were ....14.... about having to leave all of our school friends.

4 How might you feel if you said these things? The words in the box may help you. Example:

What was that noise? surprised or afraid

| afraid | amused | angry | cross | pleased |
| relaxed | sad | surprised | upset | worried |

1. Where have you been?
2. Isn't that nice!
3. Damn you!
4. He should be more careful.
5. Oh dear!
6. What a lovely idea!
7. You're kidding!
8. You'd better not do that again.
9. I can't see a thing.

Now invent a short conversation using at least two of the sentences above.

PEMBROKE, IF YOU CAN LEARN TO CONTROL YOUR EMOTIONS I'LL MAKE YOU A BRANCH MANAGER.

OH BOY, OH BOY!

5 Find Lesson C1, Exercise 6 on the Student's Cassette. Listen and answer the questions.

1. Which speaker has got children?
2. Which speaker expresses his/her feelings quite easily?
3. Which speaker is occasionally upset by small things?
4. Someone wouldn't be able to cope with being told about a serious problem. Who is it?

6 Read the poem and/or the 'strange tales', using a dictionary if you wish.

JOHN HEGLEY

TALKING ABOUT MY FEELINGS AIN'T MY CUP OF TEA

Please don't do the third degree
about the two of us
or the one of me
'cos I ain't one for talking about my
    feelings,
I just get these mental blocks
if it's insecurity the box it's in is ever
    so secure
with a very well kept key
I used to be closer to my emotions
or maybe they were close to me,
in the past I've been very open
the last time was when I was 3
    months.
They say bashing pillows is beneficial
and it helps to hug a tree
they say problems shared are
    problems halved
but they don't say it to me.
Revealing how I'm feeling
it isn't my Darjeeling
it ain't my cup of tea.

(John Hegley)

ain't: isn't *or* am not
ain't my cup of tea: If something 'isn't your cup of tea' it means you don't like it
do the third degree: ask a lot of questions like a policeman
Darjeeling: a kind of tea

Strange tales indeed!

In May 1957 seven people were sitting in a dining room just after lunch. Suddenly a man in brown walked past the open door into the kitchen. Four of the people saw him, and one got up to ask him what he wanted. The man had vanished, yet he could not have left the house unseen. Only then did the people realise that they must have seen a ghost.

This happened near Sydney, Australia, one evening in 1873. Six weeks after Captain Towns died, his married daughter entered a bedroom where there was a burning gas lamp. Reflected in the shiny surface of the wardrobe was a 'portrait' of her father. His thin, pale face, and grey flannel jacket were unmistakable. A young lady who was with the daughter saw the image too. They called other members of the household. Altogether eight people came and marvelled at the apparition. But when the Captain's widow tried to touch it, the image faded away.

An old man was seen trudging home through a stormy night, dressed only in pyjamas. The driver who passed him on the road discovered that the old man had died three weeks before.

One night in 1976, a woman awoke to see a tall, thin, female figure in her bedroom. The phantom pressed skinny fingers around the woman's throat as if to strangle her. Then the grip relaxed, and the figure faded. Later, the victim described the ghost to her fiancé. The description fitted his long-dead Malaysian grandmother.

In 1964 a huge press was accidentally set moving inside a Detroit car factory. A nearby worker claimed his life was saved only by a tall, scarred black man who pushed him clear of the machinery. No one with him saw that person, but some recognised the description. It fitted a black worker accidentally killed there 20 years before.

In the middle 1800s, a young girl was walking down an English country lane. Suddenly she seemed to see her mother lying on a bedroom floor. The girl fetched a doctor and they found her mother exactly as the girl described her. The woman had fallen with a heart attack. Luckily the doctor arrived in time to save her life.

In 1926, two women on a country walk near Bury St Edmunds in Suffolk, England, saw a big house in a garden surrounded by a high wall. Soon afterwards they passed that way again. They found only overgrown waste land that had not been disturbed for years.

(from *The Piccolo Explorer Book of Mysteries*)

7 Read the first text and then complete the second one.

A

I'm not exactly calm. In fact, I'm a fairly emotional person. I express my emotions easily, and never let them build up inside me. I enjoy the good times more, and get over the bad times more quickly, when I can talk or shout or cry about them. So people around me usually know what kind of mood I'm in. Strangely enough, this helped me keep a secret once. I had a problem that upset me terribly, and for once I didn't want to share it with anyone. No one ever imagined that I was hiding anything!

B

I'm not a very ......1...... person; I'm ......2...... calm and easy-going. I don't often ......3...... angry – I don't really see the point of it. And I almost never ......4...... or ......5....... When something ......6...... me, I just try to see how I can change it. I don't let the people around me know how I ......7...... unless there is a good reason for it. My emotions take a long time to ......8......, but they are strong and lasting.

Now *either* write a text based on the notes in the box, *or* write a few sentences about yourself or someone you know. Write about your/their emotions and how they are expressed.

> NOTES
> emotional but don't share moods
> when upset, usually keep it inside instead of shouting/crying
> would like to be more open about emotions
> would feel more comfortable if I could express more
> have never learnt to

"My goodness, getting mad won't help."

"Fear? He doesn't know the meaning of the word!"

C2 Focus on systems

1 Grammar: Future Progressive tense. Look at the pictures and write sentences to say what the person will be doing at the different times. Example:

This time tomorrow he will be flying to the USA.

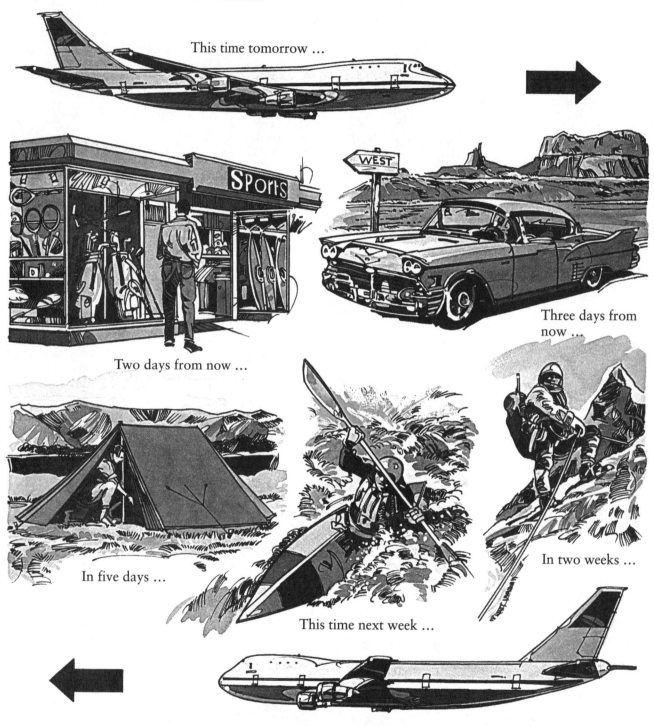

This time tomorrow …
Two days from now …
Three days from now …
In five days …
This time next week …
In two weeks …
Three weeks today …

2 Grammar. Write what you will (or might) be doing at some of these times:

in two hours' time
eight hours from now
this time tomorrow
this time next Tuesday
three weeks tomorrow

in six months
this time next year
two years from now
five years from now

3 Grammar: Future Perfect tense. Look at the work schedule and write what the situation will be at the following times: mid-March, the end of April, mid-June, early September. Example:

<u>By mid-February they will just have started the runways, they will have built most of the approach road, they will have finished the foundations for Terminal 1, but they won't have started Terminal 2.</u>

EAST MERTON AIRPORT WORK SCHEDULE

OCT	NOV	DEC	JAN	FEB	MAR	APR	MAY	JUN	JUL	AUG	SEPT	OCT	NOV	DEC	JAN
work on approach road →															
				work on runways →											
	foundations for Terminal 1 →														
					construction of Terminal 1 building →										
							foundations for Terminal 2 →								
											construction of Terminal 2 building →				
								control tower →							

4 Grammar. Write sentences about things which you will have started or finished by some of the following times (or other times if you prefer):

three hours from now
three months from now
by next year
two years from now
five years from now
ten years from now

5 Spelling revision. Write the *-ing* forms. What are the rules? Check on page 144 if you are not sure.

start	<u>starting</u>	take
hope	<u>hoping</u>	wait
stop	<u>stopping</u>	send
get		run
jump		come
like		sit
rub		

"I regret to announce that this morning, at fifteen minutes past ten o'clock, on the Cross Bronx Expressway, Professor Cramer was struck and seriously injured by a three thousand pound tuna fish."

6 Read your horoscope, using a dictionary if you wish.

YOUR STARS

AQUARIUS (Jan 21–Feb 18)
This time tomorrow you'll be doing something you've never done in your life before. Try to get it right. Money could be a problem towards the end of the week. Look out for trouble from small animals.

PISCES (Feb 19–Mar 20)
Stop being so sorry for yourself. Everybody's getting fed up with you. Even the cat is getting fed up with you. If you go on like this, you'll have lost all your friends by the end of the year.

ARIES (Mar 21–Apr 20)
Wonderful things are going to happen to you this week. One of your poems will be published in a gardening magazine. A friend will send you a postcard. Friday will bring an invitation to a folk concert. Enjoy the excitement while it lasts; next week everything will be back to normal.

TAURUS (Apr 21–May 21)
Years ago, you treated somebody very badly. You thought they'd forgotten? No. They'll be looking for revenge this week. Don't try to get away: there is no place to hide.

GEMINI (May 22–Jun 21)
Prepare for travel. Some very strange things are going to happen, and you are suddenly going to become President of a small distant oil-rich country. This time next week you'll be sitting in the Palace drinking champagne.

CANCER (June 22–July 22)
This week's problem will be children. By the end of the week you'll be wishing they had all been drowned at birth. Try to be patient; next week will bring more children.

LEO (July 23–Aug 23)
A tall handsome man wearing a uniform will come into your life. This may mean a visit to the police station. Tell the truth – it's better in the end.

VIRGO (Aug 24–Sept 23)
First, the good news. Somebody you have always been strongly attracted to will be sending you an invitation. Now the bad news: it's to a wedding. Not yours.

LIBRA (Sept 24–Oct 23)
At last your talent, beauty, intelligence and human warmth are going to be properly recognised. By Friday you'll be rich and famous; by Saturday you'll already have been on TV three times; this time next week you'll be starting a glamorous new career.

SCORPIO (Oct 24–Nov 22)
Tomorrow will bring an enormous sum of money out of the blue. It's a pity you're so extravagant – by this time next week you'll probably have spent it all.

SAGITTARIUS (Nov 23–Dec 21)
Be careful in your relationships. In the great supermarket of life, you have to pay for anything you break – including hearts. Try to say 'No' more often. You are too attractive for your own good.

CAPRICORN (Dec 22–Jan 20)
Thursday is a bad day for travel. Friday is a bad day for meetings. Saturday is a bad day for everything. You'll have got over the worst by Sunday, but stay cautious – fate could still have a few unpleasant surprises for you.

7 Do one of these writing tasks. Write at least 150 words.

1. Look again at Exercise 6 and then write a horoscope for somebody you don't like, and one for somebody you like.
2. Imagine that you are a young man or woman who has just arrived in an English-speaking country. Write a letter about your plans to a friend back home. Use the structures you have practised in this lesson. You must also use at least six of the following words and expressions.

actress	bathroom	cat	European	excellent	fetch	in bed
in time	mad	promise	taxi	terrible	zoo	

C3 I'm a bit short of time

1 Vocabulary revision. Write each of the times in two ways. Example:

1. three ten OR ten past three

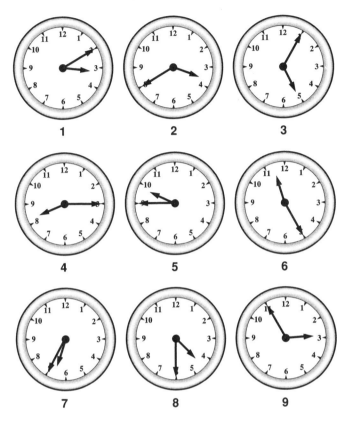

2 Vocabulary revision. If today is Tuesday August 9, what day and date are the following?

1. the day after tomorrow
2. a week today
3. tomorrow week
4. Thursday week
5. three weeks tomorrow
6. a week ago yesterday
7. a week ago tomorrow
8. two weeks from now

If today is Monday August 15, then Wednesday August 17 is the day after tomorrow. What expressions could you use to talk about the following days?

1. Saturday August 13
2. Tuesday August 23
3. Thursday August 25
4. Tuesday August 30
5. Monday August 8
6. Sunday August 7
7. Tuesday August 9

3 Andy had two phone calls this evening: one from Beth and one from Cathy. The two phone calls have been mixed up and the speeches put in the wrong order. Write out one of the conversations. Note that some of the speeches can be used in either phone call (as in the examples). Examples:

Beth's call to Andy
ANDY: Hello. Camford 49330.
BETH: Hello. Is that Andy?
ANDY: ....
BETH: ....

Cathy's call to Andy
ANDY: Hello. Camford 49330.
CATHY: Hello. Is that Andy?
ANDY: ....
CATHY: ....

Hi, Andy. This is Cathy. How are you?
I can't remember, actually. Why?
Look, I've got two tickets for the Mozart concert at the Mandela Centre tonight. Would you like to come with me?
OK. Bye.
8 o'clock. I'll come round to your place at 7 o'clock, shall I?
Yes, I think so.
Bye.
Fine thanks. What about you?
No, I'm afraid I'm away this weekend. Listen, Beth, I'm really a bit busy at the moment. You know how it is. I'll give you a ring in a couple of weeks. OK?
Fine. See you then.
Hello. Camford 49330.
I haven't seen you for ages. I thought we might go out for a drink somewhere.
This is Beth. How are you?
Hello. Is that Andy?
Let me just look in my diary. ... Sorry, it looks as if I'm not free.
That's difficult. Could we make it 7.15?
See you. Bye.
Well, what about at the weekend?
Yes, who's that?
Mozart? Cathy, that would be really lovely! What time does it start?
Pretty well thanks. Look, are you free this evening?

4 Grammar revision. Put in *always, ever, never, already* or *yet*.

1. Have you .... been to Australia?
2. I don't think she's .... got up before nine o'clock in her life.
3. Is Granny here ....?
4. 'Would you like a drink?' 'I've .... got one, thanks.'
6. If you are .... in New York, do come and stay.
7. .... lend money to strangers.
8. 'Is breakfast ready?' 'Not ....'
9. I .... know what I'm going to get for Christmas.
10. Do you .... have bad dreams?

5 Read one or more of these three texts, using a dictionary if you wish.

DAYS

MONDAY
You'd better not try anything
just don't try anything
that's all.
You're all the same
you days.
Give you an inch ...
Well
I've got my eye on you
and I'm feeling light
fast
and full of aggro
so just watch it
OK?

TUESDAY
Listen, Tuesday
I'm sorry
I wasn't very nice to you.
It was *sweet* of you
to give me all those stars
when you said goodbye.
They must have cost a fortune
and they really were
just
what I've always wanted.

WEDNESDAY
Cracks, spills, burns, bills, broken
   cups, stains, wrong numbers,
   missed trains:
you're doing it on purpose
aren't you?
Trying it on
to see how far you can go.
I swear to you
if the phone rings again
while I'm in the bath
I'll pull it out
and ram it down your throat.

THURSDAY
'A difficult day for Aries
caution is advisable
in business dealings
setbacks possible
in affairs of the heart.'
Thursday, my friend
if we've got to get
through all these hours together
we might as well do it
with as little trouble as possible.
You keep to your side of the
   horoscope
and I'll keep to mine.

FRIDAY
Day like a shroud
ten feet down
black
in an airless coffin
you wrap me
in my own
clinging
loathsome
sticky skin.
I scream
and you laugh.

SATURDAY
Day
oh day
I love your perfume
(you put on daffodils
just for me)
and your yellow eye
sparkling
and the sexy way
you rub up
against me
day
I love you.

SUNDAY
Sunday and I
got drunk together
and you know
it turns out
we went to the same school.
He's a bit strange at first
but actually
he's not a bad chap
when you get to know him
old Sunday.

(Lewis Mancha)

aggro: aggression

Days

What are days for?
Days are where we live.
They come, they wake us
Time and time over.
They are to be happy in:
Where can we live but days?

Ah, solving that question
Brings the priest and the doctor
In their long coats
Running over the fields.

(Philip Larkin)

New Year's Day

THE YEAR is a perfect circle, and it can begin on any day you like; it was a mere accident of Roman politics that bequeathed us January 1st.

In the very early years of the Roman Republic, the newly elected consuls took up office in the month of March – and that dictated when the year began. Then in 153 BC, this transfer of power was rescheduled to January, and the first of that month became New Year's Day throughout the western regions of the Roman Empire.

This convention survived the change to the Julian calendar in 46 BC, and even the subsequent adoption of Gregorian refinements some 1600 years later.

But in the north of Europe the situation was a mite confused. Prior to the Norman conquest of England, the New Year in these parts began on Christmas Day, December 25th. In 1066 the Normans brought with them the Roman habit of beginning the year on January 1st – but this continental affectation barely lasted for a century. From 1155 onwards New Year's Day was Lady Day, March 25th, and it was only with the legal adoption of the Gregorian calendar in Britain and Ireland in 1752 that it reverted again to January 1st.

The French tried a different scheme when they had their Revolution. Their new calendar, introduced to coincide with "the year of liberty" in 1792, had the year beginning on September 22nd, the day on which the republic was proclaimed – but 14 years later they too went back to January 1st, in 1806.

There are yet many other New Year's Days. The ancient Greeks, for example, preoccupied with sport, reckoned their calendar from the first Olympiad in 766 BC. This required their year to begin with the first moon after the summer solstice – around the beginning of July.

The Chinese also watch the sun and moon; the Chinese New Year coincides with the second new moon after the winter solstice – which drops it somewhere between January 21st, and February 19th.

(Brendan McWilliams, *The Irish Times*)

a mite: a little bit

6 Write at least 150 words about your plans for the next five years. Try to include some words and expressions from the Student's Book lesson.

"Yes, it has been a long time. I'm just calling to see if I could tear you out of my address book."

"Are we doing anything on Tuesday week?"

C4 We regret ...

1 Grammar revision. Complete the text using *could* or *would* + the verbs in the box. You might need to use some of the verbs more than once.

| be able | be useful | find out | prefer |
| read | see | want | |

Imagine you ...1... people's minds, so that you always knew what they were thinking. You ...2... when people were lying to you, or if they wanted to cheat you, for example. And you ...3... to see what politicians really meant when they were making all their promises. It ...4... in exams, too, because you could find out the answers by reading the examiners' minds. And when people said 'I love you', you ...5... if they really meant it. But in general I think I ...6... not to know things that people wanted to keep secret. And I'm not sure that I ...7... to know everything that people thought about me.

2 Grammar revision: word order. Make questions for these answers. Each question should end in a preposition (e.g. *Where does your cousin come from?*).

1. I sent it to Mary. (*Who ...?*)
2. I was thinking about you.
3. You should eat it with a fork.
4. He bought it for his sister.
5. You can put them in that big vase, if you want to.
6. I'm looking for the toilets.
7. He's looking after his mother.
8. It was directed by Spielberg.

3 Vocabulary revision. Which is the odd one out in each group? Put it in the correct group.

1. *Do*: nothing, homework, a decision, something interesting
2. *Get*: undressed, a letter, a plane, lost, a mistake
3. *Have*: lunch, coffee, a photo, a rest, a sandwich
4. *Make*: a holiday, a plan, a pizza, a bed, tea
5. *Take*: a bus, size 7 shoes, changed, a rest, a train

4 Vocabulary revision. What are these things made of? Can you write the names of all the materials? Use a dictionary if necessary.

54

5 Read the quotations, using a dictionary if you wish.

The first casualty when war comes is truth.

(Hiram Johnson)

For secrets are edged tools
And must be kept from children and from fools.

(Dryden)

In England it is bad manners to be clever, to assert something confidently. It may be your personal view that two and two make four, but you must not state it in a self-assured way, because this is a democratic country and others may be of a different opinion.

... People on the Continent either tell you the truth or lie; in England they hardly ever lie, but they would not dream of telling you the truth.

(George Mikes)

The problems of policing Calne were discussed at a secret meeting last night between local councillors, Mayor Mr Ted Cooper and Chief Superintendent Sam Ashley, divisional head of Chippenham police. But no one would release any information today. Mr Cooper said 'It was conducted in private because it concerned the public so much.'

(from *The Bristol Evening Post*)

Have you ever noticed, friend, that when you are sleeping happily and the telephone rings and you reach an arm from under the blanket and say 'Hello' into the mouthpiece, the voice on the telephone always says 'Did I wake you up?'

And have you ever noticed how you immediately and invariably reply? You lie. 'Of course not,' you say, or 'Are you kidding? I've been up for hours.'

Scientific studies with laboratory mice have not yet shown how many persons will answer candidly – 'Yes, you woke me up, and I hope you're satisfied' – but I bet it is fewer than three in a million.

(Russell Baker)

6 You work for a publishing firm. An old friend of your mother's has sent you his collected poems and asked you to consider them for publication. A typical poem goes:

'While I was eating a fried egg
I thought of you
and began to cry.
Life is so sad.'

You do not feel able to publish the poems. Write a letter to your mother's friend telling him so. Try to include some words and expressions from the Student's Book lesson as well as some of the following:

Thank you for ...ing
I/We have considered ... very carefully
but (I) regret that ...
I am unable to ...
While ...
I do/did not feel that ...
In addition ...
May I suggest that ...

"You have an honest face, sir – open 'em up!"

7 Try to solve at least one of the detective problems. (The answers are on page 144.)

How good a detective are you?

1 One evening late in 1941, Colonel Montgomery of Scotland Yard found himself standing before the members of the London Mystery Club, a group that enjoyed discussing mystery novels.

"I wouldn't be asking for your help if it wasn't important," the colonel said. "Recently a stranger arrived in London from South America. Our intelligence sources have informed us that this man is probably a Nazi agent. We believe that he is a courier of a great deal of wealth with which to finance espionage in Britain.

"A few hours after he stepped off the boat, we arranged a car accident that sent him to hospital with a fractured arm. Our staff searched his clothes and luggage, which consisted of only a briefcase with letters from his friends in British Guiana. We discovered nothing. Either this man is not an enemy agent, or he is an exceedingly clever one.

"We considered a number of possible ploys. He could have posted counterfeit British currency to himself, but the irregularity of wartime mail makes this rather unlikely. He could have had diamonds implanted in his body surgically, but an X-ray machine eliminated that possibility. Tomorrow morning this man will walk out of the hospital and merge with our populace. Do you have any suggestions as to how he might be concealing something like a hundred thousand pounds?"

The members turned to one another and whispered for a few moments. Several heads nodded, and then the president turned and said, "Colonel, we think you have overlooked a rather obvious possibility."

Can you work out what it is?

2 "Mr Reilly? This is Colonel Montgomery of Scotland Yard. I'm afraid I have some bad news for you. Your brother-in-law has just been murdered."

"Oh my God," said the voice on the other end of the line. "I only saw Micky last night. I can't believe this is true. Are you sure it's him?"

"The identification is positive, Mr Reilly. I would like to come straight over and talk to you about who would have a motive for killing him."

An hour later, Colonel Montgomery was seated in Reilly's flat.

"It's no secret that Micky had enemies," said Reilly. "His business partner, Harold Smith, once accused him of stealing money from their business. They had some violent arguments. Then there's my sister's husband, Charles Jones, who accused Micky of having an affair with his wife. Charles, I'm embarrassed to say, is associated with the underworld. Another person who could have killed Micky is my wife's brother Billy. I know he hated Micky. I can give you his address, if you promise not to tell him I did."

"No, thank you, Mr Reilly. From what you've told me, it's rather obvious that you killed Micky."

How did Montgomery know this?

3 Alphonso, the spy, was being questioned at Scotland Yard. "All right, Alphonso," said Colonel Montgomery. "Where did you hide the secret document you stole from the Foreign Office?"

"I was afraid of being caught with it," Alphonso replied. "When I saw your man trailing me, I ran into a library and hid it in a book. I put it between pages 123 and 124 so I would remember where it was, but I was so intent on remembering those numbers that now I've forgotten the book's name."

"You're lying, Alphonso," said Colonel Montgomery. "Where did you really put it?"

How could Colonel Montgomery tell Alphonso was lying?

(from *The Reader's Digest*)

C5 The voice of democracy

1 Grammar. Choose the correct tenses.

1. 'Look! I *found / 've found* a £20 note!' 'It's probably mine. Where *did you find / have you found* it?'
2. 'Alice *bought / has bought* a new car.' 'Really? Where *did she get / has she got* the money?'
3. 'I'm sorry. I *broke / 've broken* a cup.' 'How *did you manage / have you managed* to do that?'
4. My father *just had / has just had* a car accident, but he *wasn't / hasn't been* badly hurt.
5. News *just came in / has just come in* of an earthquake in Southern Mangrovia. According to first reports, the quake *struck / has struck* just after midnight last night.
6. 'Mummy! Look what I *did / 've done*!' 'Oh, my God! What *did you do / have you done* that for?'
7. 'Did you know Henry *went / has gone* to California?' 'Oh, yes? He *probably wanted / has probably wanted* to get away from Bill for a bit.'
8. '*What happened / What's happened* here?' 'It looks as if he *came / has come* round the corner too fast.'
9. 'You know those young trees we *planted / have planted*? They *all died / have all died*.' 'You probably *didn't water / haven't watered* them enough.'

2 Grammar. Which tense would you probably use with these time-expressions – Simple Past or Present Perfect? Write an example sentence using each expression. Examples:

yesterday: Simple Past (I saw Gill yesterday.)
all this year: Present Perfect (She's been ill all this year.)

last week
ten years ago
since Tuesday
all my life
when I first met you
the day before yesterday
once upon a time
for the last few weeks
after we got married
since we got married
during my childhood
up to now

3 Grammar revision. How long is it since you last did these things? Use the structure *I haven't ... since/for ...* Examples:

eaten an ice cream
I haven't eaten an ice cream for weeks.
been shopping
I haven't been shopping since yesterday.

travelled by train
read a novel
been to the cinema
played football
stayed up all night
fallen in love
been ill
been in hospital
done an examination
spoken to a policeman

4 Grammar revision. Choose a word from the box to put into each blank, using some words more than once.

| about | at | by | for | in | of | on |
| through | to | | | | | |

1. That's very kind .... you.
2. Are you interested .... politics?
3. How can I find out .... things to do in the area?
4. I didn't know Adrian was married .... Gloria.
5. I only listen .... the radio when I'm in the car.
6. Do you believe .... God?
7. What was the reason .... the delay?
8. What do you think .... the US's latest move in the Middle East?
9. What time we get there will depend .... how bad the traffic is.
10. I sometimes dream .... having enough free time to travel all over Europe.
11. Unemployment in this area has risen .... 10% this year, because .... the factory closures.
12. Some birds, ... example the robin, stay in Britain all year round.
13. Going .... customs can take quite a while in America.
14. I really didn't do it .... purpose, but I know she thinks I did.
15. How did Marco Polo travel – .... land or .... sea?
16. Are you coming .... car or .... foot?
17. I'm really proud .... my mother, being so independent at her age.
18. Are you any good .... repairing cars?
19. We'll try to come earlier, but we'll be there .... eight o'clock at the latest.
20. What did you talk .... ?

5 Try to complete the transcript from memory (or use the *Learn/revise* box in the Student's Book if you need to). Then find Lesson C5, Exercise 3 on the Student's Cassette and check your answers.

'Democratic Fantasian Radio – the voice of ......1...... . Ten a.m. Here is the news, read by Aldo Fisk.'

'According to the organisers, at least 200,000 people ......2...... in yesterday's ......3...... against the government's economic ......4...... . After marching through the city centre, demonstrators gathered in Wesk Square to hear speeches by ......5...... leaders. The demonstration remained calm, ...6...... aggressive behaviour by the police. Two people are reported to have been ......7...... in fighting which ......8...... briefly after the demonstration.

'Economics ......9...... say that ......10...... earnings have gone down by 12% since this time last year. Critics of the government say that its economic policies ......11...... to inefficient management and lower ......12...... . Industrial ......13...... has fallen by 27% over the year, and exports are down by nearly 40%. Inflation ......14...... to 37%, and the Fantasian grotnik now stands at 374 to the US dollar.

'Widespread floods in Southern Fantasia have made ......15...... 80,000 people ......16...... . Help by the army came ......17...... to prevent serious damage to buildings and farmland. Damage is estimated at three billion grotniks.

'News has just come in that Dr Amelia Musk ......18...... of a heart attack at her home in Chingport. Dr Musk, who was ......19...... for her ......20...... writings, had been ill for some time. She was 62.

'And now the ......21...... . It will be cold and wet, with strong winds. There may be some snow on ......22...... ground. The weekend will be very cold, with maximum temperatures ......23...... five degrees Celsius.'

6 Read Jim's letter. Then write your own letter giving news about yourself to a friend or relation. Use the 'skeleton' letter as a basis. You can change the order of words, and make any other changes you need to, but you must use plenty of the words and expressions in the skeleton, and some other words and expressions from Jim's letter.

```
                    18 Marble Lane
                    Penygroes
                    North Wales LL6 7AQ
                    14 July 1992

Dear Bernard,
   Thanks for your letter. It was good to hear from you
and get all your news.
   We've just started work on the new building. It will
take approximately six months to get it finished, if all
goes well. It's an exciting project, and we're all very
pleased that we got the contract.
   I've found a nice place to live — just outside the
village, on the edge of a small lake. It's an old house,
but it's in very good condition, and extremely
comfortable. There's plenty of spare room, so why don't
you and Janice come up one weekend?
   The only problem here is the weather. According to the
locals, this is the wettest summer in living memory, and
I can quite believe it. It's rained every day since I got
here, and it shows no signs of stopping.
   Still, in spite of the weather I'm enjoying myself.
The people here are very friendly, and I've been elected
to the darts team in the village pub. Apparently they've
lost their last sixteen matches, and they're hoping that
a bit of outside talent may improve their record.
   I'll try to get down to London some time in the next
couple of months, but I don't think I'll have time for a
bit. I'm going to have to spend at least three weeks here
getting the work and the house organised before I can get
away.
   No more news for the moment. Write soon and let me
know what's going on back in the big city.
      Love to Janice,
      Yours,

      Jim
```

ADDRESS
DATE

Dear ...,

Thanks ...
I've just started ...
It will take approximately ... to ...

I've found ...
Why don't you ...?

The only problem ...
According to ...
I can quite believe it.

In spite of ...
It's/I've ... every day since ...

I'll try ...
but I don't think ...
I'm going to have to ...

No more news for the moment.
Write soon and ...

Love/Yours,

C6 Focus on systems

1 Grammar: relative clauses. Make sentences using *that/which*. (Both are possible in all cases.) Example:

Animals that/which eat meat are called 'carnivores'.

Animals	is on the table	are called	down.
The book	run on electricity	has all	the cat.
The snow	runs our heating	is for	melted.
Water	fell last night	is called	motors.
The pump	falls from the sky	has broken	'carnivores'.
The letter	is in that saucer	wasn't for	'rain'.
Engines	eat meat	are called	Helen.
The milk	came this morning	is for	me.

2 Grammar. Rewrite these sentences adding the reduced relative clauses in the right places. You will not need to use all the reduced relative clauses.

1. The government has announced that anybody will be arrested.
   The government has announced that anybody found on the streets after 10 p.m. will be arrested.
2. People will not be allowed in until the interval.
3. Two paintings were recovered by police today.
4. The person is unfortunately unable to talk to you at the moment.
5. Unemployment figures show that nearly three million people are now out of work.
6. Who's that woman?
7. Ten men and eight women were slightly injured and had to be taken to hospital.
8. I'm afraid he hasn't got the qualifications.

> talking to my husband
> required for the job
> dealing with your application
> stolen last year from the National Gallery
> turning up late for the start of the concert
> found on the streets after 10 p.m.
> taking part in yesterday's anti-war demonstration
> released this morning
> hoping to catch the twelve o'clock train

3 Grammar revision. Fill in the table of irregular verbs. Learn the ones you are unsure of.

PRESENT	PAST TENSE	PAST PARTICIPLE
beat	....	....
....	bit	....
....	....	dealt
fall	....	....
....	felt	....
....	....	hidden
hold	....	....
....	led	....
....	....	left
mean	....	....
....	met	....
....	....	risen
spend	....	....
....	stole	....
....	....	struck
tear	....	....
....	threw	....
....	....	worn

4 Read and pronounce all the words in the box. Then see how many of the tasks you can do in five minutes. (You may use the same words for more than one answer.)

> absolutely   artificial   break   bring   build
> call   decision   delicious   drugstore
> economic   energetic   experience   fight
> furniture   hurt   keep   law   lonely
> marriage   noise   north   organisation
> personality   pleasure   productivity
> responsibility   smile   sociable   story
> towards   unattractive   walk   warm

1. Find five words which contain a 'silent *e*'.
2. Find one American English word.
3. Find five irregular verbs.
4. Find three words where the main stress is on the third syllable.
5. Find one word where the main stress is on the fourth syllable.
6. Find three words in which the last syllable contains the /ə/ sound.
7. Find five words which contain the vowel /ɔː/ (as in *short, talk, caught*).

59

5 Translate these into your language.

1. The book you are reading was written by a friend of mine.
2. She passed that examination she sat last month.
3. Have you ever been rude to anybody?
4. When I was a child, my parents made me go to bed at nine o'clock during the week but let me stay up later at the weekend.
5. She was delighted but he was absolutely furious.
6. This time tomorrow I'll be flying to Japan.
7. By the end of the month we will have spent all our money.
8. I'll give you a ring the day after tomorrow.
9. I thought we might go to the theatre together.
10. On the other hand I mightn't tell the truth if I thought it would hurt someone.
11. He wrote to me twice last week but I haven't heard from him at all this week.
12. All the people injured in last Monday's plane crash have now left hospital.

6 Read the two texts and then decide where the sentences (a–h) should be added.

Beatrice and the nightingale

One warm May night in 1924, the cellist Beatrice Harrison went out to play her cello in the woods behind her cottage in Surrey, in the south of England. ......1...... To her surprise, she heard a bird echoing her playing. She started again, and the bird sang with her. The sound was incredibly beautiful, and she knew it could only be a nightingale.

The next night, and nearly every night after that, the nightingale was there again. Beatrice Harrison could hardly believe what was happening: she was playing duets with a wild bird! ......2......

At that time, broadcasting was just becoming popular, and many people in Europe had radios. Beatrice Harrison decided to try to persuade the BBC to set up their microphones in her garden. ......3...... The BBC had never before tried an outside broadcast of this kind, and the distance between Beatrice Harrison's home and London made things more complicated. But the sound engineers made careful preparations, and one night in May 1924 everything was ready.

For a long time it seemed as if the nightingale was not going to come. Beatrice Harrison played for nearly two hours with no reaction. ......4...... The duet of the musician and the nightingale was heard in London, in Paris, even in Italy.

Several more broadcasts were made, and the following year HMV made a record of Beatrice and the Nightingale, which became one of the most successful records sold in the 1930s.

The worst musical trio

......5...... This happened about thirty years ago to the son of a Romanian gentleman who was owed a personal favour by Georges Enesco, the celebrated violinist. Enesco agreed to give lessons to the son, who was quite unhampered by musical talent.

Three years later the boy's father insisted that he gave a public concert. 'His aunt said that nobody plays the violin better than he does. A cousin heard him the other day and screamed with enthusiasm.' Although Enesco feared the consequences, he arranged a recital at the Salle Gaveau in Paris. ......6......

'Then you must accompany him on the piano,' said the boy's father, 'and it will be a sellout.'

Reluctantly, Enesco agreed and it was. ......7...... Before the concert began Enesco became nervous and asked for someone to turn his pages.

In the audience was Alfred Cortot, the brilliant pianist, who volunteered and made his way to the stage.

The soloist was of uniformly low standard and next morning the music critic of *Le Figaro* wrote: '......8...... The man whom we adore when he plays the violin played the piano. Another whom we adore when he plays the piano turned the pages. But the man who should have turned the pages played the violin.'

(from *The Book of Heroic Failures* by Stephen Pile)

---

a. After playing for some time in the moonlight, she paused.
b. But suddenly, to everybody's relief, the wonderful liquid notes began to fill the night.
c. However, nobody bought a ticket since the soloist was unknown.
d. It was an astonishing experience, and she wished that she could share her pleasure with other people.
e. On the night an excited audience gathered.
f. There are few bad musicians who have a chance to give a recital at a famous concert hall while still learning the rudiments of their instrument.
g. There was a strange concert at the Salle Gaveau last night.
h. With the technology of the time, this was no easy task.

7 Answer at least five of the following questions and use your answers to write a paragraph or two about your tastes in music.

1. What is your favourite sort of music?
2. Do you have an ear for music?
3. Do the people you live with and your close friends share the same tastes in music as you?
4. Where do you listen to music most – at home, in the car, …?
5. If you could choose one musical instrument to be able to play brilliantly, what instrument would you choose?
6. Do you like having background music while you are working?
7. When do you tend to listen to music?
8. How often do you go to concerts?
9. Do you buy records, cassettes or CDs? If so, how often?
10. What usually makes you decide that you want to buy a certain record (or disc or cassette)?
11. Have you got one or two favourite performers (or groups or orchestras) at the moment? If so, who?
12. Have your musical tastes changed since you were younger? If so, in what way?
13. What instrument do you most like the sound of?
14. Do you ever sing in the bath or while you are working?
15. Would you like a child of yours to be a professional musician?

C7 People going hungry

1 Grammar revision. Make one sentence out of each pair.

1. I gave the money to a man. I can't see him. (Begin *I can't* …)
   I can't see the man (that) I gave the money to.
2. The money was in a box. The box is still here. (Begin *The box* …)
   The box (that) the money was in is still here.
3. Ethiopia gets aid from some countries. These countries are mainly in the northern hemisphere. (Begin *The countries (that) Ethiopia* …)
4. Emergency food is carried in trucks. Some of them are very old. (Begin *Some of the trucks* …)
5. I give money to some charities. I'm careful about which charities. (Begin *I'm careful about* …)
6. She took the papers out of a file. I don't know which file. (Begin *I don't know* …)
7. The Patels live on a small farm. It has been flooded three times in three years. (Begin *The small farm (that) the Patels* …)
8. War on Want puts its money into projects. The projects are designed to help poor women especially. (Begin *The projects (that) War* …)

2 Grammar revision. Make each pair of sentences into one sentence. Use words from the box to join the halves; you can take out some words and change the word order and verb tenses if necessary. In some cases more than one solution is possible.

although	as	as soon as	because	since	unless	until	when	while

1. We in Oxfam don't work through governments. We can work on both sides of a struggle in a circumstance like the civil war in Ethiopia.
   We in Oxfam don't work through governments, since/because we can work on both sides of a struggle in a circumstance like the civil war in Ethiopia.
2. We have field officers. They do not start projects, but wait for local people to come to them with ideas.
3. We don't have Oxfam people working on projects in the field. We don't believe that Westerners can come into other countries and tell people there what they need.
4. Britain is financing big projects like hydroelectric power stations in third world countries. People in these same countries are dying from the need for smaller projects like clean-water programmes.
5. Everyone in the world will have clean water one day. Up to that time, hundreds of thousands of babies die every year.
6. 'Aid' from Britain often involves buying advice or goods from British firms. The 'aid' is really going to Britain!
7. The British people might demand that their politicians change the way aid is given. If not, nothing will ever change.
8. Oxfam gives poor people more control over their own lives. Immediately, they gain a sense of self-respect and work hard to succeed.
9. Sir Winston Churchill heard about Oxfam's being founded. He said it was unpatriotic.

3 Vocabulary. Can you divide these into groups?

1. Essential, useful or not very useful (to you).

| ashtray   button   cushion   feather   fork
| hat   knife   paper   pencil   picture
| plate   safety-pin   soap   stone
| toothpaste   towel   typewriter |

2. Good, bad or neither.

| asleep   egg-shaped   frightened   hard
| hollow   liquid   long   loud   loving
| pretty   relaxed   sexy   six-legged   soft
| ugly   useful   wooden |

4 Vocabulary revision and extension. Add as many words as you can to these two vocabulary networks.

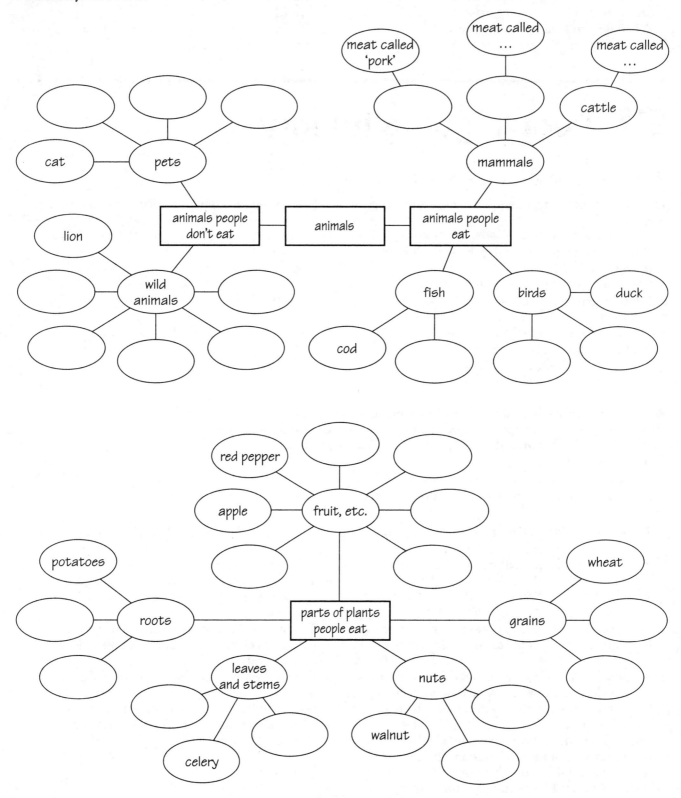

5 🔊 Find Lesson C7, Exercise 4 on the Student's Cassette. Which of the words in the box do you hear? Use the words to fill in the blanks in the two texts. (You may need to make some changes and use some words more than once.)

borrow	capital	cattle	consumption	debt	development	interest
international	lend	milk	peanuts	repay	rise	surplus	village

When a bank ....1.... you money, your ....2.... usually consists of two things: the ....3.... (the sum you originally borrowed), and the ....4.... (a percentage of the original sum). If you are unlucky, ...5.... rates may ....6.... before you finish ....7.... the entire sum.

....8.... are raised for meat and for ....9..... This is not as economical a way of using land as growing food like wheat or ....10..... Additionally, production is much greater than ....11.... in many Western countries, and the result is a ....12.... of ....13.... and butter.

6 Read the two texts. When you read the first time, put a circle around the words you don't know but can guess the meaning of; put a line under the words you must look up to understand the text. Look up the underlined words in the dictionary and read the texts again.

THE COMMISSION

In this poem there is a table
Groaning with food.
There is also a child
Groaning for lack of food.
The food is beautifully photographed
The meat more succulent
The fruit as juicy
As you are likely to see.
(The child is sketched in lightly
She is not important.)
The photograph is to be used
In a glossy magazine
As part of a campaign
Advertising after-dinner mints.

This evening the photographer
In receipt of his fee
Celebrates by dining with friends
In a famous West End restaurant.
Doodling on the napkin between courses
The photographer, always creative,
Draws a little Asian girl,
Naked, wide-eyed, pleading.
The photographer is pleased.
He has an idea for the next commission,
The one for famine relief.
The tandoori arrives
He puts away his pen
And picks up a fork.

(Roger McGough)

West End: a wealthy area of central London, famous for its restaurants, theatres, cinemas, etc.
doodling: drawing small pictures when you are feeling bored
tandoori: food cooked in a North Indian way

Good food dustbin guide

TWO high school students from the Norwegian oil capital of Stavanger have recently completed a fortnight's holiday living out of other people's dustbins. They report that it was a very tasty gastronomic tour.

Torbjoern Groenning, 16, and Kolbjoern Opstad, 18, had planned to live as cheaply as possible. They travelled by bike with their fishing rods, intending to live off what they caught and wild berries, buying only strict essentials. They claim it was "just a coincidence" that led them to look into one of the dustbins by the roadside: "Before we went to fish for our supper on the first afternoon, we threw away some rubbish."

Inside the dustbin near Helleland, they discovered four eggs, half a packet of paprika-flavoured crisps, four ham sandwiches, a tin of mackerel, two litres of skimmed sour milk, three different cheeses, one kilo of strawberries and an unopened can of Californian fruit salad. They also found a tube of sausage meat, half a kilo of margarine, a jar of plum jam and several loaves of bread.

The boys decided to turn their holiday into an investigative dustbin crawl. Their journey at the height of the tourist season took them from Stavanger, on Norway's south-west coast, to Mandel, a resort 180 miles further south, and their revelations have since shocked Norwegians into thinking about how much they waste.

On one occasion they discovered 20 freshly cooked crabs in a picnic site dustbin. They ate them with a fresh loaf and some mayonnaise found at the same spot. Budding experts on dustbin survival, they collected deposits on empty bottles to buy themselves fresh milk. And to celebrate their best haul of bottles, worth £5, they bought themselves soft drinks and cream cakes.

There was one recurring practical problem: the heat. Torbjoern explains: "We could feel the asphalt melting under our bikes. So we never touched food that was not well-wrapped. We preferred unopened things and submitted anything else to a strict smelling-test."

Torbjoern and Kolbjoern are now active members of an ecological pressure group, called The Future in Your Hands, which claims 7,000 members. The boys are already planning next year's holiday. They are considering a dustbin tour of Europe – to find out how much other holiday-makers throw away.

(Alex Finer, *The Sunday Times*)

7

You are a millionaire and you have decided to use £10 million of your own money to start a charity to help hungry people in the Third World. Write a plan for your charity, making sure you cover all of the points below. Try to include some words and expressions from the Student's Book lesson.

1. Choose a country or countries to help.
2. Will you concentrate on certain sorts of projects? How will you decide which individual projects to support?
3. About how much of the £10 million will go on setting up the head office? How much on administration? How much on raising more money? How much on educating people in the West to help change government policies that hurt the Third World?
4. Of the money that goes directly as aid to the Third World, what percentage will be used for emergency relief and what percentage for long-term projects?
5. How many employees will your charity have?
6. Give your charity a name, and think of a motto.

"That's our problem, Charlie – the more we get, the more we want."

"I hope you don't mind me saying so, but it's been a pleasure to watch you eat."

C8 A lot needs doing to it

1 Grammar. Look at the picture and write at least five things that need doing. Use the verbs in the box. Example:

His shoes need mending.

| cut   clean   mend   polish   press |
| sew on   wash |

2 Grammar. Look at the illustration. It shows two memo lists – one written by a rich and lazy person, who does nothing for herself, the other written by a poorer person, who does everything for herself. Write a list of things that you must remember to do or to have done during the next week or so.

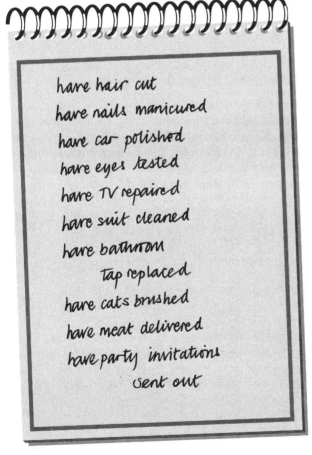

have hair cut
have nails manicured
have car polished
have eyes tested
have TV repaired
have suit cleaned
have bathroom tap replaced
have cats brushed
have meat delivered
have party invitations sent out

cut hair
buy soap
oil bicycle
see doctor
try to repair radio
clean and press overalls
repair kitchen tap
bath dog
buy potatoes
invite Helen to tea

3 Vocabulary revision. Label as many of these objects as you can.

4 Find Lesson C8, Exercise 3 on the Student's Cassette. Listen and answer the questions.

1. What do the owners of the house use the main downstairs room as?
2. How old is the fireplace?
3. Why did they have the study doorway raised?
4. How did one of the windows in the main bedroom get broken?
5. Why is the kitchen in rather a mess?
6. Where do the owners spend most of their time when they are not working?
7. Why did they have built-in cupboards made for the small, upstairs bedroom?
8. What could be done with the store room?

"Mind you, sir, it needs a bit doing to it."

5 Read the text, using a dictionary only when really necessary, and then decide whether the sentences which follow are true or false.

The day the ceiling caught fire

I never did like polystyrene ceiling tiles. Quite apart from the fire hazard, they don't look very good. So when I moved into a house whose previous owner had covered every ceiling with polystyrene tiles, I fully intended to take the lot down. I really did. It was just that there always seemed to be other things to do that were more urgent.

Now I can tell you that nothing is more urgent. If you have such tiles on your ceiling, take them down now. Tomorrow may be too late.

For that's the other thing about polystyrene tiles. They can turn a small fire into a killer. On the whole, we can congratulate ourselves on a very lucky escape.

Saturday, May 17, began as a fairly ordinary day. I got up at about 7 o'clock, took my wife Jean a cup of tea in bed, then set off for the south coast on business.

Jean rose shortly afterwards, did a few domestic chores, then left the house to make one or two family calls.

It was just as well that she did, for within an hour the house was filled with lethal black smoke and fumes. Burning plastic dripped from the ceiling, starting little fires in carpets or furniture.

A neighbour spotted the smoke pouring out of the shattered dining room window and called the fire brigade. Another neighbour managed to locate Jean, and she and the firemen arrived more or less simultaneously.

This was another piece of good luck, because it meant that they didn't have to break down a door to get in. Once inside, they put out the flames in what seemed a remarkably short time and without a mess; in fact, the only evidence that the fire brigade had been inside the house was that the fire was out.

They also called the electricity and gas boards, who sent representatives to check the safety of their respective installations. 'The wiring's all right – must have been a gas leak,' said the man from the electricity board. 'Nothing wrong with the gas – must have been an electrical fault,' said the gas man. Both were right, in a way. The trouble seems to have started in the electrical wiring of the cooker clock.

One thing is certain: without those ceiling tiles, it would have been a very localised fire, and might even have gone out by itself. As it was, the fire spread from the kitchen to the adjoining dining room. The heat shattered seven panes of glass, and charred one window frame so badly that it had to be replaced.

Two elderly armchairs in the dining room were destroyed, but the sofa escaped, as did the dining table. The fire brigade put out the flames before they reached the hall and stairwell, or it might have been a much more serious matter.

But the smoke damage …

Everything in the house was covered with an oily black film, almost impossible to remove. Every single item of clothing and bedding in the house needed to be washed, even those in drawers and cupboards.

There seemed to be nowhere the smoke hadn't penetrated. Everything we owned had to be sorted out into one of three categories: ruined, cleanable, or useable immediately (well, more or less). All the goods in category two – by far the largest – we bundled into a spare bedroom, and we're still working our way through the contents.

The insurance company paid up, with no more than the ordinary delay, for the damage to the house and the interior decoration. The ceilings have been covered with an ornamental plaster which has approved fire resistant qualities.

Now, four months later, things are slowly returning to normal. We feel we can invite people into our home again. But nothing can make us forget that we had a very lucky escape. The fire could have started at any time. Had it broken out during the night we would undoubtedly have been killed by the fumes long before anyone raised the alarm.

The discovery that you aren't fireproof is a very frightening one.

(from *Property Mover* – adapted)

1. Polystyrene tiles are dangerous.
2. The author and his wife realise they were wrong to put them on the kitchen ceiling.
3. One day when they were both out a fire broke out.
4. It started with a gas leak in the cooker.
5. A neighbour saw flames coming out of the kitchen window and called the fire brigade.
6. Another neighbour told Jean that her house was on fire.
7. Luckily she had left the door unlocked, so the firemen didn't have to break it down.
8. The fire brigade didn't make a mess.
9. Two chairs in the dining room escaped damage.
10. But the dining room table was badly damaged.
11. Most of their possessions were ruined by smoke.
12. They were lucky the fire didn't start at night.

6 Write at least 200 words describing the house you are living in at the moment. Say what changes you would like to make. Try to include some words and expressions from the Student's Book lesson.

7 Try the crossword.

ACROSS

1. Make stronger.
7. Do you keep all your letters or do you .... them up?
9. What you do at an election.
11. The colour you see when you are angry.
12. Wet (weather).
15. In an .... you need to keep calm and think quickly.
17. I'm a bit busy .... the moment.
19. If I eat a lot of sugar I often get a .... or two on my face.
21. Sometimes cheerful, sometimes bad-tempered.
23. Between nine and eleven.
25. I was .... in Dublin in 1956.
26. Many people keep this kind of animal as a pet.
28. Her brother died three years ....
30. *20 down* backwards.
33. 'I've just broken my china fruit bowl!' 'Perhaps you could .... it back together again.'
34. The opposite of *down*.
35. The Simple Past of *lend*.
36. Between your hip and your foot.
37. Change from a solid into a liquid.
38. Don't let anybody see you.
41. The past participle of *spend*.
44. .... least 1000 people took part in the anti-war demonstration.
46. We had a new floor put .... downstairs.
47. Have you got a computer .... home?
48. I'll hold your hand if you .... afraid.
49. On your own.
51. I love you whether you are rich .... poor.
52. Most people have .... fingers and two thumbs.
56. I .... getting headaches.
58. 'Did you?' '..............., I didn't.'
59. *30 across* backwards.
60. Feeling unhappy about something.

DOWN

1. You might do this if you are very frightened.
2. You do this on a horse or a bicycle.
3. The opposite of *unpleasant*.
4. The past participle of *teach*.
5. Between afternoon and night.
6. Negative answer.
7. A popular drink taken with milk or lemon.
8. A girl's name.
10. Make an effort to do something.
13. Get better.
14. You haven't finished this crossword ....
16. Not on the right, not on the left – in the ....
18. I'm .... tired to go out tonight.
19. She's got two daughters and one ....
20. .... the other hand.
22. Not old enough = too ....
24. The opposite of *later*.
27. Hurry up and .... dressed!
29. If you are feeling ill, you .... to take the day off.
31. You usually go into a garden through a ....
32. A freezer is a .... for keeping food cold in.
33. Pleased.
37. Breakfast is the first .... of the day.
39. Just let me look .... my diary.
40. Almost the same as *every*.
42. I left my car in the car ....
43. Most Moslems .... drink alcohol.
45. A measure of weight.
49. A banana, a pear, ... apple.
50. Way out.
53. We went for a walk .... spite of the rain.
54. Everything seems to .... wrong for him.
55. *Must* is never followed by ....
57. Did anybody turn .... for the meeting?

(Solution on page 144.)

"I hope the children aren't bothering you."

D1 What do they look like?

1 Vocabulary revision and extension. Do you know the names of all the articles of clothing in the picture? Can you write the names of ten more articles of clothing?

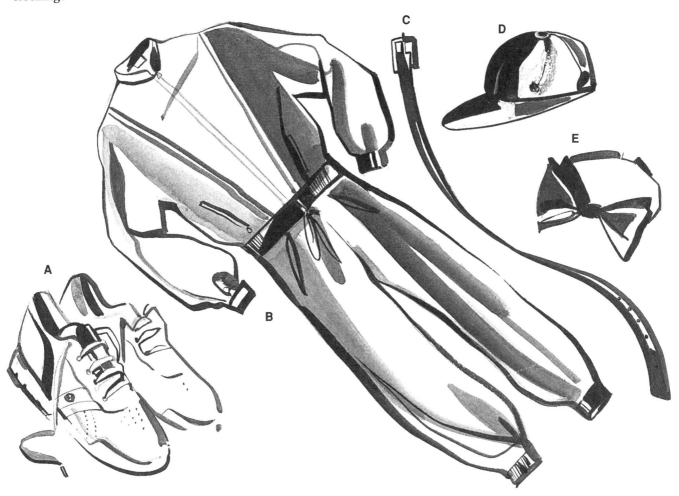

2 Grammar. What is the difference between *so* and *such*? Look at the examples and then choose the best rule. Check the answer on page 144. Examples:

I'm so tired.
I've got such a headache.
I've got such a bad headache.
My headache's so bad.

Rule 1: *such* is more emphatic than *so*.
Rule 2: *such* is used before nouns; *so* is used before adjectives.
Rule 3: *such* is used before a noun, or before adjective + noun. *So* is used before an adjective without a noun.
Rule 4: *such* is used after *have*; *so* is used after *be*.
Rule 5: the difference is a question of style.

3 Grammar. Put in *such* or *so*.

1. I'm .... handsome.
2. And I'm .... intelligent.
3. I've got .... a sense of humour.
4. And .... interesting ideas.
5. I'm .... a brilliant dancer.
6. And .... superior in every way.
7. It's really .... a pleasure to be with me.
8. I can't understand why I have .... trouble keeping my girlfriends.

4 Grammar. Put in *so much, so many, so few* or *so little*.

When I agreed to serve on the committee, I didn't realise there would be ....1.... meetings – they take up ....2.... of my time that I think I'm going to have to resign. The meetings are completely useless anyway – people put ....3.... energy into arguing for hours and hours about things that have ....4.... importance that they weren't worth discussing in the first place. And ....5.... of the committee members are actually the kind of people I really want to get to know. I'm sure I'll be ....6.... happier if I give it up.

5 Grammar revision: modification of *too* and comparatives. Use expressions from the table to describe some of your features and parts of your body (or somebody else's). You can add other adjectives if you like. Examples:

*My eyes are possibly **a little too small**.*
*I wish my nose was **a bit shorter**.*
*It would be nice if my feet were **rather narrower**.*
*My mouth is **just right**.*

a bit	longer
a little	shorter
a fraction	wider
rather	narrower
a lot	bigger
much	smaller
far	*etc.*

	too long
	too short
	too wide
	etc.

| just right |

6 📼 Find Lesson D1, Exercise 1 on the Student's Cassette. Listen to the song and write down all the parts of the body that you hear.

"Gerald, do you remember how I used to say your head was shaped like an onion?"

"See what I mean? No sense of humour."

7 Read the descriptions, and then write a paragraph saying which of the four women you think has the most interesting personality, and why.

Lily Smalls

(She is looking in the mirror and talking to herself.)

Oh, there's a face. Where you get that hair from? Got it from old tom cat. Give it back, then, love. Oh, there's a perm. Where you get that nose from, Lily? Got it from my father, silly. You've got it on upside down. Oh, there's a conk. Look at your complexion. No, you look. Needs a bit of make-up. Needs a veil. Oh, there's glamour. Where you get that smile, Lil? Never you mind, girl. Nobody loves you. That's what you think. Who is it loves you? Shan't tell.

(from *Under Milk Wood* by Dylan Thomas)

perm: longlasting waves or curls put into hair at a hairdresser's
conk: nose

PREHISTORIC WOMAN

She was just over four and a half feet tall, large boned, stocky, and bow-legged, but walked upright on strong muscular legs and flat bare feet. Her arms, long in proportion to her body, were bowed like her legs. She had a large beaky nose, a prognathous jaw jutting out like a muzzle, and no chin. Her low forehead sloped back into a long, large head, resting on a short thick neck. At the back of her head was a bony knob, an occipital bun, that emphasised its length.

A soft down of short brown hair, tending to curl, covered her legs and shoulders and ran along the upper spine of her back. It thickened into a head of heavy, long, rather bushy hair. She was already losing her winter pallor to a summer tan. Big, round, intelligent, dark brown eyes were deep set below overhanging brow ridges.

(from *The Clan of the Cave Bear* by Jean M. Auel)

four and a half feet: 1m 37

THE TRANSLATOR

The woman is watching me. She smiles sympathetically then goes back to her work. She is reading through a stack of foreign newspapers and occasionally marking an item with a thick black pencil. She is a linguist, fluent in most European languages. During the night the marked passages will be translated and Fidel will read them with his breakfast. She is not attractive. Her face is dominated by a large forehead and nose. Her neck is short and her shoulders box-like. But she is very intelligent. I wonder if she would trade her intelligence for beauty. But naturally. Stupid people never realise their stupidity. Beautiful people enjoy their attraction every waking moment. But the ultimate is to be beautiful and intelligent.

(from *Siege of Silence* by A.J. Quinnell)

On the river bank

The girl lay back on the slope of the river bank, her eyes closed against the sun. Her dark hair fanned out on each side of her face, her white, even teeth biting on a long stalk of grass as the young man looked down at her. Her skin was pale despite the freckles on her neat, pert nose, but her mouth was poppy red, full and tempting.

The young man's hair was almost white and it lifted softly in the breeze off the river. He was reading silently from an open book that was resting on the girl's stomach.

(from *Codeword Cromwell* by Ted Allbeury)

"Denis is trying to grow a beard."

D2 Focus on systems

1 Grammar: tenses after *I wish* and *If only*. Put in the right tenses.

1. I wish I (*can*) speak more languages.
2. If only I (*know*) what she was thinking!
3. Don't you wish you (*have*) a sweater like this?
4. I wish weekends (*come*) more often.
5. If only it (*not be*) so cold we could go for a walk.
6. I wish I (*be*) a cat – it must be a nice life.
7. I wish I (*pass*) my exams when I was at school.
8. Do you ever wish you (*not be*) born?
9. If only I (*not start*) smoking!
10. I wish I (*never meet*) you.
11. I wish I (*spend*) my money on something else instead of buying that car.

2 Grammar revision: relative clauses without *that/which*. Make sentences as in the example. Don't use *it* or *them*. Example:

I've lost the book Alice lent me.

BEGINNINGS	ENDS
I've lost the book	she had it last year
That's the same coat	Mary gave it to him
What's that picture	Alice lent it to me
Where are the papers	my doctor told me to take them
These are the pills	you're looking at it
He's wearing the ring	I put them on the table

3 Grammar revision. Complete the sentences with the prepositions from the box.

at behind by in front of inside off on out of over through under

1. 'Could I use your phone?' 'Yes, it's over there .... the window.'
2. I think that picture would look better .... the fireplace.
3. How did those black marks get .... the ceiling?
4. I've just found your address book. It was .... your chair.
5. Could you tell the children to get their toys .... my bed and come .... my bedroom?
6. When we redecorated the living room we found an old cupboard .... the plaster.
7. It's colder .... this house than outside.
8. The windows are so dirty you can't see .... them.
9. If everybody will sit down .... the table, we can start eating.
10. That boy spends at least six hours a day .... the TV.

4 Spelling. Check that you know all the adjectives in the box and then turn them into adverbs. Examples:

quick <u>quickly</u>   final   <u>finally</u>
nice   <u>nicely</u>   possible <u>possibly</u>
easy   <u>easily</u>

complete definite deliberate extreme fortunate full happy heavy high hopeful idle kind light probable real short slow terrible tidy total useful wide

Write sentences using five of the adverbs you have made.

5 Vocabulary study. Look at the words in the box and the things in the pictures. Find out the meanings or names of any that you don't know. Then choose one of the pictures and write down all the words from the box that could be used to describe what is in the picture (or part of it).

big   blunt   cheap   cold   dull   expensive   fast   flat   flexible fragile   hard   heavy   light   long   medium-sized   narrow   pointed rigid   rough   sharp   shiny   short   slow   small   smooth   soft transparent   unbreakable   warm   waterproof   wide

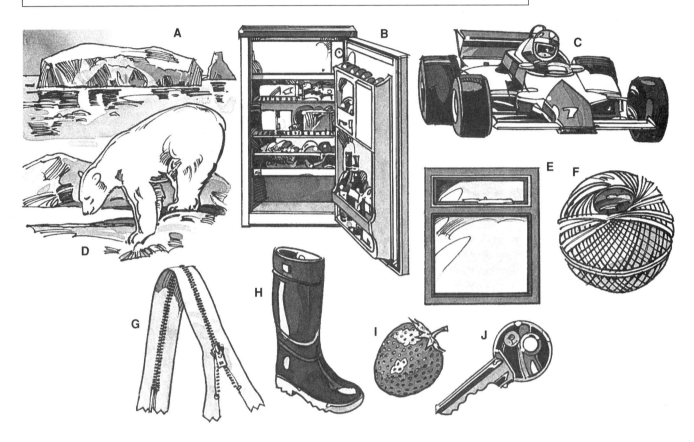

6 Read the poem, using a dictionary if you wish.

Conversations with my Fairy Godmother

I

You deaf cow.
I said bold, not bald.
You can forget the other two wishes.

II

'Hello, Fairy Godmother. You again.'

'Hello, son.
I'll give you a choice
Twenty pounds now
or you can be recognised after your death
as the greatest poet of the century.'

'Make it twenty-five.'

III

'So that's the baby.'

'It is indeed,
Fairy Godmother.'

'Very nice.
Would you prefer it to have beauty
or intelligence
or fame?'

'Gosh
Fairy Godmother
can we think it over?'

'Or regular meals?'

(H. Highwater)

7 Do one of these writing tasks.

1. Invent the missing parts of this story and then write it out in full.

A visit from my fairy godmother

I had a visit from my fairy godmother yesterday evening. I looked up from my newspaper, and there she was standing by the window.

'Hello,' she said. 'I'm your fairy godmother.' She didn't look quite as I expected. ....

'What do you want?' I asked.

'Well,' she said. 'I've come to give you three wishes. That's what fairy godmothers do. They give you three wishes, don't they? What's your first wish?'

'OK,' I said. 'I'd like ....'

'That's a bit of an unusual wish,' she said. 'I don't think I've ever heard that one before. Anyway, if that's what you want – '
....

'Actually,' I said, 'I think that wish was a bit of a mistake. I'm sorry I wished that wish. Can I have my next one?'

'OK,' she said. 'What is it?'
....

'Are you sure?' she asked.
....

'Right,' I said. 'That was much more satisfactory. Now for my last wish, ...'

'That's going to be a bit difficult to manage,' she said. 'but I'll see what I can do.'
....

'Well, thanks for everything,' I said. 'Is there anything you'd like before you go?'
....

2. Write your own story about a visit from your fairy godmother.

"In all my years as a fairy, that's the silliest use of three wishes I've ever seen."

"By God, Mumford, I wish you'd do something about that bad breath of yours."

D3 I don't like playtime

1 Grammar revision. Put in *each, all, some, any, no* or *none*.

1. The teacher is careful to give .... time to .... child during the day.
2. .... children are a bit noisy, but most of them behave quite well, and there are .... serious discipline problems.
3. .... of the children can read and do simple maths, but .... of them still find it difficult to write.
4. The teacher would like to use computers for maths, but there aren't .... in her classroom – in fact, there are .... in the school.
5. .... child has his or her own likes and dislikes.
6. Peggy likes .... the things they do at school.
7. Ben doesn't like .... of the school activities at all.

2 Grammar revision. Put in *there is, there was, there has been, there will be*, etc. (You may need to use question forms and contracted forms.)

1. Do you think .... a teachers' strike next week?
2. Why .... a dustbin in the living room?
3. .... two policemen at the back door. They say they want to see you.
4. When I got home, ... a letter from Charlie on the doormat.
5. Quick! Phone for an ambulance! .... an accident!
6. How many general elections .... since the war?
7. I used to enjoy cycling when I was younger, but ....n't so many cars then.
8. If food was properly distributed .... enough for everybody.

3 Vocabulary revision. Find words from the two boxes that belong together. Example:

<u>singing songs</u>

asking	doing	drawing	listening to
making	playing	reading	singing
solving	telling	watching	working
writing			

books	games	hard	letters	maths
pictures	plans	problems	questions	
songs	stories	the radio	TV	

4 Vocabulary revision. Use these words and expressions to help you complete the text. You may need to make some small changes. If necessary, look back at the Student's Book lesson to see what the words and expressions mean and how they are used.

critical	each	enthusiastic	examination
explain	fair	job	least
(*no*) point (*in ...ing*)		on strike	patient
private	size	subject	unco-operative
useless			

Caroline's favourite ...1... at school was maths: she enjoyed solving problems, and was ...2... about the teaching methods. But most of her friends tended to find maths very difficult, and because they thought it was a ...3... subject they saw no ...4... in working at it, and were ...5... and ...6... in the lessons. Maths was, in fact, the ...7... popular subject in Caroline's class.

During Caroline's last year at school the teachers went ...8... for two months, to protest against the ...9... of classes (30–35 was typical). ...10... morning, Caroline gave ...11... maths lessons to three of her friends, so that they would have a chance of passing their ...12... . She's ...13..., and good at ...14... things to people, and the lessons went well: Caroline and her three friends all passed. They offered to pay her for the lessons, but she refused: she sympathised with the teachers' strike, and did not think it would be ...15... if she took money for doing their ...16... .

"*Look, if you have five pocket calculators and I take two away, how many have you got left?*"

5 Look at the statistics. Then complete the following sentences with some of these words and expressions. You may need to use some of them more than once.

| very few   not many   some   a quarter   three quarters   nearly all |
| more   far more   nearly   less than |

1. .... British pupils go to private schools.
2. .... British pupils go to state schools.
3. .... American than British pupils go to private schools.
4. Almost .... of British pupils leave school at 16.
5. .... American pupils leave school at 16.
6. .... 55% of American pupils go on to full-time higher education.
7. .... 10% of British pupils go on to full-time higher education.
8. .... of American pupils obtain the High School Diploma.
9. .... of British pupils pass A Level.
10. .... American than British pupils go on to full-time higher education.

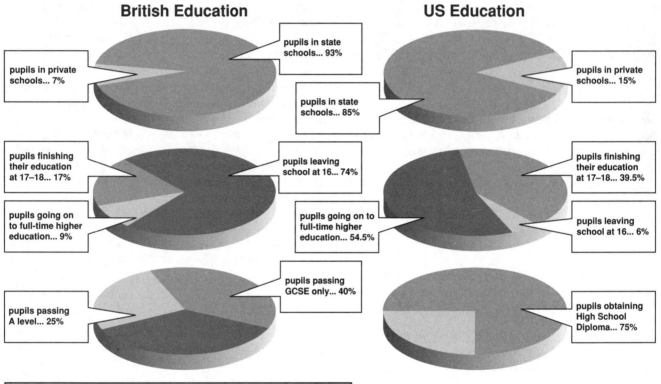

GCSE: General Certificate of Secondary Education – taken at age 16.
A Level: Advanced Level – taken at age 18.

"I often say, Mrs Dent, I'd rather have your little Christopher in my class than all the bright, clever ones!"

"Oh, by the way ... according to my teacher I'm suffering from a lack of discipline in the home. See to it, will you?"

6 Read one or more of the texts, using a dictionary if you wish.

First Day at School

A millionbillionwillion miles from home
Waiting for the bell to go. (To go where?)
Why are they all so big, other children?
So noisy? So much at home they
must have been born in uniform
Lived all their lives in playgrounds
Spent the years inventing games
that don't let me in. Games
that are rough, that swallow you up.
And the railings.
All around, the railings.
Are they to keep out wolves and monsters?
Things that carry off and eat children?
Things you don't take sweets from?
Perhaps they're to stop us getting out
Running away from the lessins. Lessin.
What does a lessin look like?
Sounds small and slimy.
They keep them in glassrooms.
Whole rooms made out of glass. Imagine.
I wish I could remember my name
Mummy said it would come in useful.
Like wellies. When there's puddles.
Yellowwellies. I wish she was here.
I think my name is sewn on somewhere
Perhaps the teacher will read it for me.
Tea-cher. The one who makes the tea.

(Roger McGough)

Children's jokes

The absent-minded professor said to another professor, 'I'd hardly recognise you. You've changed so much. You've put on a great deal of weight and your hair has turned grey and you don't wear glasses any longer. What has happened to you, Professor Dixon?'
   'But I'm not Professor Dixon,' came the answer.
   'Remarkable. You've even changed your name.'

A lion was walking through the jungle when he came across a deer eating grass in a clearing. The lion roared, 'Who is the King of the jungle?' and the deer replied, 'Oh, you are, Master.' The lion walked off pleased. Soon he came across a zebra drinking at a water hole. The lion roared, 'Who is the King of the jungle?' and the zebra replied, 'Oh, you are, Master.' The lion walked off pleased. Then he came across an elephant. 'Who is the King of the jungle?' he roared. With that the elephant threw the lion across a tree trunk and jumped on him. The lion scraped himself up off the ground and said, 'Okay, okay, there's no need to get mad just because you don't know the answer.'

First day at school

But I was still shy and half paralysed when in the presence of a crowd, and my first day at the new school made me the laughing stock of the classroom. I was sent to the blackboard to write my name and address; I knew my name and address, knew how to write it, knew how to spell it; but standing at the blackboard with the eyes of the many girls and boys looking at my back made me freeze inside and I was unable to write a single letter.
   'Write your name,' the teacher called to me.
   I lifted the white chalk to the blackboard and, as I was about to write my mind went blank, empty; I could not remember my name, not even the first letter. Somebody giggled and I stiffened.
   'Just forget us and write your name and address,' the teacher coaxed.
   An impulse to write would flash through me, but my hand would refuse to move. The children began to titter and I flushed hotly.
   'Don't you know your name?' the teacher asked.
   I looked at her and could not answer. The teacher rose and walked to my side, smiling at me to give me confidence. She placed her hand tenderly upon my shoulder.
   'What's your name?' she asked.
   'Richard.' I whispered.
   'Richard what?'
   'Richard Wright.'
   'Spell it.'
   I spelled my name in a wild rush of letters, trying desperately to redeem my paralysing shyness.
   'Spell it slowly so I can hear it,' she directed me.
   I did.
   'Now can you write?'
   'Yes, ma'am.'
   'Then write it.'
   Again I turned to the blackboard and lifted my hand to write, then I was blank and void within. I tried frantically to collect my senses but I could remember nothing. A sense of the girls and boys behind me filled me to the exclusion of everything. I realised how utterly I was failing and I grew weak and leaned my hot forehead against the cold blackboard. The room burst into a loud and prolonged laugh and my muscles froze.
   'You may go to your seat,' the teacher said.
   I sat and cursed myself. Why did I always appear so dumb when I was called to perform something in a crowd? I knew how to write as well as any pupil in the classroom, and no doubt I could read better than any of them, and I could talk fluently and expressively when I was sure of myself. Then why did strange faces make me freeze? I sat with my ears and neck burning, hearing the pupils whisper about me, hating myself, hating them.

(from *Black Boy* by Richard Wright)

7 Do one of these writing tasks. Write at least 200 words and try to include some words and expressions from the Student's Book lesson.

1. Write how you feel about the subjects in the box. Use one of these expressions in each answer (but write more if you want to).

   I really enjoy …
   I'm extremely interested in …
   I'm fascinated by …
   I'm quite interested in …
   I'd like to know more about …
   I don't know anything about …
   I've always wanted to learn something about …
   I'm not very interested in …
   I'm not in the least interested in …
   I don't much like …
   I don't like … at all.
   I'm bored by …
   I hate …
   I think … is a complete waste of time.
   I used to like …, but I've lost interest in it.
   I used to think … was boring, but now I'm getting interested in it.

archaeology	art	biology
classical music	computing	cooking
economics	folk dancing	history
maths	philosophy	poetry	pop music
psychology	religion	wild life

2. Write about the education system in your country. Is it different from the British and American systems (see Exercise 5)?

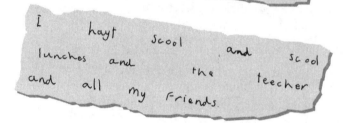

(from *Lots of Love* and *The Facts of Love*, compiled by Nanette Newman)

"Girls, girls! – A little less noise, please."

D4 I knew everyone

1 Vocabulary revision. How quickly can you answer these questions?

Your father's or mother's brother is called your *uncle*. What is the word for each of these?

1. your father's or mother's sister
2. your uncle's wife
3. your brother's or sister's son
4. your brother's or sister's daughter
5. your sister's husband
6. your brother's wife
7. your son's wife
8. your wife's or husband's father
9. your uncle's son or daughter

2 Grammar revision: possessives. How quickly can you write the answers?

Your nephew is your brother's or sister's son. How could you describe each of these?

1. your aunt
2. your uncle
3. your niece
4. your cousin
5. your grandson
6. your mother-in-law
7. your sister-in-law

3 Grammar: word order. We often put prepositions at the ends of questions in English. Look at the examples and then make questions for the other answers.

1. I come from Burma.
   Where do you come from?
2. She lives with her aunt.
   Who does she live with?
3. I'm writing to my mother.
4. I'm thinking about my childhood.
5. We live in a small country town.
   (*What sort of ...?*)
6. We're talking about our families.
7. She comes from Scotland.
8. He works for an insurance company.

4 Grammar: word order. There are two ways of making relative clauses with prepositions. Look at the examples and then change the other sentences from formal to informal.

1. I did not like the people **with whom I was at school**. (*formal*)
   I didn't like the people I *was at school with*. (*informal*)
2. I have never been back to the town **in which I was born**. (*formal*)
   I've never been back to the town **I *was born in***. (*informal*)
3. He is one of the people with whom I used to work.
4. I do not much like the town in which I live.
5. My family is the only thing for which I would fight.
6. John is the only person to whom I write.
7. The house in which I grew up no longer exists.
8. He has had a terrible quarrel with the woman with whom he lives.

5 Grammar revision. Put in *for*, *since*, *from* or *ago*.

1. I've known her .... seven years.
2. But I've only known her well .... last year.
3. She joined my firm about ten years ....
4. But she was away at the New York branch .... 1988 to 1991.
5. .... January she's been in charge of the marketing division.
6. I had known .... some time that she was going to get the job.
7. In fact, she should have had it years ...., but they couldn't get old Harrison out.
8. It was pretty obvious .... her first few weeks in the new job that she was going to be first class.
9. In fact, she should turn out to be the best marketing manager the firm's had .... a very long time – maybe .... the 1960s.

6 Read this without a dictionary if possible. (*Alien* means 'foreigner'.)

Once a foreigner, always a foreigner

I believe, without undue modesty, that I have certain qualifications to write on 'how to be an alien'. I am an alien myself. What is more, I have been an alien all my life. Only during the first twenty-six years of my life I was not aware of this plain fact. I was living in my own country, a country full of aliens, and I noticed nothing peculiar or irregular about myself; then I came to England, and you can imagine my painful surprise.

Like all great and important discoveries it was a matter of a few seconds. You probably all know from your schooldays how Isaac Newton discovered the law of gravitation. An apple fell on his head. This incident set him thinking for a minute or two, then he exclaimed joyfully: 'Of course! The gravitation constant is the acceleration per second that a mass of one gram causes at a distance of one centimetre.' You were also taught that James Watt one day went into the kitchen where cabbage was cooking and saw the lid of the saucepan rise and fall. 'Now let me think,' he murmured – 'let me think.' Then he struck his forehead and the steam engine was discovered. It was the same with me, although circumstances were rather different.

It was like this. Some years ago I spent a lot of time with a young lady who was very proud and conscious of being English. Once she asked me – to my great surprise – whether I would marry her. 'No,' I replied, 'I will not. My mother would never agree to my marrying a foreigner.' She looked at me a little surprised and irritated, and retorted: 'I, a foreigner? What a silly thing to say. I am English. You are the foreigner. And your mother too.' I did not give in. 'In Budapest, too?' I asked her. 'Everywhere,' she declared with determination. 'Truth does not depend on geography. What is true in England is also true in Hungary and in North Borneo and Venezuela and everywhere.'

I saw that this truth was as irrefutable as it was simple. I was startled and upset. Mainly because of my mother whom I loved and respected. Now, I suddenly learned what she really was.

It was a shame and bad taste to be an alien, and it is no use pretending otherwise. There is no way out of it. A criminal may improve and become a decent member of society. A foreigner cannot improve. Once a foreigner, always a foreigner. There is no way out for him. He may become British; he can never become English.

(from *How to be an Alien* by George Mikes)

7 Write an imaginary letter home from an English or American immigrant who has been in your country for a year, saying what he/she likes, dislikes, finds easy and finds difficult. Try to include some words and expressions from the Student's Book lesson.

D5 A beautiful place

1 Grammar: Past Perfect tense. Imagine that a forgetful old lady went out one evening to see some friends. She had a number of problems. Find reasons for them, using the Past Perfect tense. Example:

Why didn't she get to her friends' house?
Because she had forgotten their address.

1. Why didn't she look in her address book?
2. Why didn't she phone home and ask her daughter for their address?
3. Why didn't she go back home?
4. Why couldn't she get a hotel room?
5. Why did she get wet?
6. When she found her home, why couldn't she open the front door?
7. Why did her daughter take a long time to let her in?

2 Grammar: Past Perfect tense (continued). Put together the following ideas to make sentences about a burglary. Use *although* or *because* + Past Perfect in each sentence. Example:

we thought might be burgled – neighbours burgled week before
We thought we might be burgled because our neighbours had been burgled the week before.

1. burgled last Saturday; burglar obviously knew we were out – we left lights on
2. he got in easily – we locked door
3. got in without making noise – we forgot to switch on burglar alarm
4. burglar didn't find jewels – we hid them
5. got money – we put in safe
6. found passports and credit cards – left in desk drawer
7. burglary very expensive for us – forgot to renew insurance

3 Vocabulary revision. Match the words in the box with the pictures.

| bridge | field | gate | glacier | hill | island | lake | mountain | path |
| river | road | rocks | stream | valley | waterfall | wood | | |

4 Find Lesson D5, Exercise 5C on the Student's Cassette. Which of the words in the box are *not* in the song?

| eagle | flying | lake | river | sea | shade | skiing | sky | snow | trees | waves | wind |

5 Decide where the four lettered sentences (*a* to *d*) should be added to the eleven numbered sentences of the text. (For example, you might decide that sentence *a* should come after sentence *1*.)

1. She comes from Houston, Texas and I come from Oxford, England.
2. Being on the coast of the Gulf of Mexico, it's both hot and humid, and there's bad atmospheric pollution from the oil refineries.
3. She thinks Oxford is pretty depressing: it's cold most of the year, there's no sun and it rains a lot.
4. So we have more or less decided to live somewhere else.
5. Our physical environment is important to both of us, and we both love beautiful landscapes.
6. I especially like mountains, and feel good at a high altitude; she gets altitude sickness if she goes upstairs.
7. I like a cool damp climate; she doesn't like rain.
8. She likes deserts; I can't stand heat.
9. We both need space, and feel happy in wild areas a long way from civilisation; we also both like cinemas, theatres, art galleries, concerts and good food and wine.
10. I hate big cities; she loves pavements and crowds.
11. However, we'd quite like to stay together, so we have this problem.

a. Does anybody know a hot flat cool mountainous desert with no people, plenty of culture and some good restaurants?
b. I think Houston has a horrible climate.
c. Probably if we weren't together, I would live in North Wales and she would divide her time between Paris and Texas.
d. What we haven't decided yet is exactly where.

6 Do one of these writing tasks. Try to include some words and expressions from the Student's Book lesson.

1. Write a description of a place that you like or dislike very much.
2. Describe a place on earth as seen from the point of view of an explorer from another planet.

"I don't care what planet you're from, you can't run around earth stark naked!"

"You have a go in ours, and we'll have a go in yours, okay?"

7 Read two or more of these poems, using a dictionary if you wish.
Write how you feel about them.

Curaçao

I think I am going to love it here.

I ask the man in the telegraph office
the way to the bank.
He locks the door and walks with me
insisting he needs the exercise.

When I ask the lady at my hotel desk
what bus to take to the beach
she gives me a lift with her beautiful sister
who is just driving by in a sports job.

And already I have thought of something
I want to ask the sister.

(Earle Birney)

Stopping by woods on a snowy evening

Whose woods these are I think I know.
His house is in the village though;
He will not see me stopping here
To watch his woods fill up with snow.

My little horse must think it queer
To stop without a farmhouse near
Between the woods and frozen lake
The darkest evening of the year.

He gives his harness bells a shake
To ask if there is some mistake.
The only other sound's the sweep
Of easy wind and downy flake.

The woods are lovely, dark and deep,
But I have promises to keep,
And miles to go before I sleep,
And miles to go before I sleep.

(Robert Frost)

I dreamed I was

Oh I dreamed I was walking alone
In a city of sadness,
And I wandered thro' deserts of stone,
In a jungle of drabness.
I saw children in rows were reciting the rules,
And the railings were high that surrounded the
   schools,
And I knew that it wasn't a dream,
Slabs of stone where the grass should have been.

And the walls were a wilderness high,
And the sun was in hiding,
And the clouds were tearing the sky,
Where the smoke clouds were writhing,
And the God of the city had iron jaws,
A ragged monster with jagged claws,
And I knew that it wasn't a dream,
Smoke and dust where the heart should have been.

In the markets where daydreams were sold
The blind men were masters,
Turning all that they touched into gold,
The blind men were masters.
I saw a million doorways and a million rooms,
A million mourners and a million tombs,
And I knew it wasn't a dream,
A million masks where the faces should have been.

Then at last the sun shone in my dream,
And toppled each tower,
There where the stone slabs had been,
The earth was in flower.
And the iron bars melted every one,
The stone walls quivered and cracked in the sun,
And I saw that it couldn't have been,
And I knew it was only a dream.

(Leon Rosselson)

Coming down

Coming down from the summit
it was all different.
Suddenly the world was tame
and upside-down.
We began to talk about work
mortgages
children
wives.
Then, below the first ice-field
Bellini stopped, and said
'Next year
we do the East Face direct.'
We looked back
and everything was all right again.

(Lewis Mancha)

D6 Focus on systems

1 Grammar revision. Put in *that/which* or *whose*. Then match the definitions to the words in the box. (There are more words than you will need.)

1. a farm animal .... provides milk
2. an animal .... meat is called pork
3. a bird .... eggs people often eat
4. a mammal .... lives in holes in the ground
5. an animal .... neck is longer than its legs
6. an animal .... ears are longer than its tail
7. a bird .... can talk
8. a fish .... lives in fresh water

| cobra | cow | crocodile | fox | frog | giraffe | hen | parrot | pig |
| rabbit | squirrel | tiger | trout | whale | | | | |

2 Grammar: identifying expressions. Choose five or more of the adjectives and make sentences to explain what they mean. Use the structure *A ... person is somebody who ...* Examples:

A bright person is somebody who thinks quickly.
A shy person is somebody who is afraid of contact with other people.

| affectionate | argumentative | bright | dull | faithful | friendly |
| homosexual | honest | humorous | moody | shy | sociable | tolerant |

3 Grammar: non-identifying expressions. Join these sentences together with *which*. Use a comma (,) before and after the relative clause. Can you replace *which* by *that* in any of the sentences?

1. My house needs a lot doing to it. It is about 40 years old.
   My house, which needs a lot doing to it, is about 40 years old.
2. His violin is worth over £20,000. It once belonged to Beethoven.
3. Yesterday's meeting lasted six hours. It was a complete waste of time.
4. The average weekly wage used to be about £6. It is now about £280.
5. Penguins are completely unable to fly. They have no natural enemies.
6. This car keeps breaking down. I bought it from an ex-friend of mine.
   This car, which I bought from an ex-friend of mine, keeps breaking down.
7. My novel is going to be published next autumn. You didn't like it at all.
8. These glasses give me a headache. I have to wear them for reading.
9. Your letter took nine days to get here. You posted it on the seventeenth.
10. Folk music has gone out of fashion. I like it enormously.

4 Translate these into your language.

1. One of the window panes needs replacing and the frame needs painting.
2. We've had the downstairs store-room converted into an office.
3. My brother's the large fair-haired one with the beard standing next to Sarah.
4. If only I hadn't eaten those shrimps!
5. I wish I could find my glasses.
6. If only she would stop complaining!
7. I did French at school for six years and I've been learning Spanish since September.
8. What do you mean by 'training for jobs'?
9. His parents gave him a good upbringing but unfortunately he didn't have a very good education.
10. By the time we arrived everyone else had already gone home.
11. Tony, whose wife is a Member of Parliament, isn't interested in politics at all.
12. The party which I supported was unsuccessful in the last election.

5 Pronunciation. Say the words, then copy them and underline the stressed syllables.

advertisement   atmosphere   casually   convince   definitely   economics
elderly   environment   generally   horizon   horizontal   increasingly
majority   muscular   obviously   rectangular   redecorate   several
strengthen   successful   undervalued   variety   volunteers

6 Read the article; as you read, write your answers to the questions. Only use a dictionary if you are really stuck.

DEFENCE AND POVERTY

On present trends Britain will, just after the turn of the century, be the poorest nation in the whole of Europe apart from Albania. But at least, on present policy, it will have Trident to defend its increasingly run-down and divided society. This is the result of British policy making since 1945, with its emphasis on the symbols of great power and status. The demands of the defence community have continually been put before the needs of the rest of society.

Trident: a type of nuclear missile

1. Do you think the author of this article is in favour of spending large sums of money on defence?
2. Why do you think the author speaks of a 'divided' society?

On the latest figures Britain spends 5.5 per cent of its national wealth on defence compared with 4 per cent in France, just over 3 per cent in Germany and just under 3 per cent in Italy. The pattern has been the same for the last 30 years, as Britain has tied up more of its resources unproductively in the defence field than any of our competitors. But what would happen if Britain were to reduce its defence expenditure to the level of say Germany and Italy? This would involve fundamental changes in policy, such as ending any pretence at having a world-wide Navy, together with huge cuts in the equipment programme and buying more equipment from abroad.

3. Who are some of Britain's competitors? What do you think they are competing for?
4. Why do you think Britain maintains a world-wide Navy?

The extra government spending that would be possible on schools, hospitals and schemes to reduce unemployment would be massive; but so would the major dislocation in huge areas of British industry. Unfortunately for those who want to change defence policy towards a more realistic structure and at the same time to improve British economic performance, the military-industrial complex is extremely powerful and includes not just military planners and industrial bosses but also trade unions and a huge number of jobs, probably as many as 800,000.

5. Why are some trade union leaders against spending less on defence?

Is there no way out of this dilemma? Some have suggested that it should be possible to wind down the defence industries and redeploy the effort to civil work just as was done after 1945. The problem is that then it was easy to demobilise the forces and rebuild civilian industry because there was a vast demand for its products after wartime shortages, and massive new programmes in areas like housing to employ ex-servicemen. And the government had enough power over the economy to control the rate of transition.

6. Was there big growth in civilian industry in your country after the Second World War?

To undertake a similar programme now, when there are nearly four million unemployed, in the hope that somehow new demand for British products will emerge, would be economic and political suicide. But what about starting with the industrial base – the research and development (R and D) effort? Britain puts more of its R and D money into the defence field than any other country, including the US. The latest figures show that almost 30 per cent of British R and D spending is on defence compared with 23 per cent in the US.
In Germany it is about six per cent and in Japan about 0.5 per cent. In Britain far too much of our best scientific effort is going into new military equipment and not enough into developing new products that might help revitalise the economy.

7. If you were Prime Minister of Britain, would you try and reduce the amount of money Britain spends on military research and development?
8. Why do you think Germany and Japan spend so little on military R and D?

Past experience suggests that just gradually cutting back on military spending will get nowhere. A major reorganisation of parts of the economy would be involved, and today's British industry could not carry out this reorganisation without government intervention. This sort of programme in today's circumstances can only be achieved by much greater state control of the whole process.
But is there any sign that a Labour government is prepared to face all the problems that such a policy involves?

(from an article by Clive Ponting – adapted)

9. Do you think government should have a lot of control over private industry?

7 Write at least 200 words giving your views on at least one of these questions. Try to include some words and expressions from the Student's Book lesson.

1. Which politician (in your country / in the world) do you admire most? Why?
2. What do you think are the two or three most important qualities for a successful politician?
3. Do you think politicians should have jobs other than their political jobs?
4. Do you think politicians should vote the way their party expects them to vote, even if their own opinion is different?
5. Should Members of Parliament be paid more or less than: doctors, heads of universities, senior executives in industry?

D7 Boy meets girl

1 Grammar revision: quantifiers with and without *of*. Choose suitable expressions from the box to complete the text. More than one answer is possible in some cases. You may not need to use all the expressions.

any (of)	each (of)	every	every one of
more (of)	most (of)	neither (of)	no
none (of)	several (of)	some (of)	

I've got two daughters; ....1.... them is married. My younger daughter, Ann, has had ....2.... boyfriends already than I've had in my whole life. I'm quite envious. She's got ....3.... boyfriends at the moment. I don't know how she does it, but she somehow manages to give ....4.... the boys the impression that he's the only one. I don't think ....5.... them knows about the others. ....6.... her boyfriends are very good-looking. But I don't think ....7.... boy who goes out with Ann can be very bright.

My other daughter is quite different – much more the faithful type. She's had ....8.... boyfriends, but always one at a time. And ....9.... relationship is very serious while it lasts. The two girls have quite a lot of arguments, of course. The older one always says that you need complete trust and honesty for ....10.... real relationship. Her sister says that ....11.... relationship is perfect all the time, so you might as well have a lot and get something different out of ....12.... them. ....13.... people criticise my younger daughter and say that her sister is right, but I'm not so sure. I think ....14.... her ideas are quite interesting, and if I was her age again I might behave in the same way.

2 Grammar revision: position of frequency adverbs. Use the adverbs from the box to say how often you do some of these things. Put the adverb in the right place (before the verb). Example:

I often write to my parents.

always	very often	often	quite often
sometimes	occasionally	hardly ever	
never			

How often do you:
- write to your mother/father/son/daughter?
- write to your brother/sister?
- buy flowers for people?
- start conversations with strangers?
- talk about your deepest feelings?
- lose your temper?
- kiss people?
- get attracted to people?
- fall in love?
- get depressed?
- cry?
- say 'I love you'?
- mean it?

3 Grammar: position of frequency adverbs (continued). Use the same adverbs to say how often you have done some of these things. Put the adverb after the first auxiliary verb. Examples:

I have often wished I could be alone.
I have never been hurt by somebody I loved.

How often have you:
- fallen in love with the wrong person?
- deliberately ended a relationship?
- been unhappy in a relationship?
- been happy in a relationship?
- wanted more friends?
- wanted fewer friends?
- wished you could be completely alone?
- been unpleasant to somebody you loved?
- been badly hurt by somebody you loved?

4 Grammar. Write sentences using *had better* (*'d better*).

1. 'My car has been stolen.' '................'
2. 'Barry's been late for work every day this month.' '................'
3. 'My sister's had a high temperature for two days.' '................'
4. 'You've parked your car in a dangerous place.' '................'
5. 'It's late, and the children are very tired.' '................'
6. 'My car has been making a funny noise lately.' '................'
7. 'Your sister has phoned three times this morning.' '................'
8. 'I'm afraid we're going to miss the train.' '................'
9. 'These tomatoes don't look very good – what do you think I should do?' '................'

5 Read the letters. Which letter does each of the following sentences summarise best, in your opinion?

1. I live in a terrible world and nobody really understands my problems.
2. It's not their business.
3. What am I doing here?
4. Should I behave like everybody else?
5. Our attitudes are very different.
6. He's not good for her.
7. I don't believe her promises.

Falling to pieces

My family seem to be falling to pieces. My parents argue over the silliest things. I'm sure they'll split up soon. And my four brothers really go on at me because I haven't got a job and have to keep borrowing money from Mum. But I never have any luck with jobs. I feel so lonely, I spend all my time just sitting at home.

Rich, London

I want to go home

I've been living in Italy for the past two years because of my husband's job. As far as he's concerned we're here for good. He's very happy and so are our children. But I can't seem to settle down. I just wait for each day to pass so that the time when we might move back to England comes nearer. Will things get better?

J.L., Rome

Rude question

I am a 58-year-old accountant. I had a couple of heart attacks in the past, but I've had no problems for several years. I do a lot of sport and keep very fit. My weight hasn't changed since I was 20.

My problem is people who say 'By the way, Joe, how old are you?' The question never has anything to do with our conversation. I don't care how old they are, so why should they worry about my age? I would like to tell them it's none of their business. Is there a tactful way to say it?

Joe, Edinburgh

She must end it

Some weeks ago my sister-in-law told me she was having an affair. My brother has his faults, but I love him. She and I are also very close. I told her she must end the relationship. The man is married with a loving wife and three wonderful children.

She promised it would stop but it is still going on. She even had a weekend away with him – thanks to my covering up – so that she could finish the affair. But it seems they just had a great time together instead.

What should I do to end this situation before someone is hurt?

C.C., London

Will he be faithful?

My lover and I are in our early forties and we are both divorced. We intend to get married but I'm not sure that he'll be a faithful husband.

As well as his ex-wife, he has two other women friends whom he sees quite often. When I object, he says his friends are not my business and he'll keep on seeing them when we're married.

I have one or two men friends, who he says are no concern of his, but I plan to give them up if we get married. And that's the difference between us.

Should we get married?

Rosemary, Cambridge

What's wrong with me?

All my friends say they've had sex with boys, but I haven't. They keep saying there's something wrong with me. If there is, can you tell me what it is and what I can do about it? I've been out with plenty of boys but I just haven't wanted to have sex.

J.D., Norwich

Should I tell my father?

Some time ago my father went to live with another woman. But my parents are still good friends and my father is very good about looking after us.

A few months ago my mother met another man. I was glad at the time because she was very lonely. Now I don't think it was quite such a good idea. He has a horrible temper and the other night he actually hit my mother. She begged me not to tell my father, which I wanted to do.

She refuses to give the man up and says I don't understand, even though I'm fourteen. She must be really lonely to want to go out with such a pig. I know my father is still fond of her and I think that if he knew what was happening he might even come back. Do you think I should disobey her and tell him?

Becky, Chester

6 Do one of the following writing tasks.

1. Write an answer to one of the letters in Exercise 5. Use some of the words and expressions in Exercise 7 in the Student's Book lesson.
2. Write a few paragraphs about a relationship between two people that you know well. Use plenty of words and expressions from the lesson.
3. Find Lesson D7, Exercises 1 to 5 on the Student's Cassette and listen to the recording one more time before writing a short story about 'a first meeting'.

I know what love is, it's the stuff they sell on the telly

If you dont want to have a baby you have to wear a safety belt

You must take care of Love — if You Dont it goes bad

kittens

My cat falls in love and stays out all night and then he brings a lot of kittens back.

(from *God Bless Love*, *Lots of Love* and *Vote for Love*, compiled by Nanette Newman)

"And now, my darling, make my happiness complete by helping me to get up."

D8 Different kinds

1 Vocabulary. Complete the text with words and expressions from the box.

| all   although   belong (*twice*)   completely   different (*twice*)   divided
family   for example   including   languages   main   most   related
ways   world |

......1...... of the languages of Europe – and some Middle-Eastern and Indian ......2...... – are ......3...... to each other. They ......4...... to a large family which linguists call the 'Indo-European' ......5...... of languages. ......6...... they may look and sound completely ......7...... from each other, linguists can show that their grammar and vocabulary are similar in many ......8....... The Indo-European languages can be ......9...... into eight ......10...... groups: Germanic (......11...... English); Romance (the languages which are descended from Latin, for example Spanish); Celtic (for example Scottish Gaelic); Balto-Slavonic (for example Russian); Indo-Iranian (for example Hindi, Farsi); Greek, Albanian and Armenian. Not ......12...... European languages ......13...... to the Indo-European family. Finnish and Hungarian, ...14......, are members of a quite ......15...... language family, and Basque (spoken in northern Spain and south-western France) seems to be ......16...... different from all the other languages in the ......17.......

Russian — odin, dra, tri
Greek — ena, dio, tria
English — one, two, three
Hungarian — egy, kettö, harom
Hindi — ek, do, tin
Spanish — uno, dos, tres
Welsh — un, dau, tri

2 Read the text about the Romance languages. Then write a text about the Germanic and Celtic languages. Use the notes to help you.

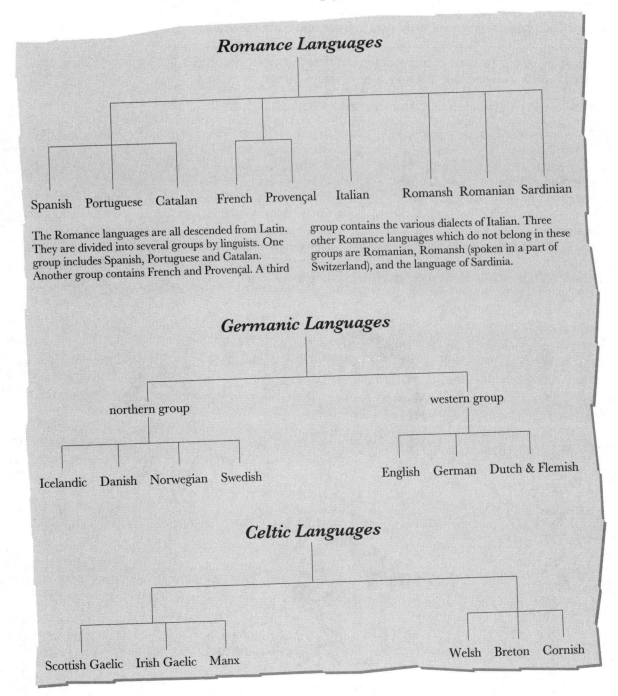

The Romance languages are all descended from Latin. They are divided into several groups by linguists. One group includes Spanish, Portuguese and Catalan. Another group contains French and Provençal. A third group contains the various dialects of Italian. Three other Romance languages which do not belong in these groups are Romanian, Romansh (spoken in a part of Switzerland), and the language of Sardinia.

NOTES

GERMANIC LANGUAGES descended from Primitive Germanic.
2 main groups: northern & western.
northern group incl. Icel., Dutch, Norw., Swedish.
west. gp incl. English, German, Dutch/Flemish.

CELTIC LANG. distantly related to Germanic lang.
2 main groups
- one contains Scottish Gaelic, Irish G. and Manx (spoken in the Isle of Man)
- the other contains Welsh (sp. in Wales), Breton (sp. in Britanny, in north-west France) and Cornish (spoken in Cornwall until the 18th century).

So English closely related to German, but only distantly related to other languages of Britain.

3 Try to match the different kinds of animals to their descriptions. Then find Lesson D8, Exercise 2 on the Student's Cassette and check your answers with the information on the recording.

invertebrates	cold-blooded; no longer the most important animals
insects	warm-blooded; like reptiles in many ways; can fly
vertebrates	cannot live on land; the largest group of vertebrates
fish	soft insides; external skeletons or shells
amphibians	don't lay eggs; warm-blooded; a few fly
reptiles	internal skeletons; soft outsides; in the minority
birds	happy in the water; also on the land
mammals	no backbone; majority of animals; many more to be discovered

4 Put the sentences into the correct order. Then divide the text into three paragraphs (and give it a title if you wish).

A: Human beings are mammals, belonging to the order called primates.
B: Most primates live in trees.
C: The first skeletons which are certainly of modern humans date from about half a million years ago.
D: One and a half million years ago there were meat-eating primates which were very like us.
E: Nobody knows exactly when the first people appeared, but four to five million years ago there were human-like primates in Africa.
F: There are about 4,500 kinds of mammals.
G: There are several different kinds of primates, including monkeys (which have tails), and apes (which do not).
H: These can be divided into nineteen groups – scientists call them orders – for instance the carnivores, or meat-eaters.
I: They have hands and large brains, and can communicate very well.
J: Typical carnivores are dogs, tigers or polar bears.
K: We are closely related to apes, and are very like them in most ways.

5 Vocabulary. Look at the example and then answer one or more of the questions, using as many of the words and expressions in the box as possible.

| add   lengthen   make ... smaller/bigger/fatter   remove   shorten
| straighten   strengthen   turn ... into ...   widen |

Example:
Suppose you wanted to turn a giraffe into a fox – what would you have to do?
You would have to make the body much smaller; shorten the neck; shorten the legs; lengthen the tail; lengthen the nose; add more hair; change the animal's colour; and make a number of other changes.

What would you have to do if you wanted to:
1. change a rabbit into an elephant?
2. change a cow into a blackbird?
3. change a pig into a horse?
4. change a chicken into a lion?
5. change a shark into a butterfly?
6. change another creature (you choose) into something else?

6 Read this, using a dictionary if you wish.

TRACING OUR ANCESTORS

Imagine that the names on a page of a city telephone directory are those of your ancestors in chronological order. The first name is your own, the second is your mother's, the third is your mother's mother and so on. If your ancestors could be traced back over the whole of human history their names would occupy about 100 such pages. But all those who lived within the period of written history would be listed on the first page alone. Most of modern science would effectively be covered by the life-spans of the first seven names – about 200 years. At the bottom of the first column would appear the name of your ancestor who lived in the Iron Age (about 720 BC – the time that Shalmaneser V deported the Hebrews from Israel). The horse would have come into service some way down the second column. The name at the bottom of the first page would be that of an ancestor who lived about the time the first sizeable city was founded (approximately 5200 BC). Around the bottom of the second page, the dog would have been domesticated (about 15000 BC). All the names occupying the following 98 pages would be those of ancestors who lived in small bands. Such is the time scale of human social history.

(from *The Joy of Knowledge Encyclopaedia* by Dr Alex Comfort – adapted)

7 Try the crossword.

ACROSS
1. The gases surrounding the earth.
7. Excuse ....
9. Can you .... your car, please? It's in the way.
10. Without any hair.
11. You and I.
12. A rugby ball is this shape.
13. Go in.
14. The Present Simple of *worn*.
15. This is hard, but you can eat it. It grows on trees.
16. This is stronger than *want*.
18. Will you .... after the children while I do the shopping?
20. Who does this camera belong ....?
21. Hair on a (man's) face.
23. You might take one if you have a headache.
24. I don't think I'll ever get .... my shyness with men.
26. This involves working with figures.
28. The Simple Past of *die*.
31. A valuable black liquid.
32. This sounds like *hour*.
34. .... many ways.
36. You have to obey this.
38. You have one of these to earn money.
39. Not high.
40. What are you laughing ....?
41. Which party is .... power at the moment?
42. The opposite of *fat*.
43. It's .... since I've seen her.
45. What's he like: young .... old?
46. Her company trained her to .... a computer.
47. What is he scared ....?
48. The Simple Past of *hold*.

DOWN
1. Current/deposit ....
2. Succeed at doing something.
3. Smaller than a star.
4. Quite old.
5. Feelings.
6. Finished.
8. A chance to change the government.
15. This sounds like *know*.
17. The end of life.
19. This looks rather like a bat, but it isn't a mammal.
20. We met yesterday for the first ....
21. You need this to think.
22. What .... you mean by that?
23. You shoot this with a bow.
25. Smaller than a town.
27. I suppose ....
29. Hurt.
30. What you owe.
33. Govern.
34. The house has been divided .... three flats.
35. The Simple Past of *win*.
37. eat, ..., eaten.
39. His moustache covered his top ....
43. We'll come .... soon .... possible.
44. I couldn't wait to tell her .... I rang her at the office.
45. '................, dear.' 'What's wrong?'

(*Solution on page 145.*)

E1 They saw wonderful things

1 Grammar revision. Can you put in the right prepositions?

1. Nicolo and Maffeo Polo stayed in China .... a long time.
2. Marco kept a diary .... his experiences.
3. They landed .... the Turkish coast.
4. They rode .... Iran, Afghanistan and Mongolia.
5. Marco's illness delayed them .... a year.
6. .... the way they saw wonderful things which were unknown .... Europe.
7. They saw a liquid that came .... the ground and could be used .... fuel.
8. .... 1275 they arrived .... China.
9. Marco was amazed to find a country that was far more civilised .... Italy.
10. .... his diary he described cities .... Hangzhou.
11. There were bridges high enough .... ships to go ....
12. The emperor took a special interest .... Marco.
13. When they arrived back .... Italy, they told their friends .... their experiences.
14. Nobody would believe their stories .... the strange countries .... the east.

2 Find Lesson E1 on the Student's Cassette. Listen to the recording as many times as you like and write down as much as you can.

3 Grammar: Present Perfect Progressive. What do you think these people have been doing? Example:

A: She's been playing tennis.

4 Vocabulary: words that are easily confused. Choose the right word for each sentence (using a dictionary if you wish), and then make a sentence using the other of the two words.

1. Sorry, Patricia isn't here at the moment. She's gone on a business *trip/voyage* to Prague.
2. Did you have a good *journey/travel*?
3. Would you like me to *bring/take* your letters to the post office?
4. Chess is a very complicated *game/play*.
5. Shakespeare *dead/died* in 1616.
6. There's a flower shop *in front of / opposite* our house.
7. She works very *hard/hardly*.
8. Who do you think will get the Nobel *price/prize* for physics?
9. The only traffic you ever get on our *road/street* is tractors from the local farm.
10. She's a very *sensible/sensitive* child – she loves nature and poetry and music.
11. 'How are you?' 'Well, *actually / at the moment*, I've been feeling rather tired lately.'

5 Vocabulary revision. The following words and expressions are all connected with travel. Can you divide them into three groups, under the headings 'road', 'rail' and 'air'? Some of them will go in more than one group.

| boarding pass   change   check-in   check the oil   compartment |
| crossroads   delay   driver   emergency exit   flight   map   motorway |
| no smoking   petrol station   pilot   platform   return ticket   roadworks |
| seat belt   security check   stewardess   speed limit   ticket collector |

ROAD
check the oil

RAIL
compartment

AIR
boarding pass

6 Guessing unknown words. Read the text, and then try and find words to match the definitions.

This is your captain speaking

[1] 'Ladies and gentlemen, this is your captain speaking. I regret to tell you that the aircraft is on fire, and we are about to make an emergency landing. Now there is absolutely nothing to worry about. I would like you all to remain seated, with your seatbelts fastened, until the aircraft comes to a complete stop, and then leave via the emergency exits. If you haven't already read the leaflet in the seat pocket in front of you, I suggest now would be a good time. Oh, and by the way, you should have ninety seconds to get out.

[2] 'Look, I know there are 450 of you back there, and ninety seconds may not seem too long, but it can be done. If it makes you feel any better, I can tell you that when this plane was built they got 450 people out of the factory and sat them down where you're sitting, and then shouted "fire". *They* all got out within ninety seconds, otherwise the FAA would never have given this thing a licence. Okay, so there wasn't any real fire, and maybe they could use all the exits, but they didn't have your motivation, now did they?

[3] 'I suppose some of you must be wondering what happens if you don't make it in ninety seconds. Yes, well, I'm glad you asked that question. You may have noticed that there is quite a lot of plastic in this aeroplane, and your seats are filled with polyurethane foam. Now it doesn't burn very easily, but I have to tell you that when it does catch fire it gives off rather a lot of smoke and a few gases. Carbon monoxide, hydrogen cyanide; stuff like that. It does get a bit hot, too. About 1000 degrees Centigrade after two minutes, if you really want to know. So if I were you I'd try to make it in ninety seconds.

[4] 'Just a couple of other things you ought to know. About your duty-free purchases: I expect most of you have got bottles of whiskey and brandy in the overhead lockers and we'll just have to hope those bottles don't break, won't we, because boy does that stuff burn! And then there are your clothes. I noticed most of you were wearing some when you came on board, which is a bit of a pity, really. There's nothing like a good woollen suit for generating hydrogen cyanide when the fire really gets going.

[5] 'Now, if you sit tight I'm going to try to get this thing on the ground without breaking anything. And, er, in case I don't get another opportunity, thank you for flying with ____ Airlines.'

[6] Fictional, of course, but those are the odds which face a passenger unlucky enough to be caught in an in-flight fire. Time is the vital factor. If the fire cannot be traced and extinguished by the crew, and fairly quickly at that, the aircraft has to be landed as rapidly as possible. Once on the ground, hopefully intact, evacuation must be immediate and swift before smoke and gas snuff out the lives of all on board. Many have died because they did not get to the emergency exits in time.

(from *The Unsafe Sky* by William Norris)

First paragraph:
1. stay
2. sheet of printed paper, usually given free to the public

Second paragraph:
3. government body that can give a plane the right to fly
4. ways of getting out of somewhere
5. reason for doing something

Third paragraph:
6. material that has air bubbles in it

Fourth paragraph:
7. things you have bought
8. small place for storing things, with a door or lid
9. making

Sixth paragraph:
10. found
11. stopped (used about fires)
12. people getting out of a place

94

7 Read the letter. Then write another letter of complaint to a tour operator, constructed in the same way. You can base your letter on the notes, or imagine your own situation.

---

19 Coniston Way
Hemel Hempstead
Herts WD4 8MY

15 October 1992

Sunway Tours Ltd
33 Brooklands Avenue
Watford
Herts WD1 2NP

Dear Sir or Madam,

In April I booked a villa party holiday in the Algarve with your company for October 3–10. I paid £450 for the holiday, including breakfast and dinner provided by a cook, plus £41 for a single room supplement.

Two days before my departure, someone from your office phoned me to say that the villa was overbooked, and to ask if I would accept a four-star hotel instead. I replied that I would rather not go abroad. I was reassured later that same day (October 1) that my original booking still stood. On my arrival at the airport your representative said that there was no problem.

On arriving at the villa, however, I found that it had been fully booked by a family group and that I had been moved into a nearby bungalow without being asked. I was given meal vouchers for meals at a nearby hotel, but these did not cover the full cost of meals.

You advertised, and I paid for, a specific type of holiday. This holiday was not available, and I was forced under protest to accept inferior accommodation. I have booked with your company twice before, and have always been very happy with my holidays; I am very surprised that this has happened. I am sure you will agree that it is only fair that I be offered compensation for my inconvenience. Could you let me know as soon as possible what compensation you plan to give me?

I look forward to hearing from you soon.

Yours faithfully,

Sandra Banarjee

Sandra Banarjee (Ms)

Notes:
- rented cottage for one week, May 9–16 (£225)
- 'The Yews' near Lake Windermere
- Lakeland Leisure Ltd, P.O. Box 32, Kendal, Cumbria
- advertisement: 'charming cottage, newly furnished and carpeted throughout'
- arrival: damp and mould (downstairs very bad); dirty; vacuum cleaner didn't work; overflowing dustbins
- no other accommodation available, so stayed
- 21 May: wrote asking for compensation for poor state of cottage and loss of enjoyment
- 28 May: still no reply

E2 Focus on systems

1 Vocabulary revision. What are these things called, and what are they used for? Match the nouns, the verbs and the pictures. Example:

A: saucepan – boil

| bowl | cloth | food processor | frying pan |
| grater | knife | mug | oven | saucepan |
| sink |

| boil | cut | drink | fry | grate | mix |
| prepare | roast/bake | wash up | wipe |

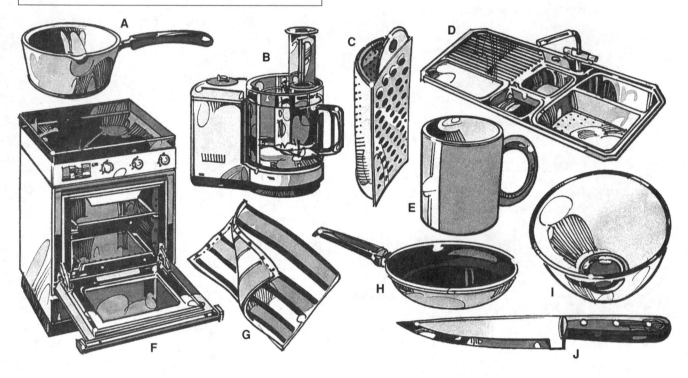

2 Vocabulary revision. Do you know what all these verbs mean? Match the words and the pictures.

| bend | break | cut | hit | mend | scratch | slice | squeeze | twist | turn |

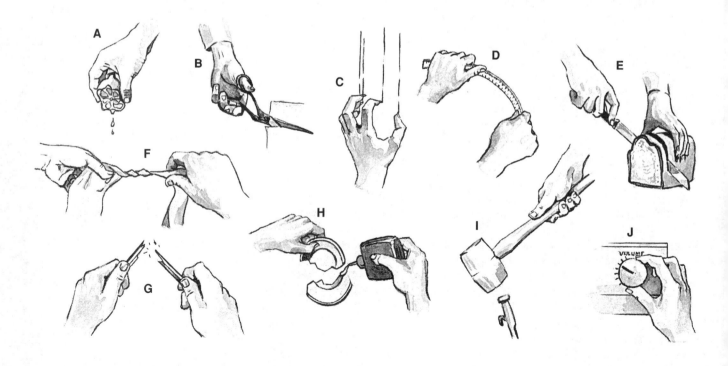

96

3 Vocabulary study. Match tools and instruments from the left-hand column with the descriptions of their uses from the right-hand column, and with the pictures. Use a dictionary if necessary. Then make sentences like the one in the example, to say what the tools/instruments are used for. Example:

A: A screwdriver is a tool which is used to turn screws.

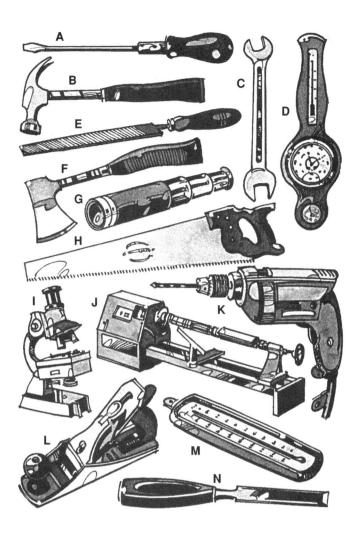

TOOLS AND INSTRUMENTS	USES
axe	shape lengths of wood
barometer	turn screws
chisel	turn nuts
drill	hit nails
file	smooth wood
hammer	make holes
lathe	measure air pressure
microscope	cut down trees
plane	measure temperature
saw	cut pieces out of wood
screwdriver	cut lengths of wood
spanner	see distant things
telescope	see small things
thermometer	smooth metal

4 Grammar. Join the beginnings and ends together to make sensible sentences.

BEGINNINGS	ENDS
Although I loved her,	I took an aspirin.
When it started raining,	you won't arrive before dark.
Unless you start now,	I switched on the radio.
After I'd finished the housework,	I decided not to see her again.
Before you start your new job,	I went to the pub.
Until you've seen it yourself,	write and tell me how you are.
Because I had a headache,	you ought to have a holiday.
As soon as I got up,	you won't believe how big it is.
If you have time,	I closed the windows.

5 Grammar. Complete the sentences with *although*, *in case*, *so that*, *unless* and *whether*.

1. .... we have a change of government, everything will stay the same as it always has been.
2. They don't care .... they pass or fail their exams.
3. .... they are very rich, they never give anything to charity.
4. Close the door .... the heat doesn't escape.
5. You'd better stay in .... she gives you a ring.
6. Do you know .... he wanted his coffee black or white?
7. Take your swimming trunks .... the weather is good enough for us to use the pool.
8. You'll miss your train .... you hurry up.
9. Everyone had a dessert .... we had all said we weren't hungry.
10. Let me write your name down .... I don't forget it.

6 Do two of the following three reading tasks (A, B or C).

A. Read the text. Then write down as quickly as you can words or expressions in the text which correspond to the words and expressions listed after it.

Why Men Make Rotten Patients

[1] Most men make dreadful patients. When they have a headache there is trouble if anyone makes a sound.

[2] When a man has flu he lies in bed while his wife waits on him hand and foot.

[3] When she has a pain in her chest she happily accepts being told that there is nothing seriously wrong. He remains miserable and convinced that he has heart trouble.

[4] When he has been ordered to rest that's just what he does, complaining bitterly if there is no one around to stir his tea or find him a handkerchief. She is expected to carry on looking after the rest of the family – even though she has been told to take things easy.

[5] In addition to being mentally less able to cope with illness men are physically not as fit as women. Men are more likely to drink, smoke and eat too much and take too little exercise.

[6] The man who dons his tracksuit and jogs to the pub every night still does far less exercise than his wife who has to cart the groceries from the shops, handle the washing and lug the vacuum cleaner up and down stairs.

[7] Most men know they aren't as fit as women. So when they're ill they're frightened. Their fear is reinforced by the knowledge that a woman's life expectation is longer than a man's. Although today's women drink and smoke more and take on greater responsibility than in the past, the number of years by which they can expect to outlive a man is increasing.

[8] Men are more likely to die in accidents and of lung cancer. They're more likely to commit suicide and die of heart disease.

[9] It's not just illness that makes men such rotten patients – it's fear!

(Dr Vernon Coleman, *The Daily Mirror*)

1. certain (*paragraph 3*)
2. mix milk/sugar into (*paragraph 4*)
3. as well as (*paragraph 5*)
4. puts on (*paragraph 6*)
5. pull (*paragraph 6*)
6. strengthened (*paragraph 7*)
7. live longer than (*paragraph 7*)
8. kill themselves (*paragraph 8*)

B. Read these without a dictionary.

DOCTOR, DOCTOR (Children's jokes)

'Doctor, please come over quickly. My wife's broken a leg.'
'But I'm a doctor of music.'
'That's OK. It's the piano leg.'

'Tell me, doctor. Is it serious?'
'Well, I wouldn't advise you to start watching any serials on TV.'

'Doctor, doctor, I keep thinking I'm a dustbin.'
'Don't talk such rubbish.'

'Which do you want first – the good news or the bad news?'
'The good news, please, doctor.'
'Our tests show that you only have 24 hours to live.'
'My God – what's the bad news?'
'I should have told you last night, but I forgot.'

'Doctor, I can't stop stealing things.'
'Take these pills. They should help you.'
'But what if they don't?'
'Pick up a Rolls for me.'

'Doctor, I feel as if nobody ever listens to me.'
'Next, please.'

'What seems to be the trouble?'
'Doctor, I keep getting the feeling that nobody can hear what I say.'
'What seems to be the trouble?'

'Doctor, I ate a dozen oysters yesterday and I've had stomachache ever since.'
'Were they fresh?'
'I don't know.'
'Well, how did they look when you opened them up?'
'You mean you're supposed to open the shells?'

'Doctor, I think I need glasses.'
'You certainly do. This is a bank.'

'Did you take those pills I gave you to improve your memory?'
'What pills?'

C. Read the texts and answer the questions as quickly as you can.

'Drowned' people could recover safely

STORIES about seamen, apparently drowned, staying under water for far longer than the traditional four minutes and coming back to life without any brain damage, may be true.

Doctors at St Bartholomew's Medical College in London have discovered that human beings have a "diving response", like that of sea mammals, which is triggered by a surprise fall into water – especially cold water.

By closing off most of the needs of the body for blood supply, reducing the heart rate and power to a very low level but concentrating the emergency blood supply on the brain, humans can survive being under water for more than half an hour – and probably much longer – without brain damage.

In infants and children, it seems the diving response is especially powerful.

(from *The Guardian* – adapted)

ZZZZZZ ...

Insomnia isn't good for you. Complete lack of sleep will kill you more quickly than complete lack of food. Elephants and dolphins can survive happily with 2 hours of sleep out of every 24, but the average night's sleep among normal human beings is now reckoned to be 7 hours 36 minutes.

People in their fifties tend to sleep less than those in their twenties, but people in their sixties get more sleep than at any time since childhood. Men sleep 10 minutes more than women, and the difference rises to 20 minutes more in the fifties and 50 minutes more in the seventies.

(by Gyles Brandreth – adapted)

WHEN A CUPPA COULD KILL

A screech of brakes, a deafening crash ... and you realise there's a road accident just outside your front door. You've phoned for the police and an ambulance. What's your next step – put on a pot of tea or break out the brandy bottle?

That could be the most dangerous thing possible, say the experts who deal with accidents.

Nothing at all must be taken by mouth – not even tea. Mr D. J. Fuller, consultant orthopaedic surgeon at the Radcliffe Infirmary, Oxford, said: "Anyone involved in an accident, even injured in a fall down the stairs, may need an operation. To give a general anaesthetic after drinking or eating could be very dangerous."

BED REST IS BAD FOR YOU

Ever noticed how you seem to take longer to get over an illness if you take to your bed for a few days instead of struggling on? The reason, according to the leading American health magazine *Prevention*, is that a whole range of bodily functions begin to weaken after as short a time as *one* day in bed.

Muscle tissue starts to break down, robbing the body of important minerals and leading to substantial weakness in just a few days; bones start to break down and lose calcium; the body is unable to use food efficiently; heart and blood vessels get weak after a couple of days, which can lead to a rise in pulse rate and a drop in blood volume; joint stiffness and constipation are also common.

'Prolonged bed rest is not to be taken lightly,' says Dr Benjamin Natelson, professor of neurosciences at New Jersey Medical School. And that's why doctors these days make every effort to get patients up and moving as soon as possible after heart attacks and operations.

(from *Living Magazine* – adapted)

1. What groups of people are most likely to survive near-drowning without brain damage?
2. The average 55-year-old man sleeps longer each night than the average 55-year-old woman: how much longer?
3. What is the best drink to give to someone who has had an accident?
4. What happens to your bones if you stay in bed too long?

"First the good news. His temperature has gone down."

"Don't worry, Sister! He can't get far without a heart!"

E3 Looking forward

1 Grammar revision. Put in the right tenses.

1. When I (*be*) an old woman I shall wear purple.
2. Will you tell me as soon as the bell (*ring*)?
3. I'll be interested to see whether John (*come*) tomorrow or not.
4. After we've finished the building work, things (*be*) easier.
5. I'll have the letter finished before the postman (*get*) here.
6. I hope you (*tell*) me all about the holiday when you (*get*) back.
7. Next time you come I (*take*) you to see my mother.
8. I don't know if I (*be*) here when you (*phone*) tomorrow morning.

2 Grammar. Put in the Future Progressive or the Future Perfect.

1. What will you *be doing / have done* this time tomorrow?
2. How soon will the builders *be finishing / have finished* laying the foundations?
3. Do you think you'll *be making / have made* a decision by next July?
4. Next Sunday morning I'll *be sitting / have sat* on a beach doing nothing.
5. By the end of the year I'll .... 20,000 miles on business. (*drive*)
6. We'll .... for you at the station when you arrive. (*wait*)
7. Jennie and I .... here for twenty years next September. (*be*)
8. I think when I'm 80 I'll probably still .... to understand what goes on in your head. (*try*)

3 Grammar. Say when you will, may or might do some of the following things. Use some or all of the expressions in the box.

| soon | one day | one of these days |
| sometime | sooner or later | never |

learn Russian/Chinese/Japanese/Latin/ ...
learn the piano/violin/trumpet/ ...
travel to Australia/Canada/India/ ...
take up jogging/parachuting/hang-gliding/ ...
write a novel / play / short story / ...
take a long holiday
get married (again) / have (more) children / get divorced
give up smoking/drinking/gambling/ ...

4 Grammar and vocabulary revision: two- and three-word verbs. Use the expressions in the box to complete the sentences. You may have to make some small changes. There is one extra expression – can you make a sentence with it?

get on	get on with	get up	go on
look after	look at	look out	put off
put on	ring back	run out of	slow down
turn on			

1. If you .... talking like that I'm leaving.
2. She's really nice – she .... everybody.
3. You're going too fast – could you .... a bit?
4. I'll have to .... going to the dentist – I haven't got time this week.
5. Could you .... the radio so that we can hear the news?
6. ....! You're going to knock that glass off the table.
7. I don't much like .... children.
8. After we had been travelling for about half an hour, I began to realise that I .... the wrong train.
9. I'm a bit busy just now. Can I .... in ten minutes?
10. It's cold outside. I think I'll .... a sweater.
11. .... those clouds. I think it's going to rain.
12. I've .... sugar. Could you lend me some?

"Old age is his trouble – he used to leap through them!"

5 Read the poems, using a dictionary if you wish. Write a few sentences saying what you think of each poem.

Fire and ice

Some say the world will end in fire
Some say in ice.
From what I've tasted of desire
I hold with those who favour fire.
But if it had to perish twice
I think I know enough of hate
To say that for destruction ice
Is also great
And would suffice.

(Robert Frost)

Heaven

The god-men say when die go sky
Through pearly gates where river flow,
The god-men say when die we fly
Just like eagle, hawk and crow.
Might be, might be –
But I don't know.

(Australian aborigine's comment on Christianity)

New Year Resolutions

This year
I shall lock next year in a cupboard
with last year
and feed them on bread and water.

This year
I shall let in
what is worth letting in only
(but for that
my door is wide open).

This year
earth and air
fire and water
will be welcome at my breakfast table
(and so will you).

This year
I shall amass the world's largest collection
of unburst soap-bubbles.

This year
the rain and I
will dance together
on several occasions.

This year
I shall change the world with a poem.

This year
I shall give you starring roles
in many of my dreams.

This year
dogs that chase me
while I am out jogging
will wish they hadn't.
(I refuse to give details
for security reasons.)

This year
I shall chat up all my wrong numbers
and make new friends.

This year
I shall teach the baby to dance
and play poker.

This year
I shall find the end of the rainbow
dig up the pot of gold
and buy dresses for you
and jewellery
(and you shall have the rainbow for your hair
and the crescent moon
as a pendant).

(Lewis Mancha)

6 Add a verse or two of your own to the poem 'New Year Resolutions'.

E4 Coincidences

1 Grammar. Use one of the structures in the box to introduce the sentences, as in the examples.

> It seems/seemed obvious that ... (not) ...
> It seems/seemed (un)likely that ...
> It seems/seemed possible that ...
> It looks/looked as if ...
> It doesn't/didn't look as if ...
> It sounds/sounded as if ...
> It doesn't/didn't sound as if ...
> I wonder/wondered whether ...

1. We are alone in the universe.
   It seems unlikely that we are alone in the universe.
2. There are living creatures on other planets.
   It seems obvious that there are living creatures on other planets.
3. We will make contact with creatures from other worlds in the next twenty years.
4. They will be very like us.
5. We will get on well together.
6. The weather was going to get worse.
7. It was going to snow.
8. We would have trouble getting home.
9. The road over the mountains was open.
10. The thunder was right over our heads.
11. We would be struck by lightning.

2 Grammar: revision of tenses.

1. If I arrive before you, *I'll/I'd* wait for you.
2. Suppose you had to change your job. What *will/would* you do?
3. If I were you, *I'll/I'd* try to save some money.
4. I'll telephone you as soon as I *know / will know* something.
5. We can't go out until the rain *stops / will stop*.
6. I would have helped her if she *asked / had asked* me.
7. If I'd known you were coming, *I'll buy / I'd buy / I'll have bought / I'd have bought* some champagne.
8. It would have been better if you *didn't say / hadn't said / wouldn't have said* anything.
9. As soon as I saw him, I knew that *we met / have met / had met* before.
10. Excuse me. I *ordered / had ordered* a coffee half an hour ago. Is it ready yet?
11. 'Is she an old friend of yours?' '*I know / I've known* her since we were children.'
12. A friend of mine *was hurt / has hurt / has been hurt* in a car crash yesterday.
13. I'm afraid I can't come and see you. My car *is repaired / is being repaired / is repairing* today.

3 Vocabulary. Each of the words in the box is linked in some way with one of the other words. Try to find all the pairs. Example:

ambulance → injured

> ambulance booking cancel carriage
> cliff coal coffee cream date diary
> edge election fuel injured lip
> majority moustache passenger shine
> star

4 Vocabulary revision: words that are easily confused. Choose the right word for each sentence. (You may have to change the words slightly.)

(*say* or *tell*)
1. He .... that he would be late.
2. He .... me that he would be late.
3. Please .... us when you're ready.

(*listen (to)* or *hear*)
4. I like to .... the radio when I'm driving.
5. Speak a bit louder – I can't .... you.
6. ....! I can .... somebody moving about downstairs.

(*look (at)*, *watch* or *see*)
7. ....! I've had my hair done. Do you like it?
8. I don't .... TV much: I haven't got the time.
9. '............... that big bird!' 'Where? I can't .... a bird.'

(*good* or *well*)
10. You speak very .... English.
11. You speak English very ....
12. 'She's got a new job.' 'That's ....'
13. He's always very .... dressed.

(*borrow* or *lend*)
14. 'Could you .... me your cassette player for a couple of hours?' 'OK, but don't forget to give it back. Last time you .... it you kept it for six weeks.'
15. I don't like .... money from people and I don't like .... money to people.

(*put on* or *wear*)
16. What did you .... at the interview?
17. Why have you .... your coat? It's really warm outside.

(*asleep*, *go to sleep*, or *sleep*)
18. I never .... before 10.30.
19. Is she .... already?
20. I usually .... about seven and a half hours a night.

5 Spelling. Put the missing letters (*a, e, i, o, u, y*) in the right places.

-ppr--ch   j--c-
b---t-   -cc-r
b-sc--t   r--t-
f-v--r-t-   s-c--t-
-nst--d   -s--l

6 Read at least two of these five texts, using a dictionary if you wish.

CHANCE ENCOUNTERS?

There can be few stories as enigmatic as the following. Erskine Lawrence Ebbin was knocked off his moped by a taxi and killed in Hamilton, Bermuda. It was the same taxi with the same driver, carrying the same passenger, that killed his brother Neville in July the previous year. Both brothers were 17 when they died, and had been riding the same moped in the same street. Ah! but history never quite repeats itself – the time of both accidents differed by (only) 50 minutes.

But perhaps the most remarkable tale of a chance encounter is that of young Roger Lausier. When he was four years old he strayed away from his mother along the beach at Salem, Massachusetts. He paddled for a while and then got caught by a powerful undercurrent, and would have drowned but for a woman who brought him ashore and revived him. The rescuer refused all rewards, and left wishing the infant luck. Nine years later, Roger was a strong swimmer and was tracking a shoal of bluefish when he heard a woman scream: 'My husband is drowning! My husband is drowning!' Roger saw that a heavily-built man had fallen from his powerboat and was floundering helplessly. He paddled his inflated raft over in time to clutch the drowning man's hand, and kept him afloat until another boat got to them, and they went safely ashore. In the hospital the grateful woman kissed the boy: 'I'm Alice Blaise, and I can't thank you enough for saving my Bob.' Roger had no idea who Mrs Blaise was until the story came out during a presentation to him by the Massachusetts Humane Society. He had saved the husband of the woman who had saved him on the same beach nine years previously.

(from *The Best of Fortean Times*)

SAME NAMES

• Confusion reigned in Bulawayo Magistrates' Court. Smart Ngwenya, waiting to give evidence in a different case, was brought into the court room. The mistake was realised after the charge had been read and denied. Embarrassed court officials hustled him out and led in another Smart Ngwenya (ngwenya means crocodile) who also turned out to be the wrong man. The 'correct' Smart Ngwenya was brought in at the third attempt.

• Patricia Kern of Colorado was sent a tax demand for $3000 from a job she had held in Oregon, a state in which she had never set foot. Inquiries showed that Patricia DiBiasi of Oregon owed the taxes. Both were born Patricia Ann Campbell, on 13 March 1941, and shared a social security number. Both had fathers called Robert, both married military men within 11 days of each other, both worked as bookkeepers and had children of 21 and 19.

• In January 1985 Peter Bacon of Eyam, Derbyshire, crashed into a car driven by Peter Bacon of North Anston, Sheffield. A couple of months later, John Stott, whose car crash was witnessed by Bernard Stott (no relation), and investigated by a police officer called Tina Stott, was taken back to a police station where the three people were met by desk sergeant Walter Stott.

(from *The Best of Fortean Times*)

Love will find a way

In New York on business in 1980, writer Ian Livingston was invited by a friend to spend a week in Cape Cod.

On the second night there, they went to a local bar, where they met two girls, and Ian ended up talking to Jane. 'The four of us spent a lot of the remainder of the week together. Although Jane was English, she was spending an indefinite time in the USA, and we did not bother to exchange addresses.

'The next holiday I had was in Corfu in late August. There I met an Irish girl, Elizabeth. At the end of the holiday we did exchange addresses, as she was living in Manchester; my parents live in Manchester.

'At the end of October I phoned Elizabeth, told her I was coming to visit them, and suggested we go out for a drink. She agreed. So it was that on a wet, early November night I rang the bell of a flat in Manchester. The door opened and there, looking as aghast as I was, stood Jane. Elizabeth and Jane shared a flat.'

(from *Coincidence* by Brian Inglis)

No escape from love

'Over 50 years ago – when I was a very young man – I had an intense affair with a beautiful woman somewhat older than myself,' Michael Relph nostalgically recalls.

The woman told her husband she was leaving; drunk and emotional, he stormed off threatening to take his life. Back at Relph's flat, she seemed unmoved, 'but I found the responsibility too great. I told her that at all costs she must find him and stop him committing suicide.' She left the flat to look for her husband.

Such was Relph's distress over losing her that he decided he must go somewhere with no associations which could remind him of the ignominious end of his first love affair; and this prompted him to visit a distant relative, a bank manager in a small Sussex town.

'He invited me to luncheon. As he took me across the deserted market square to his local pub for a pre-lunch drink, my gloom lifted a little in the knowledge that there was nothing here to remind me of my lost love and no possibility of a chance encounter.

'A hotel stood centrally in the square and at its entrance a car drew up. The two people who got out as we approached were my lover and her husband. We were the only people in the little square.'

Many years later, when the romance was briefly rekindled, she told Relph how much she, too, had dreaded such an encounter. 'She and her husband had only decided to eat at the hotel because they had taken the wrong road. Neither of us had ever been in the town before, and had she or I been one minute earlier or later, we would have missed one another.'

(from *Coincidence* by Brian Inglis)

Like father, like son

A few years ago Mary Taylor had gone to London with her son to see the Chinese Exhibition then at the British Museum.

Her son, then aged 19, had not seen his father since he was 18 months old. In the exhibition, he returned to me, ashen white, and said, 'Don't think me silly, but I have just met my father. I know it is him. We just came face to face and I knew.' I went across with my son and realised that it was indeed my one-time lover, and that he, too, from the expression of shock on his face, had recognised my son. (They are actually very similar in appearance, and were even wearing identical spectacle-frames.)

'We all went for a drink, and he told us that he had been in London for a meeting and had suddenly had a compulsive urge to leave it and go to the exhibition, taking a taxi to reach it.'

(from *Coincidence* by Brian Inglis)

7 Write at least 200 words about one of the following subjects. Try to include some words and expressions from the Student's Book lesson.

1. How (or why) do you think coincidences happen?
2. Do you believe in ghosts or in life after death? Why (not)?
3. Do you believe the earth has been visited by creatures from other parts of space? Why (not)?
4. Do you think it is ever possible for people to see into the future? Why (not)?

"The practice of astrology took a major step toward achieving credibility today when, as predicted, everyone born under the sign of Scorpio was run over by an egg lorry."

E5 I don't know much about art, ...

1 Grammar. Some of these sentences have got words in the wrong order. Correct the sentences that are wrong and put *OK* after the correct sentences.

1. I like (very much) modern art.
2. Of all the impressionists, I like Manet best.
3. I don't like Giacometti's statues much.
4. I don't like very much Van Gogh.
5. I like best Picasso's early paintings.
6. I like some abstract paintings a lot.

Now write these sentences in the right order.

7. very much I like going to museums .
8. best I like Renaissance paintings .
9. very much I don't like religious paintings .
10. a lot I like medieval churches .

2 Grammar revision. Put in *very* or *too*.

1. I really love the people in this picture: they are *very* well painted.
2. I don't like the colours in this one: they're *too* strong, I feel.
3. You are looking .... beautiful this evening.
4. Oh no! We're .... late! The museum's closed!
5. You are .... young to remember how beautiful this city was before the war.
6. Leonardo da Vinci was not only a .... great painter; he was also a scientist and an engineer.
7. I'm .... pleased that we were able to see those Nigerian statues.
8. Is Geoffrey .... upset about not getting into art school?
9. There were .... many people at the exhibition: I couldn't see anything!

3 EITHER: See if you can make up some questions ending in *by* for these answers.

1. Charlotte Brontë.
   Who was 'Jane Eyre' written by?
2. Gustave Eiffel.
3. Michelangelo.
4. Shakespeare.
5. Tolstoy.
6. Alfred Hitchcock.

OR: Write similar questions about books, paintings, sculptures, buildings or films that you know.

4 Vocabulary revision. Circle the one that is different (and say why).

1. painting   statue   (switch)   drawing
2. jazz   rock   folk music   violin
3. swim   eat   run   jump
4. hungry   tired   thirsty   exciting
5. laugh   frown   worried   smile
6. glove   shoe   chair   sock
7. England   Scotland   Ireland   Wales
8. hair dryer   vacuum cleaner   hairbrush   food mixer
9. bottom   inside out   face downwards   sideways

5 Find Lesson E5, Exercise 1, Part 1 on the Student's Cassette. Listen and answer the questions.

1. True, false or we don't know? The first speaker likes the way the picture has been painted, its colours and its atmosphere.
2. Why does the second speaker enjoy looking closely at the picture?
3. Why doesn't the third speaker like the picture?

"*I like this one – it has a message.*"

6 Read this, using a dictionary if you wish.

Strange but true!

The largest picture ever painted measures 6,727.56m². It shows a 'smiley' face on a brightly coloured background and was painted in Australia in 1990 by students and schoolchildren and by artist Ken Done.

Velasquez' painting *Portrait of Juan de Pareja* was sold for £2,310,000 in 1970. In 1801 the same painting had been sold for £40.95.

Picasso produced about 13,500 paintings and drawings, as well as large numbers of book illustrations, prints, sculptures and ceramics.

If you visit all the parts of the Hermitage Museum in St. Petersburg you have to walk 24 kilometres.

Paintings have been found in caves in France that are 27,000 years old.

The Museum of Modern Art in New York hung *Le Bateau* by Matisse upside down for 47 days before they discovered their mistake.

(Information from *The Guinness Book of Records*)

● Professor M. Guarducci of Rome has shown that some of the so-called 'ancient' objects in the Louvre, the British Museum, the Boston Museum of Fine Arts and Rome's Museum of Prehistory were actually made by two nineteenth-century criminals.

(Information from an article by Tana de Zulueta in *The Sunday Times*)

In 1981 a British gallery showed a work called *Room Temperature*: two dead flies and a bucket of water in which four apples and six empty balloons were floating. A gallery official was enthusiastic about the work's 'completeness, its oneness, its apparent obviousness'.

(Information from an article in *International Herald Tribune*)

7 Do one of these writing tasks. Write at least 200 words and try to include some words and expressions from the Student's Book lesson.

1. Choose one of the statements below and write your opinion, developing your argument (perhaps with examples) as much as you can.
   a. If a painting is really good, you don't have to be educated to like it.
   b. A lot of so-called 'great art' is rubbish.
   c. Too much public money is spent on art museums.
   d. No individual should be able to own a great work of art.
   e. A great photograph can be as fine a work of art as a great painting.
2. Write about your favourite sort of art or music. (How did you first become interested in it? If you had a lot of money to spend on this interest, how would you spend the money?)

E6 Focus on systems

1 Grammar: relative pronouns. Join the pairs of sentences together as in the examples.

1. She had a heart attack. It was a great shock to her family.
   She had a heart attack, which was a great shock to her family.
2. She completely recovered from her illness. Nobody had expected this.
   She completely recovered from her illness, which nobody had expected.
3. The hospital bills were $200 a day. We couldn't afford this.
4. The nurses were all very friendly. This cheered him up a good deal.
5. He broke his leg skiing. This did not surprise us in the least.
6. He has to lie in bed all day doing nothing. He hates this.
7. Cindy sold her story to a newspaper for $15,000. This paid the hospital bills.
8. He had a terrible car crash. It put him in hospital for six months.
9. Since his accident he can't play football. He finds this terribly depressing.
10. Susy's decided to be a nurse. We're quite pleased about it.

2 Grammar. Complete the sentences by putting in *that, what, which* or nothing.

1. I've already told you everything .... I know.
2. .... you need at this moment is a nice cup of tea.
3. They spend all their holidays in Corsica, ... they really enjoy.
4. That's exactly .... he said to me.
5. We're in love, ... is all .... matters.
6. .... I can't understand is why they got married in the first place.
7. I don't think she knows .... she's doing.
8. Is there nothing .... you can do for her?

3 Grammar revision. Fill in the table of irregular verbs. Learn the ones you are unsure of.

PRESENT	PAST TENSE	PAST PARTICIPLE
blow	....	....
....	chose	....
....	....	dug
eat	....	....
....	flew	....
....	....	frozen
hang	....	....
....	hit	....
....	....	laid
lie	....	....
....	lost	....
....	....	run
sell	....	....
....	shook	....
....	....	shone
show	....	....
....	sang	....
....	....	stuck
swim	....	....
....	woke	....
....	....	won
wind	....	....

4 Translate these into your language.

1. He ought to try to meet more people.
2. I hope you don't mind my asking: how old are you?
3. English and Greek both belong to the Indo-European group of languages.
4. When she was growing up, her family was very poor.
5. After I got back from my trip to the Far East, no one seemed interested in where I had been.
6. Although I'm bad at remembering people's names, I never forget a person's face.
7. I wonder whether they'll travel by train or by bus.
8. Give me a ring so that I'll know when you're coming.
9. Unless we take urgent action now, millions of people will have died of AIDS by the end of the century.
10. We had better get there early in case it gets crowded.
11. Who was this picture painted by?
12. She lived in New York when she was a child, which is why she's got an American accent.

5 Write these fractions in words and say them aloud. Be careful to pronounce *th* correctly.

$1/9$ one ninth $3/10$ three tenths

$1/7$ $1/11$ $1/10$ $1/8$ $3/7$ $4/11$ $7/10$

$5/8$ $9/13$ $11/24$ $6/15$ $2/5$

6 Read the three newspaper articles and decide which of the numbered sentences on the opposite page belongs to which article and where each should go.

A

Wedding battle smashes up marriage

Solemnly, young Hans swore undying love to his bride. Solemnly, they were pronounced man and wife.

It was nice while it lasted. Four hours approximately. Until guests were finishing the dessert course at the reception.

Then all hell broke loose. There was a bitter and bloody family battle, which left young Hans with his shirt – and his marriage – in tatters.

Today, two days after the wedding and just four days after the couple named the big day, divorce proceedings are expected to start.

It was the bride's mother and a brother of the groom who opened the fight in fine style ... The brother ripped off the dress of the bride's mother, leaving her screaming in her undies. Then, out of his corner, came the bride's father. At which point, the police were called.

But at the restaurant in Lindesberg, central Sweden, the guests weren't having the police upsetting their battle. The bride's father smashed an upper cut at policeman Gunnar Andersson. Which may have given him a points advantage, but he lost the round. Andersson hauled Dad off to the police station. His wife, wearing her husband's overcoat, went too, and was later taken to hospital to be treated for shock.

Back at the "party", the bride – a 21-year-old called Kerstin – was swinging lefts and rights like she was mad at another woman guest. But outside, the 24-year-old groom and his brother decided to celebrate in spite of everything. They were singing in the street.

Most of Lindesberg (population 7,000) had left their TV sets to watch the battle by now. They saw the Lindesberg groom – his white carnation red with blood, and with all the buttons ripped off his shirt – taken to a police cell, too. Meanwhile, the bride, scratched and bruised, and two of her sisters joined their mother in hospital.

A night to remember, certainly. Well, perhaps not.

(from *The Daily Mirror*)

all hell broke loose: suddenly there was chaos
undies: underwear
upper cut: a punch under the chin
swinging lefts and rights: hitting out in every direction

B

Couple count cost of wild wedding

THE WEDDING of William and Wendy Goodway was a day that neither will forget. But if any family snapshots have survived, there will be a noticeable absence of the usual smiling faces.

Their wedding reception ended in a fight between the two families that more resembled a brawl in a Dodge City saloon than a marriage in rural Gloucestershire.

When William Goodway regained consciousness in the ambulance he tried to get out of the vehicle while it was travelling at 50 mph, breaking a window in the process.

Yesterday the Goodways counted the cost of what was supposed to be the happiest day of their lives when they were fined £600 and ordered to pay more than £190 in compensation and costs. Goodway, 25, of Severnbank Avenue, Lydney, Gloucestershire, admitted using threatening behaviour and his wife Wendy, 33, pleaded guilty to assaulting two police officers.

Coleford magistrates heard that police arrested the groom after his attempt to get out of the ambulance, and at that point his bride struggled with the officers, drawing blood when she dug her fingernails into their hands.

Martin Brown, solicitor for Wendy Goodway, told the magistrates that the two families had been unhappy about the marriage and had gone to the reception at the Swan Hotel, Lydney, with an undercurrent of bad feeling.

Both defendants are to appeal against sentence.

(from *The Independent*)

C

That's strife over couple's wet wedding day

GAVIN CAMPBELL, a presenter of the BBC television programme *That's Life*, yesterday denied claims that he ruined the wedding of the first British couple to marry under water by being sick on the vicar.

A High Court libel jury heard that after cohabiting for 12 years, in 1989 Sue Diamond and Mark Richardson had decided to forgo a conventional wedding and fly to Florida to marry 25ft below the sea.

Mr Campbell, 45, who played the role of father of the bride, spent several hours in the witness box countering a series of allegations in the article. It had, he agreed, been necessary to go through the wedding three times, to get all the necessary shots, because there was only one camera. For example, because it is impossible to speak under water, vows had to be exchanged by ticking boxes on a slate with a waterproof pen. *That's Life* had wanted a long shot of the whole business, then a close-up on the boxes, and the couple had been shown "story boards" of their wedding the night before.

He had not forced Mr Richardson to wear a plastic top hat for the ceremony. The groom had voluntarily taken one from a pile in the boat. He had not tried to force the bride to wear a wedding dress under water.

Nor had he arranged for 20 guests unknown to the couple to attend the ceremony. There had only been seven, and they were friends of the notary, Amy Slate, or employees of the diving company.

He had not been "sick over the vicar". He had thrown up over the side of the boat just before the ceremony, and Amy Slate, playing the role of "vicar", had been in the water, but 12 feet away at the back.

The case continues today.

(from *The Independent*)

108

1. "A children's squabble turned into a fight, and rather than sweeping it under the carpet, the adults chose to use it to ignite and fuel the argument that followed," he said.
2. It had been agreed by all that she should wear a yellow wetsuit.
3. It was more interesting than their current TV programme – the wedding of Denmark's Princess Benedikte on Saturday.
4. The Virgin group had agreed to arrange it, as long as the BBC could be present.
5. The bridegroom was hit over the head with a chair and knocked out, glasses were broken and a table damaged, as a grudge between the families turned to violence.
6. One of her sons moved in, a carnation in his lapel and vengeance in his eyes.

7 Read the first dialogue and the account of it. Note the words and expressions in italics and how they correspond to the dialogue. Then read the second dialogue and write an account of it.

K: Oh, hello, Pat.
P: Hi, Kate, how's the baby?
K: Just great, thanks. Would you like a cup of tea?
P: No, thanks – no time. But could you lend me your sewing machine for an hour or two?
K: Sure, glad to. Don't forget that the pedal sticks sometimes.
P: I won't. Shall I bring it back when I've finished?
K: No, just bring it to school this afternoon and I'll get it from you there.
P: OK. Thanks a lot, Kate.
K: Don't mention it. Bye.
P: Bye.

Kate and Pat *greeted one another* and Pat asked how Kate's baby was. Kate said she was great, and *offered* Pat a cup of tea. Pat said she didn't have the time and *asked Kate to* lend her her sewing machine for an hour or two. Kate *agreed*, and *told Pat not to* forget that the pedal stuck sometimes. Pat said she wouldn't, and asked if she should bring it back when she had finished. Kate *told her to* bring it to school that afternoon and she would get it from her there. Pat *thanked* her and they *said* good-bye.

J: Oh, hello, Bill, how are you?
B: Fine, Jim. Listen, could you lend me your food processor for a couple of hours? Mine has stopped working.
J: Sure. Do you know how to work this one? Is yours the same make?
B: Let's see, no, it isn't. Could you give me a demonstration?
J: Sure, just sit down. I'll make some breadcrumbs, I need them for tonight. Or why don't you make them?
B: OK, what do I do first?
J: Put the bowl on and turn it until it clicks. Yeah, then put the blade in and push it down.
B: Does it matter which way I put it in?
J: No, just put it in any way. But don't forget to push it down until it clicks.
B: Now what?
J: Cut the bread into squares – about six squares per slice, and put them in. OK, now put the top on with the tube to the left of the front, and then turn it to the right to start it.
B: Well, that's easy enough. Mine is much more complicated.
J: Yeah, well, I don't think you'll have any problems. Do you think you could bring it back when you've finished with it?
B: Sure, don't worry. I'll have it back by eight, if that's OK.
J: Fine. See you then. Bye, Bill.
B: Bye, Jim, and thanks a lot.

"What a day! First the cement mixer breaks down ..."

E7 You can say that again

1 Grammar and vocabulary revision. Put in the right prepositions.

A: How long have you been waiting in this queue?
B: ......1...... two o'clock. How about you?
A: ......2...... about 45 minutes.
C: Next please. May I see your papers? Thank you. Oh dear. You haven't got your birth certificate. You'll have to come back. Can you be here ......3...... 3.45 p.m. ......4...... Monday?
B: That's very difficult. I work ......5...... the afternoon. Could we possibly make it one morning?
C: How about 10.15 ......6...... Tuesday?
B: I can't manage Tuesday. Suppose I could get my birth certificate to you before you close this morning? When do you close?
C: We'll be closing for lunch ......7...... about 45 minutes. But we're open this afternoon ......8...... 2.00 ......9...... 5.30.
B: I'll try to get back ......10...... one o'clock.
C: Fine, just come straight up to this window.
B: Thank you.
C: Not at all. Next please.
A: I've come to get a certificate for my mother. I think her records are here.
C: When was she born?
A: ......11...... 1916. August 16th.
C: Oh, that's all right then. You see, we have the files up to 1950, but all of the files ......12...... 1950 are at the Romford office.
A: That's a relief. I've got off work specially to come down and sort this out.
C: Just fill in this form and I'll have your certificate ready ......13...... about fifteen minutes.
A: Thank you very much.

2 Grammar revision. Write the 'short answers'.

1. 'Are you staying long?'
   'No, I'm not.'
2. 'You can get cheap flights, can't you?'
   'Yes, I can.'
3. 'You've lost the key, have you?' 'Yes, ...'
4. 'Tiring flight, isn't it?' 'Yes, ...'
5. 'Are you George Temple?' 'No, ...'
6. 'Do you fly a lot?' 'No, ...'
7. 'Drive carefully, won't you?' 'Yes, ...'
8. 'You must get ready to leave.' 'Yes, I suppose ....'
9. 'Did you know Peter Lewis?' 'No, I'm afraid ....'
10. 'It should be a quick flight.' 'Yes, I think ....'
11. 'Is there a customs check at the border?' 'Yes, ...'

3 Grammar revision. Write the 'reply questions'.

1. 'I work for BCJ Electrical Components.'
   'Oh, do you?'
2. 'He's the Deputy Sales Manager.'
   'Is he really?'
3. 'I'm off to Canada tomorrow.' 'Oh, ...?'
4. 'She runs five miles a day.' '................ really?'
5. 'The Slaters have just got divorced.' 'Oh, ...?'
6. 'It's snowing.' 'Oh, ...?'
7. 'It's getting late. I must go now.' 'Oh, ... really?'

4 Grammar revision. Write the 'question tags'.

1. It's cold, isn't it?
2. You're not ready, are you?
3. You speak Greek, ...?
4. She can't swim, ...?
5. They're late, ...?
6. The new car looks good, ...?
7. You can drive, ...?
8. Henry wasn't there yesterday, ...?
9. The grass needs cutting, ...?
10. She doesn't look at all like her sister, ...?
11. You won't tell anybody, ...?
12. Your mother lived in Japan when she was younger, ...?

5 🔊 Find Lesson E7, Exercise 1 on the Student's Cassette. How many question tags do you hear? Write them down and practise their intonation.

"No, madam, we don't expect you to stand there all day. We close in five minutes."

6 Read one or more of these, using a dictionary if you wish.

Pilot holds New York hostage

'This is the first airplane hostage situation in the history of the world with New York City as the hostage.'

That was how the police department described yesterday's bizarre incident in which a dissatisfied Australian writer threatened to crash his aircraft into a New York skyscraper.

The first word of the threat came at 10.20 a.m. when a police department official telephoned the United Nations and informed the Secretary General that a lunatic pilot in the area planned to fly his plane into the UN building.

The UN was evacuated, bomb disposal squads and fire teams moved onto the UN grounds to cope with the threatened disaster. Traffic outside the UN was rerouted and no one was allowed on First Avenue but reporters.

Then the police corrected their original report. The target of the pilot, Richard Boudin, was not the UN, but the publishing company of Harcourt Brace Jovanovich, housed in a building two blocks from the UN.

Mr Boudin apparently felt that his novel, *Confessions of a Promiscuous Counterfeiter*, was not getting enough publicity, so he chartered the plane at a New Jersey airport and radioed that he was going to destroy the publishing house.

Soon after noon the president of the publishing company agreed to talk with Mr Boudin, if he would land at La Guardia Airport. Mr Boudin accepted and flew off, the crisis over.

Police said Mr Boudin would be charged with reckless endangerment and other offences.

(Jane Rosen, *The Guardian* – adapted)

The train not stopping at platform one ...

BRITISH RAIL passengers from London to Oxford had an unscheduled detour via Swindon after a train driver forgot to stop at Didcot.

People getting ready to change for a connecting train to Oxford on Saturday evening heard the guard announce Didcot on the train intercom, only to see the station flash past them.

The 30 Oxford-bound passengers eventually reached journey's end 45 minutes late, after getting a train back from Swindon to Didcot to catch another local train home.

Mrs Jean Robinson, an Oxford health expert who was one of the passengers affected, said they had been offered no explanation or apology for what happened.

'It was fortunate the train was one that stopped at Swindon; otherwise we'd have gone to Bristol,' she said. 'When we got out at Swindon there was no one to tell us anything and we couldn't find anyone in charge.'

A British Rail spokesman said this week that the driver had simply forgotten to stop at Didcot. 'It's an error which is regretted,' he said.

(*The Oxford Times* – adapted)

Chipmunk lands in Heathrow darkness

Officials are to investigate how a light aircraft landed undetected on an unlit runway at Heathrow Airport in London.

The single engine de Havilland Chipmunk was found by a routine British Airports Authority patrol on the grass a few yards from one of Heathrow's two main runways. The runway was closed at the time.

Customs officials with dogs searched the aircraft, but police said there was no suggestion at the moment that it had been used for smuggling, or terrorist activities.

But how did the plane land unnoticed at the world's busiest airport? A spokeswoman for the Civil Aviation Authority, which is responsible for air traffic control, guessed that it must have touched down while there was 'no known traffic' – no scheduled arrivals or departures on the other runway, which remained in operation. So there was no requirement for radar monitoring.

The authorities at Heathrow automatically prepared an invoice of landing and parking charges incurred by the Chipmunk. It came to just under £37.

But the CAA's spokeswoman said: 'Until the whole matter is resolved, we don't know whether the invoice will be sent to anyone, or, if it is, to whom.'

(John Hooper, *The Guardian* – adapted)

7 Imagine that an old person is coming to visit you. He/She is travelling by air, and has never flown before. Write a letter telling him/her what to expect and giving him/her some advice. Use words and expressions from the Student's Book lesson in your writing.

"I'm not asking you to serve me – just to include me in your conversation."

E8 Who invented writing?

1 Grammar revision: conditionals. Imagine you have won a lot of money in a lottery. Here are the beginnings and ends of some sentences about the different things you can do with the money. Put the beginnings and ends together to make sensible sentences.

BEGINNINGS	ENDS
If I bet it all on a horse race	it'll certainly be safe.
If I spend it all on clothes	I may not make very much income from it.
If I give it all away	it'll be no use to anyone.
If I buy a house with it	I'll almost certainly lose it.
If I give it to my parents	I'll have lots of interesting experiences.
If I use it to travel round the world	I might be sorry afterwards.
If I bury it in a hole in the garden	I may never see it again.
If I put it in the bank	I know I'll feel wonderful.

Now complete some of these sentences. Use the structures in the box to help you.

1. If I spend it on a trip round the world …
2. If I use it to start a business …
3. If I share it with my family …
4. If I invest it in government securities …
5. If I spend it on private English lessons …
6. If I stop work …
7. If I buy a hotel …
8. If I go on living exactly as before …

> I'll …
> I won't …
> I may/might (not) …
> I'll certainly/probably …
> I certainly/probably won't …
> I will/may/might be able to …
> I will/may/might have to …

2 Grammar revision: conditionals (continued). Complete the text using verbs from the box in their past forms or using *would* + the infinitive. You can use verbs more than once, and you may need to use negative forms.

be	give up	go on	feel	have	miss
succeed	try	understand	use		

How <u>would</u> you <u>feel</u> if you <u>had</u> to live abroad for the rest of your life? Do you think you ……1…… unhappy? Are there any things that you ……2…… in particular? Suppose you ……3…… children who grew up speaking a foreign language instead of your own. How ……4…… you ……5……? Do you think that you would feel that you ……6…… them? ……7…… you ……8…… to preserve something of your culture and way of life? And ……9…… you ……10…… to pass this on to your children? Do you think you ……11……? ……12…… you ……13…… speaking your own language, or ……14…… you ……15…… using it? Would you be afraid of forgetting it if you ……16…… it?

3 Vocabulary. Match verbs from the first box with objects from the second. There may be more than one possible answer in each case. Example:

<u>take off clothes</u>

break off	bring up	cut up	give up
look up	ring up	take off	turn off
turn over	work out	write down	

an address	children	clothes	a friend
a light	meat	a page	a problem
a relationship	smoking	words	

"That's not how you spell it! There's only one owl in Tutankhamen."

4 Read and pronounce all the words in the box. Then see how many of the tasks you can do in five minutes. (You may use the same words for more than one answer.)

although   Asia   astonish   bleed   burn
cheaply   Chinese   clay   coal   compose
democratic   fail   hostess   insurance
Iraq   lamb   metal   misunderstanding
oil   pass   sculpt   seriously   shaken
sheep   shiver   situation   skeleton   sky
solve   spit   stone   strawberry
uninhabitable   unless   whether   wood

1. Find one language, one country and one continent.
2. Find two kinds of fuel and two kinds of (building) material.
3. Find two words which are opposites.
4. Find three irregular verbs.
5. Find two adverbs and two conjunctions.
6. Find two words where the main stress is on the third syllable and one where it's on the fourth syllable.
7. Find three words which contain the vowel /əʊ/ (as in *know*, *told*, *wrote*).

5 This is the text of the talk in the Student's Book. Read it, using a dictionary if you wish. (You can listen to the recording if you find Lesson E8, Exercises 3 and 4 on the Student's Cassette.)

The origins of writing

Who invented writing?

The world's earliest writing system seems to have been used by the Sumerians, who lived in the Middle East, where Iraq is today. They had a kind of picture writing, with over 1,500 signs for different objects, numbers, and other ideas. The signs were written with a piece of wood on clay tablets, which were then baked to keep them hard and preserve the writing.

Where did the complicated Sumerian writing system come from? Did they invent it, or was it developed from an earlier, simpler writing system used by somebody else? Nobody knows the answer to this question, but archaeologists have not found an earlier writing system, although they have excavated thousands of sites in the Middle East.

The archaeologist Denise Schmandt-Besserat has an interesting theory. In an article in the journal *Scientific American*, she suggests that writing may have developed from the use of stones and other objects for accounting.

In many parts of the world, people use small objects – stones, pieces of wood, etc. – for keeping records and accounts. The Romans used stones, and their word for a small stone – *calculus* – has given us our word *calculate*. Small discs or balls are used in the Chinese abacus. And in Iraq, even today, shepherds use stones to keep count of their sheep.

Almost everywhere in the Middle East, archaeologists have found small objects made of clay. These objects are of several different shapes: for example spheres, cones, discs, pyramids and cylinders. The earliest objects date from 10,500 years ago, at about the time when farming was beginning. It seems that the objects were tokens used for accounting. For instance, objects of a particular shape represented sheep. People used them to check the numbers and movements of their animals. If a lamb was born, another token was added; when an animal was killed, a token was taken away. When sheep were moved to another place, the tokens were put on a different shelf in the building where records were kept. Other objects represented other kinds of animals such as cattle or dogs, while still others stood for cloth, metals, oil and so on. Some represented numbers.

When the first cities grew up, these clay objects were used in a new way. If a farmer or cloth-maker sent animals or goods to the city, he sent with them a record to show what there was. For example, if he sent 48 sheep he would send along 48 of the tokens that represented sheep. So that nobody could steal any of the sheep, he put the 48 tokens in a hollow clay sphere, closed it up, put his personal seal – his signature – on the outside and baked it. The person who received his goods in the city would break open the sphere to check that everything was there.

Later, people had the idea of marking the outside of the clay sphere to show what tokens were inside, so that it was possible to check the goods even before breaking open the sphere. So on the outside of the sphere, they made pictures of the objects which were inside.

Later still, people realised that it was not necessary to go on using clay tokens – the pictures were just as good, and could be put on flat pieces of clay instead of spheres.

And as time went on, these pictures were used to write other kinds of messages besides business records, and more signs were invented. Writing had begun, and it soon spread all across Western Asia.

6 Do one of these writing tasks. Try to include some words and expressions from the Student's Book lesson.

1. Write in detail how your life would be different if you couldn't read or write.
2. Describe in detail when and how you learnt to read and write.

7 Try the crossword.

ACROSS

1. Someone who writes music.
6. My girlfriend's mother turned .... to be a friend of my father's.
8. Take an umbrella .... case it rains.
9. I think this painting is a real work .... art.
10. Approximately 2.5 centimetres.
12. Another way of saying hello.
14. The purpose of this exam is to .... what you have learnt this year.
16. Bigger than a village.
18. The Simple Past of *sit*.
19. Not that one – use the .... one.
20. What sculptors do.
22. The short form of Diana.
23. The verb from *operation*.
27. .... of birth: 20.10.56
30. Some people say that politicians tell these all the time.
32. She arrived late, ... usual.
34. Neither him nor her.
35. What people like the one in *28 down* do.
36. I can't wait .... go on holiday.
37. A possible explanation for something.
39. Be careful: I don't want anything to .... fire.
41. What did you .... for dessert?
43. A liquid which is both a food and a fuel.
44. What you do in the kitchen.
47. How many children .... your brother got?
48. You can do this to both *40 down* and *43 across*.
49. Purpose.
51. Something that produces heat or power by burning.
52. Neither my wife .... I can sing.
53. Someone who looks after sick animals.
55. I'll have finished this .... tomorrow, I hope.
56. Inflation has gone up by two .... cent.
57. The opposite of *plus*.

DOWN

1. A lot of people live here.
2. 1.5 = ... point five.
3. Someone who makes pottery.
4. I have a habit .... sleeping with the curtains open.
5. What will the world be like .... fifty years' time?
6. '..............., no – I can't find my keys!'
7. Not this.
10. Not outside.
11. I would if I .... but I can't.
13. Neither he nor she.
15. She took a backpack .... that she could carry all her stuff easily.
16. You might sleep in this if you go camping.
17. Either you get out .... I'm calling the police!
18. When you brush your teeth you should always .... the toothpaste out.
21. Member of Parliament.
23. Thing.
24. Do you think that ghosts actually ....?
25. 'I'm 28.' 'Are you? So .... I.'
26. He still lives with his mother and father – everyone .... has left home now.
28. A person whose job it is to pretend to be somebody else.
29. You will die if you don't do this regularly.
31. 'What did he ....?' 'He told me he loved me.'
33. You might say this when you've done something wrong.
37. Not *7 down*.
38. Happen.
40. A hard, black material which you can use to keep you warm.
41. All right.
42. Have you ever .... a Rolls-Royce?
45. She lives in Dublin – .... rather she *works* in Dublin.
46. I'm afraid I've .... got one left.
47. Good morning. Can I .... you?
48. The opposite of *cancel*.
50. Give .... a ring tomorrow. I'll be in until 11 o'clock.
51. Mend.
54. My sister doesn't mind whether her baby's a girl .... a boy.
55. The infinitive from *is/are*.

(*Solution on page 145.*)

Basic grammar revision exercises

Simple Present and Present Progressive

1 Look at the examples and think about how each tense is used.

SIMPLE PRESENT TENSE
The weather gets colder towards the end of September.
We usually go skiing in February.
Paul often plays his violin.
I never eat meat.

PRESENT PROGRESSIVE TENSE
The weather is getting colder now.
We're going skiing next week.
Listen – Paul's playing his violin.
'What are you eating?' 'Fish pie.'

Which tenses do we use to talk about the following?
A things that happen often, usually, always, never, *etc*.
B things that are happening now, these days
C plans for the future
D things that are always true
E things that are changing

2 Write the correct verb forms and decide which of the rules in Exercise 1 applies in each case.

1. Oh, dear. My work .... more and more difficult. (*get*)
2. Do you know anyone who .... cars? (*repair*)
3. Water .... to ice at 0°C. (*turn*)
4. The cost of living .... faster than people's salaries. (*increase*)
5. She .... her parents at Christmas. (*always visit*)
6. He can't speak to you at the moment – he .... a shower. (*have*)
7. 'What's that lovely music?' 'Bill .... his new CD.' (*play*)
8. .... your hands ever .... after you've been typing a lot? (*hurt*)
9. .... you .... to Newcastle by train next week? (*travel*)

> For work on possible confusions between present tenses and the Present Perfect, see page 119.
> For more about the use of present tenses to talk about the future, see pages 120–122.

3 Choose one of the people in the picture and write down what he/she is wearing and doing. Example:

A woman is sitting at a desk. She's wearing a dark suit, and she's talking to a man who ...

4 Who are these people and what are they doing? Can you write a 'riddle' like this yourself?

1. This person usually works in the open air looking after different kinds of plants and animals. But right now he is making a leather ball move from his foot into a large net. (*Answer: a farmer who is playing football*)
2. In her job this person usually spends her day looking into people's mouths and helping them if they are in pain. But right now she is standing in front of a cooker moving a large spoon around in a metal container full of a hot liquid.
3. When this person is working she usually pretends to be someone she isn't, often in front of a number of other people or in front of cameras. At the moment, though, she is wearing a special kind of clothing and is moving through a lot of water using her arms and her legs.
4. This person usually carries food and drinks to people's tables when they are having a meal away from home. But right now he is standing with a lot of other people who together are all making a very nice sound with their voices.

Simple Past and Past Progressive

1 Look at the tables and examples and try to see how each tense is used. Can you make a rule for the Past Progressive?

SIMPLE PAST TENSE

> I walked, you walked, he/she walked *etc.*
> did I walk? *etc.*
> I did not walk *etc.*

PAST PROGRESSIVE TENSE

> I was walking, you were walking *etc.*
> was I walking? *etc.*
> I was not walking *etc.*

Examples:
1. Who were you talking to at dinner last night?
2. He worked as a postman when he was younger.
3. I was finishing off a letter to my uncle and my pen ran out of ink.
4. Where did you go for your holidays this year?
5. While he was having his lunch, there was a knock at the door.
6. When the rain stopped, they both ran to the car as quickly as they could.
7. She drank too much at the party.

2 Which of the two tenses do we use for these?

A a short event that happened before or after another event
B the 'background' situation at the moment when something happened
C a long past situation, with nothing else happening in the middle of it
D the situation at a particular past moment
E a shorter event which came in the middle of a longer, 'background' event
F a short past event
G a shorter event which interrupted a longer, 'background' event

3 Write the correct verb forms and decide which of the rules in Exercise 2 applies in each case.

1. The police .... for the burglars when they .... out of the house. (*wait, come*)
2. I .... the dishes while Adam .... the children to bed. (*wash, put*)
3. When .... you .... the office this evening? (*leave*)
4. When I .... the size of the dog I .... very afraid. (*see, feel*)
5. We .... the match on the television and the picture suddenly .... (*watch, disappear*)
6. She .... voluntary work in a hospital before she .... medicine. (*do, study*)
7. I .... the crossword while I .... to work. (*finish, travel*)
8. The party .... to die as soon as Alison .... home. (*seem, go*)
9. She .... most of her childhood in Galway. (*spend*)
10. He .... up the vegetables when the cooker .... (*cut, explode*)
11. .... he .... at the bus stop at around eight o'clock this morning? (*stand*)

4 Write what you were doing, or what was happening, at three or more of these moments.

1. The last time you were really worried.
2. The last time you talked to a member of your family.
3. The last time you felt very excited.
4. The last time you felt really pleased.
5. The last time you felt very embarrassed.

5 Write questions using two of the expressions below, or write your own question(s) with Past Progressive and Simple Past verbs. Think of someone you know really well and write how they might answer the question(s).

1. when you first started school
2. at three o'clock this morning
3. before you left home yesterday
4. at lunchtime yesterday
5. when you went to bed last night

6 Find a place where you can observe a number of people doing things. Watch them for ten seconds and then sit down and write at least three things that were happening.

7 Choose the correct caption for the cartoon.

'I just was shaking his hand and he was sick.'
'I just shook his hand and he was sick.'

Present Perfect and Simple Past with time expressions

1 Look at the tables and examples. When do we use the Present Perfect with time expressions, and when do we use the Simple Past?

SIMPLE PRESENT PERFECT TENSE

> I have eaten, you have eaten *etc.*
> have I eaten? *etc.*
> I have not eaten *etc.*

SIMPLE PAST TENSE

> I ate, you ate, he/she ate *etc.*
> did I eat? *etc.*
> I did not eat *etc.*

Examples:
1. She stopped smoking when she got pregnant.
2. We've spent a lot of time in southern Italy, but we've never visited the north.
3. You haven't been at home much lately, have you?
4. Bill's eaten here several times this week.
5. I played some kind of sport every week when I was at school.
6. He's always wanted to get married, but he's never met the right person.
7. She took up the violin in 1965, and she has played it ever since.
8. They've lived here since their parents died.
9. Nobody saw the burglars enter the building.
10. 'Have you finished yet?' 'Yes, I finished ages ago, but Jill hasn't.'

2 Only one of these rules is true. Which one?

When we give the time of a past event:
A The Present Perfect is used for repeated actions; the Simple Past is used for actions that are not repeated.
B The Present Perfect is used for longer periods of time; the Simple Past is used for shorter periods.
C The Present Perfect is used when the time is not finished; the Simple Past is used when it is finished.
D The Present Perfect is used when the time is finished; the Simple Past is used when it is not finished.

3 Finished or unfinished time?

since I was four	recently/lately
after I got home	since I had lunch
ever	ten years ago
this afternoon	for the last year
for the last two days	this month
always	until I was six
in 1956	up to now
since the war	last week
never	today
yesterday	when I was two

4 Write the correct verb forms.

1. We .... a terrible night – the baby .... at three o'clock and .... crying since! (*just have, wake up, not stop*)
2. She .... to lock up last night. (*forget*)
3. He .... to her lately – have you? (*not talk*)
4. I .... too much money last month. (*spend*)
5. Since he was six he .... Mozart. (*always like*)
6. I .... as a vet until I got cancer. (*work*)
7. We .... here for the last year. (*live*)
8. We certainly .... a lot of rain this year! (*have*)
9. They .... nearly ten years ago. (*get married*)
10. '............ he .... any work at all today?' 'He .... Angie Banks a few hours ago – otherwise not a thing.' (*do; ring*)
11. 'How's the weather?' 'Great. The sun .... every day up to now.' (*shine*)
12. I .... lucky all my life. (*be*)
13. .... you ever .... what it's all about? (*wonder*)
14. I .... a lot of new people last year. (*meet*)

5 Answer these questions, giving your reasons.

1. A man says 'I worked for this company for eight years.' Does he still work for the company?
2. A woman says 'I've lived in Paris for two years.' Is she living in Paris when she says this?
3. Somebody says 'I spent three years in the army.' Is he or she still in the army?
4. You are in Japan. A friend says 'How long are you here for?' Does the person want to know when your visit started, or when it will end? How would he or she express the other meaning?
5. Somebody says 'I've been married to Alex for six years, and I was married to Chris for nine years.' Which one is he or she still married to?

6 Write two questions: use an expression from each group. Decide how a close friend of yours might answer the questions.

First group:
When you were ten …?
Last month, …?
How long ago …?
When did you last …?

Second group:
Have you … since …?
What/Who … recently?
Have you ever …?
Have you … today?

7 Complete this rule:

DON'T USE THE .... WITH EXPRESSIONS OF FINISHED TIME.

> There are separate exercises on *since* and *for* on page 120.

117

Present Perfect Progressive

1 Look at the examples. Then close your book and try to write down three of them from memory.

*Why are you so late? I **have been standing here** for ages.*
*It **has been snowing** all night.*
*'You look exhausted.' 'Yes, I've **been playing** with the children.'*
*How long **has** she **been living** here?*
*Who's **been using** my pen?*

2 Complete the sentences with Present Perfect Progressive verbs.

1. How long .... they .... in the same orchestra? (*play*)
2. I .... badly for the last month. (*sleep*)
3. Your English .... a lot lately. (*improve*)
4. 'You look happy.' 'Yes, I .... to Alison.' (*talk*)
5. They .... together since April. (*go out*)
6. 'What .... she .... all day?' 'She .... me fix the car.' (*do; help*)
7. He .... on the computer for over six hours. (*work*)

3 When do we use the Present Perfect Progressive? Use the words in the box to complete the rules. (You won't need all the words.)

| future | length | past | present | temporary |

1. The Present Perfect Progressive is used to refer to .... events or states which began in the .... and are still continuing, especially when the focus is on the .... of time involved.
2. It is also often used to refer to a recent continuing event or state which accounts for a .... situation.

Look back at Exercise 2 and decide which rule refers to each item.

4 Choose five things that you do regularly and write how long you have been doing them. Do you wish you could stop doing any of them?

5 Look at the pictures. What has the person been doing in each one?

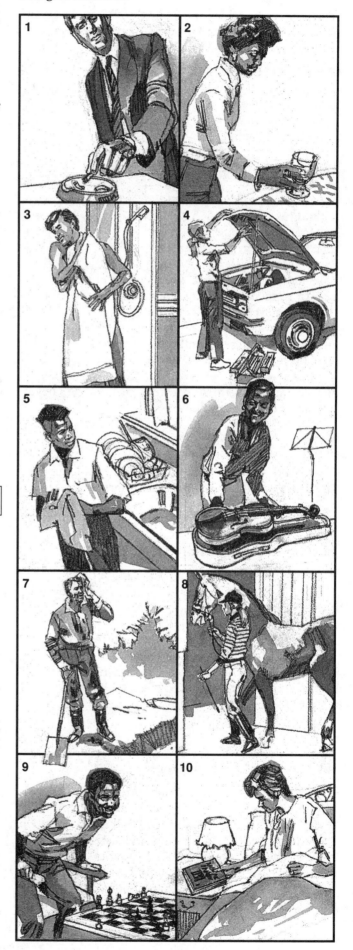

118

6
Some verbs are not used in progressive forms. Choose the correct tense (Present Perfect Simple or Progressive).

1. I have *loved / been loving* Spain since I first went there ten years ago.
2. How long has she *known / been knowing* Jane?
3. We've *tried / been trying* to talk to you since Wednesday.
4. How long has he *had / been having* his dog?
5. How long have they *learnt / been learning* Chinese?

7
Present Perfect or Present? Choose the right tense.

1. *They're / They've been* in Nairobi since March.
2. How long *are you using / have you been using* a walking stick?
3. He *is reading / has been reading* the same book for the last two weeks.
4. How long *do you have / have you had* your cold?
5. She *is writing / has been writing* a comic novel at the moment.
6. Hi! *I'm hoping / I've been hoping* you would call.
7. What's so funny? Why *are you laughing / have you been laughing* like that?
8. They *know / have known* about it for ages.

8
Choose the correct caption for the cartoon.

'We've been living together for twenty-five years, Helen. You could at least give me a chance to run for it.'

'We're living together for twenty-five years, Helen. You could at least give me a chance to run for it.'

Non-progressive verbs

1
Here are some pieces of conversation recorded at a party. Put in the right present-tense verb forms.

1. 'You .... marvellously.' 'Thanks. Unfortunately you .... standing on my toes! Ouch!!' (*dance; keep*)
2. 'Where's he from?' 'I ...., I'm afraid.' (*not remember*)
3. 'You .... me. I'm Julie's brother.' 'Ah, yes, of course. Where .... Julie .... these days?' 'She .... a flat in Norwich.' 'I ....' (*know; live; have got; see*)
4. 'He says he .... her, but I .... him.' 'I .... He .... the same thing to all the women.' (*love, not believe; agree, say*)
5. 'I .... this soup.' 'Really? I .... it .... delicious.' (*not like; think, taste*)
6. '............... anybody .... who these glasses .... to?' '............... you .... they're John's?' 'Ask him. He .... over there.' (*know, belong; think; stand*)
7. 'Why .... you .... to that man?' 'He's a friend of mine.' 'Oh? I .... him.' (*talk; not recognise*)
8. '............... you .... some more coffee?' 'No, thanks. It .... rather bitter.' (*want; taste*)
9. 'I .... him so well: lovely hair, nice eyes, ...' 'What was his name?' 'Oh, I .... actually!' (*remember; forget*)
10. 'This wine .... very strange.' 'I .... it – it was quite expensive, you ....' 'Oh, it .... Pour me another glass, will you?' (*smell; not understand, know; not matter*)
11. 'I .... you quite irresistible.' 'Excuse me. I .... another drink.' (*find; need*)
12. 'It .... very hot in here. Let's open a window.' '............... you .... to go outside for a while?' (*get; want*)
13. 'I .... you!' 'You .... that, do you?' 'Read my lips ...' (*hate; not mean*)

2
Look again at Exercise 1. Make a list of the verbs that are not usually used in progressive forms.

3
Put together some of the beginnings and ends to make sensible sentences.

BEGINNINGS	ENDS
I forget	her name.
It doesn't taste like	in God.
I don't think	it's correct.
We know	marmalade.
I love	sleeping.
We hate	to kiss you.
I want	where I put it.
I don't remember	who they are.
I understand	your wife.
I believe	your worries.

119

Since and for

1 Look at the examples. We use different kinds of expression after *since* and *for*. Complete the rule.

We've worked here since 1987.
It's been snowing since late this afternoon.
He's not been happy since he joined the company.
We've worked here for seven years.
It's been snowing since half past four.
He's not been happy since January.

Rule:
.... is followed by a reference to a period of time.
.... is followed by a reference to a 'starting point'.

2 Fill in the gaps.

since the 15th century = for 500 years
for 24 hours = since yesterday
since 1981 = for ...
for fifteen years = since ...
since last May = for ...
for the last ten months = since ...
since eleven o'clock = for ...
for the last six hours = since ...
since last Sunday = for ...
for the last two days = since ...
all his life = ... he was born
since her birthday = ... the last ... days/months

3 Put in *since* or *for*.

1. We haven't slept .... 36 hours.
2. There's been a mosque here .... the 13th century.
3. They've been together .... 1962.
4. He's been out of work .... eighteen months.
5. She hasn't stopped crying .... he left.
6. I've been waiting here .... four hours.
7. They've been away .... Tuesday evening.
8. She's been trying to sell it .... weeks.

4 Write sentences with *since* and *for* for these situations.

1. Virginie started working here two years ago.
2. Pepe lives in Madrid. He started living there at the end of last year.
3. Zara is taking ballet lessons. She started when she was five.
4. Pierre has a car in Lyons. He bought it a year ago.
5. Joe works for Bill. He began doing this in 1988.
6. Theo is visiting his family in Athens. He arrived on Tuesday.
7. Giulia plays chess. She started on her last birthday.

5 Make five questions with *How long*. Decide how a close friend of yours would answer the questions using *since* or *for*.

Talking about the future

PLANS: PRESENT PROGRESSIVE FOR FIXED ARRANGEMENTS

1 Write sentences to say what you are doing this afternoon / tomorrow morning / tomorrow lunchtime / next Monday / next Friday evening / next week.
Examples:

I'm meeting my boss this afternoon.
 (I meet my boss ...)
We're visiting Edinburgh next week. (We visit ...)

2 Look carefully at Pat's diary for next weekend and then fill in the gaps in her telephone conversation with Tim, including the Present Progressive where possible as well as phrases from the box.

Are you doing anything in the afternoon / on Saturday morning / at ... o'clock?
It depends.
Sorry, I'm not free. I'm ...ing.
Could we make it earlier/later? I'm ...ing at / until ... o'clock

TIM: Hi, Pat. This is Tim. How's it going?
PAT: Fine, thanks, Tim. You?
TIM: Oh, not too bad, I suppose. Look, are you free for a drink on Friday evening? About 8.30?
PAT: Let me just check my diary. ....1.......
TIM: Sorry, I'm afraid I'm working until eight o'clock. Oh, dear. I really do need to see you. Could I call round on Saturday morning?
PAT: ....2.......
TIM: Mm. No, sorry, I'm not free till after eleven, I'm afraid. What about lunch?
PAT: ....3.......
TIM: Have you got any time in the afternoon?
PAT: ....4.......
TIM: Yes, I'm afraid so. I'm cooking dinner for Mark and Rose on Saturday evening.
PAT: ....5.......

TIM: Yes, I'm going to church with Mum and Dad. What about the afternoon?
PAT: ......6......
TIM: And no doubt the evening's busy too?
PAT: ......7......
TIM: Well, OK – nine o'clock then. Better late than never. You see, I need to tell you about Jill. ...

PLANS: GOING TO

3 Plan your next holiday. Write sentences saying what you are going to do and what you are not going to do. Use some of the verbs in the box.

buy	drink	eat	get up	go to bed	
join	learn	meet	need	play	read
see	spend	stay	take	travel	try
use	visit	work			

PREDICTIONS ('WE CAN SEE IT COMING'): GOING TO

4 Look at the pictures. What is going to happen?

PREDICTIONS ('I THINK/HOPE/KNOW'): WILL

5 Make predictions about your life / your family / your country for the year to come. Use *I (don't) think, I'm sure, perhaps, probably*. Examples:

I don't think I'll be very rich.
Perhaps my parents will move house.
Unemployment will probably increase.

6 Put *perhaps, probably (not), certainly (not)* or *not* into the sentences to make them true for you. Add one or more sentences of your own.

1. I will visit China before the end of the year.
2. I will leave the city/town/village where I'm living in the next two years.
3. I will get married some time in the next six months.
4. I will travel to the moon before I die.
5. I will dye my hair before the end of the month.
6. I will go on a diet before the summer.
7. I will change jobs before my next birthday.
8. I will win a lot of money before the middle of next year.

PRESENT PROGRESSIVE, GOING TO OR WILL?

7 Which form would you use to talk about the following?

1. Something in the future that is obviously on the way.
2. Your plans for when you retire.
3. Something in the future that you think is probable.
4. An arrangement to meet a friend at a particular time.

8 Choose the correct forms.

1. Watch out! That car *is going to pull out* / *will pull out*!
2. There probably *isn't going to be* / *won't be* another world war before the end of the century.
3. Great news! Rupert and Joy *are going to get* / *will get* married.
4. *She's doing* / *She'll do* her driving test on Thursday.
5. I hope *I'm finding* / *I'll find* somewhere to live in London.
6. My company *is going to move* / *will move* to Liverpool at the end of the year.
7. *Are your parents doing* / *Will your parents do* anything tomorrow evening?
8. Look at the sky. The sun *is coming out* / *is going to come out* any minute now.

TENSES AFTER *IF*, *WHEN* ETC.

9 Choose the correct forms.

1. If I *hear / will hear* any news I *call / will call* you immediately.
2. We *come / will come* and see you when we *are / will be* in Moscow.
3. If he *finishes / will finish* the job early I *pay / will pay* him an extra £100.
4. Nothing *happens / will happen* until the President *makes / will make* a decision.
5. Perhaps you *like / will like* it if you *try / will try* it.
6. She *writes / will write* to us as soon as she *arrives / will arrive*.
7. The situation *is / will be* worse before it *gets / will get* better.

10 Choose the correct caption for the cartoon.

'Open a window, will you? Mr Mulliner leaves.'
'Open a window, will you? Mr Mulliner will leave.'
'Open a window, will you? Mr Mulliner is leaving.'

Infinitives with and without *to*

1 Infinitives after auxiliary verbs. Which is correct?

1. He **will to come** later.
2. He **will come** later.

These verbs are followed by the infinitive without *to*, with one exception. Which is the exception?

can could do may might must
ought shall should would

2 Infinitives after ordinary verbs. Which is correct?

1. We **need to hurry**.
2. We **need hurry**.

What kind of infinitive comes after these?

begin expect hope manage need
prefer seem start try want would like

3 Put in the correct kind of infinitive.

1. 'Is that the phone?' 'Yes, I'll *to get / get* it.'
2. She'd like *to become / become* a lawyer.
3. Could you *to tell / tell* me your address, please?
4. We didn't expect *to see / see* them there.
5. Shall I *to call / call* the doctor?
6. He hopes *to meet / meet* her tomorrow.
7. You must *to stop / stop* doing that.
8. They might not *to have / have* any left.
9. Would you prefer *to go / go* with him?
10. She managed *to fix / fix* it herself.
11. Then it began *to snow / snow*.
12. We don't *to play / play* much tennis these days.
13. They really ought not *to take / take* so long.
14. He tried *to ring / ring* her last week.
15. They shouldn't *to say / say* things like that.

4 Special structures. Which is correct?

1. Her parents never let her *to go / go* out.
2. I'm going to Paris *to learn / learn* French.
3. Would you rather *to stay / stay* here?
4. We had better *to take / take* the train.
5. 'I don't know where *to go / go* for my holidays.'
   'Why not *to visit / visit* Kenya?'
6. Do you know how *to use / use* a computer?
7. Do they have *to shout / shout* so much?
8. You can't make me *to do / do* it!

5 Complete three sentences using infinitives.

1. One of our teachers used to make us ...
2. If you want a lift with me, you had better ...
3. What are you going to Sydney for? ...
4. He doesn't know when ...
5. My parents used to let me ...
6. I don't know who ...
7. It's very late, you know. Why not ...?
8. At home, I have ...
9. Marry you?! I'd rather ...

Uses of -ing forms

1 Some of the sentences have infinitives and the others have -ing forms. Look at the rules, and decide which one gives the best explanation.

*He always wanted **to play** the violin.*
*I didn't expect **to see** so many people here.*
*We'd love **to come** and stay.*
*My father hates **flying**.*
*When did you stop **smoking**?*
*How long ago did you start **going** out together?*

Rules:
1. We use infinitives after most verbs.
2. We use -ing forms after most verbs.
3. We use infinitives after some verbs and -ing forms after others.
4. We use -ing forms to talk about the present and past, and infinitives to talk about the future.
5. We use infinitives to say what people do, and -ing forms to say what happens to people.

2 Do we normally use infinitives or -ing forms after these verbs?

agree   ask   avoid   begin   can't help
decide   dislike   feel like   finish   forget
happen   imagine   learn   manage
(don't) mind   seem   suggest

3 Do we normally use infinitives or -ing forms as subjects of sentences? Which of the following sentences seem most natural?

1. Sleeping is what I like best.
   To sleep is what I like best.
2. Learning to ski is not that difficult.
   To learn to ski is not that difficult.
3. Falling in love makes me cry.
   To fall in love makes me cry.

Give examples of: what you like best; things that are not that difficult; things that make you laugh or cry.

4 Look at these sentences. Can you make a rule?

*I'm sorry **for forgetting** your name.*
*What are you thinking **of doing** next?*
*She's interested **in studying** music.*
*We're really bad **at keeping** in touch with people.*
*He said it **without thinking**.*
*He passed his exams **by working** very hard.*
*I'm bored **with doing** the same things every day.*

Now complete these sentences:

1. We've got an excellent chance of ...ing ...
2. Thank you for ...ing ...
3. I'm fed up with ...ing ...
4. Did you ever think of ...ing ...?
5. She passed all her exams without ...ing ...

5 Look at the examples.

*I had a lovely time, **relaxing and enjoying** myself.*
*He sat there, **reading** his newspaper.*
*Write two paragraphs, **taking** special care with your spelling and punctuation.*
*She was running after me, **shouting** my name.*
*We walked past him, **not knowing** who he was.*

Now rewrite these sentences using -ing forms.

1. I stood there for an hour and waited for the bus.
2. He read his essay again and checked for mistakes.
3. The earthquake struck at 2.35; it destroyed hundreds of houses.
4. They parked the car about a kilometre away and went the rest of the way on foot.
5. She looked around the room nervously; she hoped he wouldn't be there.
6. I woke up very suddenly; I thought I'd heard a sound downstairs.
7. The river burst its banks and flooded the town.
8. She stared back at me and said nothing.

6 Infinitive or -ing form?

1. Why do you put up with .... everything? (*do*)
2. I hope .... agriculture at university. (*study*)
3. He lay on the ground, ... what had happened to him. (*wonder*)
4. .... on your own is not much fun. (*eat*)
5. I didn't expect .... such trouble. (*have*)
6. Always read the instructions before .... on any electrical appliance. (*switch*)
7. I didn't agree .... to him here. (*talk*)
8. I don't mind .... with him, but .... with him as well would be very difficult! (*work, live*)
9. Who have you decided ....? (*invite*)

7 Choose the right caption for the cartoon.

'Pembroke, have you been trying making decisions again?'
'Pembroke, have you been trying to make decisions again?'

Verbs with two objects

1 Look at the example. Some verbs (such as *buy*) can be used with two objects – an indirect object (*me*), and a direct object (*some beautiful flowers*). Example:

She bought me some beautiful flowers.

Decide which is the indirect object and which is the direct object in each of these sentences.

1. Are you sure he told her the truth?
2. Would you order me an orange juice, please?
3. Pass John the butter, will you?
4. I'd love to show you my stamp collection.

2 Make at least five sensible sentences from the table.

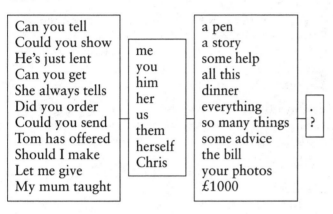

3 Change the sentences as in the examples.

1. Don't ever lend anything to her.
   Don't ever lend her anything.
2. Could you give a hand to Gill?
   Could you give Gill a hand?
3. I think you'd better write a letter to him.
4. Can you get some information about prices for us?
5. Would you mind giving this package to Alex the next time you see her?
6. Could you do a favour for my brother?
7. They keep sending the wrong newspaper to us.
8. Let me show the plans to you.
9. He's never bought a present for me before.
10. Mrs Jones used to teach some lovely poems to the children.
11. Would you pour a glass of water for me, please?
12. It's OK; I'll pass the salt to him.

4 Put each sentence into the right order.

1. her why kiss you give a didn't ?
2. the us bring could bill you ?
3. to for you like buy birthday something I'd your .
4. yet ordered we the haven't children anything .
5. you may I a offer lift ?

5 Make up appropriate requests to five of the following replies. Use the following beginnings:
Could you get/give/lend/make/tell/teach/show me ...?

Actually, I'm a bit busy at the moment.
Sorry, I don't smoke.
I'm afraid I haven't got any.
Sorry, I'm using it.
Just after six.
Yes, of course. Here you are.
I'll have a look. Just a moment.
Sure, no problem.

6 Choose the correct caption for the cartoon.

'He said they give a headache him when he takes them out.'
'He said they give him a headache when he takes them out.'

Reported speech

1 Tenses in statements and questions. Look at the examples. If the reporting verb is not past, what happens to the other verb(s)? If the reporting verb is past, what happens to the other verb(s)?

He thinks 'It's wonderful being with her.'
He thinks that it's wonderful being with her.

At this moment he will smile and say 'I **love** you and I always **have loved** you.'
At this moment he will smile and say that he **loves** her and he always **has loved** her.

He said 'I'm sure it **was** love at first sight.'
He said (that) he **was** sure (that) it **had been** love at first sight.

'I **don't remember** our first meeting,' she said.
She said (that) she **didn't remember** their first meeting.

'You **wore** that blue dress which you **have** never **worn** since,' he said.
He said (that) she **had worn** that blue dress which she **had** never **worn** since.

He said 'I'll never **forget** that day.'
He said he **would** never **forget** that day.

2 Reported statements and thoughts. What did they say?

1. He said 'I'm hungry.'
2. She said 'We've only just had lunch.'
3. She thought 'He's putting on weight.'
4. She said 'You need to go on a diet.'
5. He said 'I'm not fat.'
6. She said 'You don't do any exercise any more.'
7. He said 'I haven't got time these days.'
8. She said 'You always use the same excuse.'
9. He thought 'We'll have a row in a moment.'
10. She thought 'I made a mistake getting involved with this man.'
11. He said 'I'll start jogging again next week.'
12. She thought 'That won't make much difference.'
13. She said 'I'll believe that when I see it.'

3 Reported questions. Look at the examples. Can you make a rule about word order? When is *if/whether* used?

He said 'Why **do you keep** criticising me?'
He asked her why **she kept** criticising him.
(... why did she keep ...)

'**Have you got** something on your mind?' he asked.
He asked her if/whether **she had got** something on her mind.

She said 'What **are you talking** about?'
She asked him what **he was talking** about.
(... what was he talking about.)

He asked '**Do you still love** me?'
He asked her if/whether **she still loved** him.

She said 'Why **did you ask** that?'
She asked him why **he had asked** that.

4 Reported question-word questions. What did they ask?

1. He said 'When are you going to tell me the truth?'
2. She asked 'What do you mean?'
3. He said 'Where have you been all week?'
4. She said 'Why should I tell you?'
5. He said 'Why didn't you phone me?'
6. She asked 'Why can't you mind your own business?'
7. He said 'Who is he?'
8. 'How much has he found out?' she wondered.

5 Reported *yes/no* questions. What did they say?

1. He said 'Do you take me for a fool?'
2. She said 'Can you keep your voice down?'
3. He said 'Do you know how I'm feeling?'
4. She said 'Do you think I care?'
5. He said 'Is there nothing more between us?'
6. She said 'Has there ever really been anything at all?'
7. 'Can she be serious?' he wondered.
8. She said 'Have you anything else to say?'

6 Reported instructions and requests. Look at the examples. Can you complete the rule using some of the words in the box?

He said 'Listen to me for a moment.'
He asked her **to listen** to him for a moment.

He said 'Oh, please don't be so cruel.'
He begged her **not to be** so cruel.

She said 'Stop being so ridiculous!'
She told him **to stop** being so ridiculous.

Rule:
Instructions and requests are reported using ....
Say is replaced usually by .... or ....

| ask | infinitives | participles |
| past tenses | tell | |

7 Reported instructions and requests. What did they say?

1. He said 'Don't go.'
2. She said 'Take your hands off me.'
3. He said 'Don't leave me.'
4. She said 'Leave me alone.'
5. He said 'Please give me another chance.'
6. She said 'Drop dead.'
7. He said 'Don't say that.'
8. She said 'Get out of my way.'

8 *Say* and *tell*. Look at the examples. Complete the rules using *say* and *tell*.

She **said** 'I don't want to see you any more.'
   (She told 'I don't want to see you any more.')
He **said (to her) that** it had all been a big mistake.
   (He told (to her) that it had all been ...)
She **told him that** she had had enough.
   (She said him that she had had enough.)
She **said** 'Get out of my life.'
She **told him to get** out of her life.
   (She said him to get ...)

Rules:
1. .... (but not ....) is used when reporting direct speech.
2. Both verbs can be used in the 'reported speech' construction.
3. .... is normally followed by an object (without *to*); while .... can be followed by an object (with *to*), but doesn't have to be.
4. .... (but not ....) is used for reporting instructions and requests.

9 Change three of the sentences in Exercise 2, using *told* instead of *said*.

10 Choose the correct captions for the cartoons.

'Excuse me, can you settle an argument? My colleague here says we've scored nine goals so far but I say it's ten!'
'Excuse me, can you settle an argument? My colleague here says we've scored nine goals so far but I say it's ten!'

'Your wife rang me to remind you send me out for her birthday present from you!'
'Your wife rang me to remind you to send me out for her birthday present from you!'

Articles

1 Look at the examples. Why is *the* used in the first three and not in the last three?

*Don't forget to boil **the** water.*
*Where's **the** salt gone?*
*Are these **the** CDs you asked for?*
*We cannot live without **water**.*
*I never add **salt** to my food.*
***CDs** are clearer than tapes.*

2 Put in *the* or – (= 'no article').

1. To me .... men are a complete mystery.
2. We stayed inside because of .... sun.
3. Do you smoke .... cigars?
4. In my experience .... dogs are more friendly than .... cats.
5. It's a nice bar, but .... service is very slow.
6. I need .... time to think about this.
7. He doesn't take .... sugar in his tea.
8. Don't forget to take .... dogs for a walk.
9. I think .... skiing is my favourite sport.
10. What kind of music do you prefer – .... rock or .... jazz?

3 Look at the examples. Would any of the sentences be correct without the article *a(n)*?

*My mother's **an** accountant.*
*I hope to work as **a** mechanic.*
*Is there **an** explanation for all this?*
*They've converted my old school into **a** library.*
*You could use this nail file as **a** screwdriver.*

4 Complete some of these sentences, using nouns.

1. It would be wonderful if we could find ....
2. I'd hate to be ....
3. A(n) .... can be used as a(n) ....
4. My ambition is to become ....
5. I've never in my life had ....
6. Countries ought to spend less money on ....

5 Look at the words in the box. Eight of them cannot normally be used with *a/an*. Which are they?

ability	accent	advice	chair
examination	inflation	information	
metal	news	noise	peace	rain
trouble	violence	wind	wood

6 Make three sentences with words from the box in Exercise 5.

If

TALKING ABOUT THE FUTURE: ORDINARY TENSES

1 Look at the examples and choose the correct words to make the rule. Then close your book and write down one of the examples, and the rule, from memory.

*He's ringing me this evening **if he has time**.*
***If we see them tonight**, we'll give them your best wishes.*

Rule: In *if*-clauses, we use a *future/present/past* tense to talk about the *future/present/past*.

2 Put the beginnings and ends together to make sentences.

BEGINNINGS
If the weather is good tomorrow
If he passes his driving test
If she doesn't hurry up
If you eat all the biscuits now
If he keeps on smoking
If you're careful
If you don't stop shouting

ENDS
there won't be any left for later.
his cough will get worse and worse.
I'll call the police.
you won't have any difficulties.
I'll buy him a new car.
you'll miss your train.
we'll go for a picnic.

3 Complete the sentences with a present tense or a *will*-future.

1. If you .... to have a bath, I .... the hot water on for you. (*want, turn*)
2. If she .... got enough money, I .... her some. (*have not, lend*)
3. If the weather ...., I think I .... to the office tomorrow. (*improve, walk*)
4. His mother .... very worried if he .... home before midnight. (*be, not get*)
5. You .... it easier if you .... to relax a little more. (*find, try*)
6. If you .... that light on, you .... to see everything a lot more clearly. (*turn, be able*)
7. He .... you one if you .... him nicely. (*give, ask*)
8. If you .... your homework quickly, I .... you watch the television before you go to bed. (*finish, let*)
9. If we .... anything strange, we .... the police immediately. (*notice, phone*)
10. She .... me if she .... me here! (*kill, find*)

4 Complete these sentences.

1. If you go out in the sun without a hat, you'll get ...
2. If you don't come now, I'll ...
3. If you want to do well at this job, you'll ...
4. If you really love me, you'll ...
5. If you don't breathe, ...
6. If you're late for work more than once, ...
7. If you treat people badly, ...
8. If the weather is bad, ...

UNREAL AND IMPROBABLE PRESENT AND FUTURE SITUATIONS: PAST TENSE + WOULD

5 Look at the examples and complete the rule. Then close your book and write down one of the examples, and the rule, from memory.

*If I **lost** my job, I **would start** my own business.*
*I **would get** very lonely if I **didn't have** lots of good friends.*
*If I **were** you, I **would see** a doctor.*
*I'd **buy** a new car if I **had** enough money.*

Rule: When we talk about an unreal or improbable situation, we use *a present tense / a past tense / would* in the *if*-clause, and *a present tense / a past tense / would* in the rest of the sentence.

6 Choose the correct forms to complete the sentences.

1. If we *had / would have* more time, we *visited / would visit* lots of other places.
2. Do you think they *came / would come* if we *invited / would invite* them?
3. What *did / would* you do if you *found / would find* someone's wallet in the street?
4. If he *wasn't / wouldn't be* so lazy he *did / would do* very well.
5. How *did / would* she react if you *told / would tell* her the truth?
6. If you *caught / would catch* the last train, what time *did / would* you arrive in Manchester?
7. Even if you *were / would be* the only girl in the world, I still *didn't / wouldn't* marry you!
8. It *helped / would help* us a lot if we *knew / would know* what the thief looked like.

7 Read the sentences, and then write a similar '*if*-chain' yourself. Start '*If I moved to a different country ...*'

If I moved to a different country, I would have to get a new job.
If I got a new job, I would probably meet lots of new people.
If I met lots of new people, perhaps I would meet someone I really liked.
If I met someone I really liked, perhaps she would feel the same way about me.
If she felt the same way about me, perhaps we would fall in love.
If we fell in love, we would probably get married.
If we got married, perhaps we would have some children.
If we had some children, we would probably need to earn a lot more money.
If we needed to earn a lot of money, perhaps we would have to move to a different country.
If we moved to a different country, ...

8 Nobody is perfect. How would certain changes in your appearance, your character or your personal circumstances affect your life? Use some of the phrases below (or others of your choice) to make at least five sentences like the one in the example.
Example:

If I were slimmer I would feel a lot healthier.

have dark/fair hair
be shorter/taller
be fatter/slimmer
be older/younger
be better-looking
be more intelligent
have a better sense of humour
be more easy-going
have more patience
be less shy
be less bad-tempered
be more generous
not smoke
do more exercise
have a better job
be good at ...
be unemployed
play the guitar/piano *etc.*
read the newspaper more often
get up earlier
work harder
spend more time with ...
sleep better
eat less
grow a beard
become seriously ill
have a car accident
wear make-up

9
Write true sentences with the following beginnings.

I'd be delighted if …
I'd be very disappointed if …
I'd find it very funny if …
I'd feel very worried if …
I wouldn't like it if …
I'd love it if …
I'd be surprised if …
I wouldn't be surprised if …

10
Ordinary tenses or past + *would*? Which sentence-beginning is better?

1. a. If I get up early tomorrow …
   b. If I got up early tomorrow …
   Answer: *a* (because you may get up early tomorrow)
2. a. If I live my life again, I will …
   b. If I lived my life again, I would …
   Answer: *b* (because you won't live your life again)
3. a. If inflation goes down, the economy will …
   b. If inflation went down, the economy would …
4. a. If I meet someone really nice, I'll …
   b. If I met someone really nice, I'd …
5. a. If I get ill tomorrow, will you …?
   b. If I got ill tomorrow, would you …?
6. a. If there are no more wars, the world will be …
   b. If there were no more wars, the world would be …
7. a. If it rains tomorrow, we'll …
   b. If it rained tomorrow, we'd …
8. a. If I run out of money, will you …?
   b. If I ran out of money, would you …?
9. a. If I become blind, I won't …
   b. If I became blind, I wouldn't …
10. a. If everyone in the world speaks English, many teachers will …
    b. If everyone in the world spoke English, many teachers would …

11
Choose the correct caption for the cartoon.

'If diseases would be easier to pronounce, Mrs Jarvis, everyone will have them.'

'If diseases were easier to pronounce, Mrs Jarvis, everyone would have them.'

TALKING ABOUT THE PAST

12
Look at the examples and complete the rule. Then close your book and write down one of the examples, and the rule, from memory.

*If **we hadn't phoned him** he **wouldn't have known** about the party.*
*I **would** probably **have gone** to America if I **hadn't met** Valentina.*

Rule: When we talk about an unreal past situation, we use *a past tense / a past perfect tense / would have …* in the *if*-clause, and *a past tense / a past perfect tense / would have …* in the rest of the sentence.

13
Would or *had*?

1. If you'**d** listened more carefully, perhaps you'**d** have understood the instructions.
2. They'**d** have stayed in Egypt if they'**d** been able to get different jobs.
3. If she'**d** needed help, she'**d** have asked for it.
4. We'**d** have picked you up at the station if we'**d** known when you were coming.
5. If I'**d** been more confident I'**d** have told her how I felt about her.

14
Make sentences with *if* for these situations.

1. Tony Robson didn't play in the cup final because he wasn't fit enough.
   If he had been fit enough, perhaps …
2. A woman felt very tired this morning because she hadn't slept very well.
   If she had …
3. A man lost his job when his company went out of business.
4. A woman decided to study medicine because her grandfather had been a doctor.
5. A man was feeling very sad because his girlfriend had left him.
6. A woman worked for two years without taking a holiday and then became ill.
7. A father left a box of matches on the kitchen table and his young daughter lit a match and burnt herself.
8. A woman got lost on her way to her friend's house because she didn't have a map of the area.
9. A man forgot to lock his car, and it was stolen.

15
Complete one or more of these sentences.

If the weather hadn't been … yesterday, …
If my mother hadn't …
He would have … me if …
It would have been terrible if … yesterday.
If I had known what I do now about …, I would(n't) have …

129

Passives

1 Look at the examples and try to fill in the blanks. Can you choose the right words to complete the rule correctly?

Active: I hope somebody **will eat** the cake.
Passive: I hope the cake **will be eaten**.

Active: Somebody **is going to eat** the cake.
Passive: The cake **is going to be eaten**.

Active: Somebody **is eating** the cake.
Passive: The cake **is being eaten**.

Active: I'll be surprised if anybody **eats** the cake.
Passive: I'll be surprised if the cake **is eaten**.

Active: Somebody **has eaten** the cake.
Passive: The cake ....

Active: Somebody .... the cake.
Passive: The cake **was eaten**.

Active: When I walked into the room, somebody **was eating** the cake.
Passive: When I walked into the room, the cake ....

Active: They found that somebody .... the cake.
Passive: They found that the cake **had been eaten**.

Rule for making passive verb forms:
1. Decide what tense you want to use.
2. Put the auxiliary verb *be/have/do* in that tense.
3. Add the *infinitive / past tense / -ing form / past participle* of the verb that you want to use.

2 Change these sentences from passive to active. Example:

*The 'Moonlight Sonata' **was composed** by Beethoven.*
→ *Beethoven **composed** the 'Moonlight Sonata'.*
1. The last lecture will be given by Professor James.
2. Paris is visited by thousands of tourists each year.
3. We're being driven to the airport by my brother.
4. The ironing is usually done by my husband.
5. When she first met him he was being arrested by the police.
6. This building was designed by a German architect.

3 Change these sentences from active to passive. Example:

*Somebody **has taken** my book.* → *My book **has been taken**.*

1. Alan will paint the house for us while we're away.
2. He was sure someone had moved his papers.
3. The whole family watches this programme.
4. Somebody has drunk all the water.
5. They've found your wallet in the supermarket.
6. When she last worked with him, someone was training him to use a computer.

4 Put in passive verbs.
1. Over forty languages (*speak*) in Kenya.
2. The telephone (*invent*) by a Scotsman.
3. Walk more quickly – I think we (*follow*)!
4. Windscreens (*make*) from glass.
5. This novel (*write*) by my grandmother.
6. My new car (*deliver*) tomorrow.
7. This church (*build*) in 1365.
8. Your wedding dress (*finish*) in a couple of days.
9. Listen to this! A flying saucer (*see*) over London.

5 Have a careful look at something you own (your coat, car, pen, glasses, etc.) and then write a full description of it as in the example. Example:

*This book **was written** by three people. It **was published** in 1993 in England by Cambridge University Press. The cover **was designed** in London. It **was bought** in Paris.*

6 Put the *-ing* form (e.g. *using*) or the past participle (e.g. *used*).

1. Plastic is (*use*) in the manufacture of so many things these days.
2. We are (*turn*) the third bedroom into an office.
3. My car is (*use*) an awful lot of petrol at the moment.
4. These books are (*sell*) all over the world.
5. 'Where's John?' 'He's (*do*) the washing-up.'
6. Where was your pullover (*make*)?
7. What are they (*wait*) for?
8. The guitar has been (*play*) in Spain for many centuries.
9. He has been (*play*) the guitar since he was a teenager.

7 Choose the right caption for the cartoon.

'I've been replacing by a doormat.'
'I've been replaced by a doormat.'

130

Comparatives and superlatives

1 Look at the following comparative adjectives. Some of them are made with *-er*, and some are made with *more*. Can you complete the rule which covers most cases? Can you extend the rule to cover superlatives (*blackest, most amazing*, etc.)?

more amazing   more awful   blacker
more bored   busier   more clever   cloudier
more famous   more handsome   more honest
more important   lovelier   more professional
quicker   more romantic   safer   shorter
slimmer   sunnier   more surprised   tidier

Rule:
– Adjectives with .... have *more*.
– Adjectives with .... add *-er*; those ending in *-e* have *-r*.
– Adjectives with .... ending in *-y* have comparatives in *-ier*. Others generally have *more*.

> one syllable
> two syllables
> three or more syllables

2 Complete the following table.

	COMPARATIVE	SUPERLATIVE
....	worse	....
far	....	....
....	....	best

3 Write the comparative and superlative of:

big   crazy   deep   dirty   easy   expensive
fat   friendly   happy   important   intelligent
long   nice   old   pleasant   possible   pure
serious   straight   tall   young

4 Comparative or superlative? Look at the examples and try to complete the rule.

*He's **more amusing** than his two brothers.*
*He's **the most amusing** of the three brothers.*
*I'm **older** than everybody else in my office.*
*I'm **the oldest** person in my office.*
*We need to get a **cheaper** flat – we can't afford this one.*
*How much is **the cheapest** flat you've got?*

Rule: In general, we use *comparatives/superlatives* when we simply compare one thing or group of things with another thing or group of things. We use *comparatives/superlatives* to compare something with a group in which it is included.

5 Put in suitable words to complete the sentences.

1. Your cold seems a lot .... than mine. (*bad*)
2. He's the .... man in the world! (*attractive*)
3. This is the .... tea I've ever tasted. (*good*)
4. I'm getting .... and .... (*sleepy*)
5. He's the .... student in the school.
6. My cat is much .... than my dog.
7. Dublin is the .... city in Ireland.
8. My sister is much .... than me.
9. It was the .... exam I had ever done.
10. I'm much .... than my sister.
11. The most amazing thing in the world is ....
12. I think .... was the .... person I have ever known.

6 Think of three animals. Write a sentence about each one using a superlative.

7 *As … as*. Change the sentences as in the example.

I'm younger than him. → *I'm not as old as him.*

1. Today's exam was easier than yesterday's exam.
2. October was warmer than November.
3. Our children are quieter than theirs.
4. Their house is more expensive than ours.
5. He's shorter than his father.

8 Think of the city/town/village where you live and write five sentences comparing it with somewhere else in your country. Write sentences using comparatives or *(not) as … as*. Think of two countries or two peoples (e.g. the French, the Chinese, etc.). Write two or more sentences about differences between them.

9 Choose the correct caption for the cartoon.

'I don't want a rug that's more interesting as I am.'
'I don't want a rug that's more interesting than I am.'

Relative clauses

1 Look at the example and then make similar sentences about the other people in the table.

Alice is a woman who has brown eyes, who works as an architect, and who enjoys gardening.

NAME	SEX	APPEARANCE	JOB	INTERESTS
Alice	female	brown-eyed	architect	gardening
Bob	male	fair-haired	chef	stamps
Cathy	female	thin-faced	mechanic	skiing
Dan	male	left-handed	pilot	French

Now write sentences about three people you know.

2 How quickly can you match the words and the descriptions? (There is one word too many.)

> a beard   a bedroom   a café   a calculator
> a compact disc   a composer   a diary
> a garage   a greengrocer   a journalist
> a map   a plumber   a rubber   stairs
> a stapler   sugar   a switch   toothpaste
> a train

1. Somewhere where you can have a snack.
2. A thing that you listen to music on.
3. A person who writes music.
4. A room where you sleep.
5. A book you write your appointments in.
6. Something that you use to go up or down a floor.
7. Someone who sells vegetables.
8. Stuff which makes things sweeter.
9. A thing you turn things on and off with.
10. Something you might use if you are lost.
11. Someone who writes newspaper articles.
12. A thing which you fasten papers together with.
13. Something that removes pencil markings.
14. Hair which grows on a man's face.
15. A place where you get your car repaired.
16. Stuff you clean your teeth with.
17. A vehicle that travels on tracks.
18. A person that repairs water-pipes.

3 Look back at Exercise 2 and then decide what should go in the gaps.

1. Glue is stuff .... you stick things together with.
2. A bathroom is a place .... you have a wash.
3. My sister is someone .... takes life very seriously.
4. A microscope is an instrument .... makes tiny things appear much bigger.

> *where*   *which* or *that*
> *which* or *that* or nothing   *who* or *that*

4 Look at the examples. The first, the third and the fifth ones can be rewritten without the relative pronoun. Decide which of the other sentences can be rewritten in a similar way. Can you make a rule about when you cannot leave out the relative pronoun?

*He's the man (**who/that**) I saw outside the bank.*
*This is the place **where** I left the car.*
*A briefcase is something (**which/that**) you carry business documents in.*
*Her flat is the one **which/that** has got the red door.*
*This the pen (**which/that**) he gave me for my birthday.*

1. It's a song that always makes me think of France.
2. Willy Brandt was someone who I always admired.
3. Here's the money that I borrowed from you.
4. Aren't you the person who rang yesterday?
5. Is there something that you want to say to me?
6. You are the only one that understands me.
7. Have you got a pen which you can lend me?
8. Is this the train which goes to Durham?
9. This is the house where Shakespeare was born.
10. You're talking about the woman that I love.
11. Have you got a bag which you can put it in?
12. Is this the office where you work?

5 Put in the right prepositions.

1. a razor: something you shave ..*with*..
2. a telescope: something you look ....
3. a well: something you get water out ....
4. a dictionary: something you look words up ....
5. a pair of scissors: something you cut things up ....
6. a cow: an animal you get milk ....

Now write similar definitions for: a bin, a shelf, a sofa, a towel, a tube of toothpaste.

6 Choose the correct caption for the cartoon.

'Of course I remember you're my ex-wife – it's your name that escapes me!'

'Of course I remember you're my ex-wife – it's your name escapes me!'

Word order

1 Study the position of the words *always, usually, often, sometimes, occasionally, hardly ever, never*.

He **is always** tired.
We **are usually** at home on Monday evenings.
I **am often** ill in winter.
They **are never** very friendly to us.

She **often visits** her mother at the weekend.
We **sometimes invite** people round for dinner.
He **occasionally plays** cricket for the village team.
I **hardly ever have** any free time.

You've **never given** me a birthday present.
We **could always telephone** her.
He **must never know** anything about it.
We **are quite often given** free theatre tickets.
I **would never have recognised** you.

Can you complete the rule?

These adverbs come *after/before* am, are, is, was and were. They come *after/before* other one-part verbs. They come *after/before* the first part of longer verb phrases.

2 Make at least five true sentences.

My car	is/are	always	amusing.
My friends		usually	angry.
My home		(very/quite) often	at home.
My husband/		sometimes	boring.
wife, *etc.*		occasionally	cheerful.
My life		hardly ever	clean.
My mother/		never	depressed.
father, *etc.*			difficult.
My work			easy.
			generous.
			interesting.
			pleased to see me.
			unreliable.
			untidy.
			wonderful.
			etc.

3 Put in *always, usually, (very/quite) often, sometimes, occasionally, hardly ever* or *never*.

1. I've been out with Carol.
2. We go to the theatre on Saturdays.
3. It might take two hours.
4. I do the cooking and the cleaning.
5. We have spoken about it.
6. Everyone starts work before eight o'clock here.
7. He could remember everyone's faces.
8. They will try to help you.
9. She's been to South America.
10. I can think creatively in the evening.
11. I forget people's names.
12. We could take the train.

4 Write five sentences about yourself using *always, usually, (very/quite) often, sometimes, occasionally, hardly ever* or *never*. Example:

I hardly ever go to bed after midnight.

5 Look at these examples. Can you complete the rule?

He plays the piano very well.
   (He plays very well the piano.)
She enjoys climbing very much.
   (She enjoys very much climbing.)
You'd better clean the house quickly.
   (You'd better clean quickly the house.)
They'll probably eat everything.
   (They'll eat probably everything.)
I carelessly left the window open.
   (I left carelessly the window open.)

Rule: Don't put adverbs ....

6 Put the adverbs in the right places in the sentences.

1. He has forgotten the address. (*probably*)
2. Does she play chess? (*very well*)
3. They don't like coffee. (*very much*)
4. I heard she passed her exams. (*very easily*)
5. He did the work. (*rather carelessly*)

7 Put the words in these sentences into the correct order.

1. here usually Thursdays come doesn't on she .
2. haven't left they any probably got .
3. very before leaves he seven often home o'clock .
4. like slowly say you these I'd to words very .
5. free during we ever the hardly are week .

8 Choose the correct caption for the cartoon.

'Go and see what's wrong with him. He doesn't bark usually for nothing.'

'Go and see what's wrong with him. He doesn't usually bark for nothing.'

Language summary

This section contains the more important grammatical and functional points taught or revised in *The New Cambridge English Course*, Level 4. For a complete summary of elementary grammar, see the *Mini-grammar* at the end of *The New Cambridge English Course* Level 2 Practice Book.

Verb tenses

Past Progressive

> Used for the situation (Past Progressive) at the time when something happened (Simple Past):

In 1292, when the emperor **was getting** old, they **decided** to return home.

Present Perfect and Simple Past

> Connection with the present: Present Perfect

Average earnings **have gone up** by 60% over the last twelve months.
The government's economic policies **have led** to more efficient management and greater productivity.

> Reference to finished time: Simple Past

About 5,000 people **took part** in yesterday's anti-government demonstration. Stones and petrol bombs **were thrown** at the police.

Present Perfect Progressive and Simple Past

> Situation still going on: Present Perfect Progressive

I've been doing maths at school for seven years. *(Speaker is still at school.)*
I've been going to school for eight years.

> Situation over, finished time frame: Simple Past

I **did** English at school for three years. *(Speaker is not at school any more.)*
I **went** to school for eight years.

Past Perfect

> Used for 'second', earlier past:

After the two brothers **had returned** from China, they **planned** a new journey.
Nobody **believed** their stories about the strange countries they **had visited**.
When I was a child, I often **dreamed** of being a space explorer. (... ~~I had often dreamed~~ ...)

Talking about the future; probability

When I am old, I shall/will ...
I will not ...
I will (not) be able to ...
I will (not) have to ...
I'm sure/certain that ... will (not) ...
I (don't) suppose ... will ...
I (don't) think ... will ...
I doubt if I will ...
I am sure I will (not) ...
I might ...
It's likely   that ... will ...
   not very likely
   unlikely
   very probable
   quite probable
   possible
There will be ...

Shall and *will*

> I shall/will (I'll)
> you will (you'll)
> he/she/it will (he'll, *etc.*)
> we shall/will (we'll)
> they will (they'll)

Future Progressive

> I will (I'll) be working/seeing/...
> you will (you'll) be working/seeing/...
> *etc.*
>
> will I be working/seeing/...?
> *etc.*
>
> I will not (won't) be working/seeing/...
> *etc.*

> Used for the situation at a particular future moment:

At eight o'clock tomorrow morning **I'll be brushing** my teeth.
At half past eight tomorrow morning **I'll be driving** to work.
What **will** you **be doing** this time tomorrow?

Future Perfect

> I will (I'll) have worked/seen/...
> you will (you'll) have worked/seen/...
> etc.
>
> will I have worked/seen/...?
> etc.
>
> I will not (won't) have worked/seen/...
> etc.

Used to say what will be finished or completed at a particular future time:

In a couple of years she **will have got married** and **settled** down.
By next summer I expect **I'll have passed** all my exams.
Ten years from now, **will** you **have forgotten** me?

Non-progressive verbs

You **look** like a camel wearing a tent.
    (You're looking like ...)
I **think** the colour suits you very well, madam.
    (I'm thinking ...)
I **know** she'll be angry. (I'm knowing ...)
I **don't believe** you. (I'm not believing you.)
Do you **understand**? (Are you understanding?)

Other verbs that are not often used in progressive forms: *hope, want, like, love, need, remember, seem, feel* (meaning 'think'), *see, hear, smell, taste*.

Passives

Choosing passive verbs to get the right subject, or to avoid a change of subject

A well-made pencil looks like a single piece of wood, but actually **it is made** from two pieces of wood which have been carefully glued together.
(*Better than* ... but actually **people make it** from two pieces of wood which they have carefully glued together.)
Kellem said the man was sober and rational, but very perturbed. **He was jailed** for discharging a firearm.
(*Better than* A judge jailed him ...)
He pushed the car into a parking space, grabbed a tire iron and smashed all the windows. **He was picked up** by friends.
(*Better than* Friends picked him up ...)

Present Progressive Passive

Coffee **is being made** (at this moment).
Vegetables **are being prepared** right now.

Present Perfect Passive

Today, the transformation seems miraculous. The town **has been** completely **restored**. A new concrete and glass Town Hall **has been put up** in the central square.

Passive of verbs with two objects

They sent **me** a letter. → **I** was sent a letter.
The referee gave **him** a warning. → **He** was given a warning by the referee.

Have something done

They **had** the dining room **redecorated**.
They **had** a new staircase **put in**.

Structures with infinitives and participles

Had better

You'd **better come** in. (You had better to come in.)
Perhaps I'd **better dry** my clothes.

Ought

If you want to meet people, you **ought to join** a club.
(... you ought join a club.)
You **ought to go** dancing.

Make and let + object + infinitive

It **makes me laugh**. (It makes me laughing.)
It **makes me want** to scream.
Do you **let small things upset** you? (... to upset you.)

Need ...ing

The roof **needs repairing**. (= ... needs to be repaired)
The door **needs painting**.

Present and past participles

Sign language is **interesting**.
She's **interested** in sign language.
(She's interesting in ...)
I thought the lesson was **boring**.
I was **bored** right through the lesson. (I was boring ...)

Past structures with modal verbs

Past structures with *if* and *would*

If I **had known** her name, **I would have introduced** you to her.
If his parents **had had** more money, he **wouldn't have left** school at sixteen.
She **would have won** the race if she **hadn't fallen** over.
His life **would have been** happier if he **hadn't met** Cleo.

Past structures with other modals

Sue **could have got** married at eighteen, but she decided to go abroad and study instead.
I **should have mended** my bicycle yesterday, but I didn't.
He's late. He **may have missed** his train.
She didn't phone this morning. She **must have forgotten**.

Relative structures

Punctuation of identifying and non-identifying expressions

The biggest city in Bavaria is Munich.
Munich, in Bavaria, has a population of 1.25 million.
The village where I was born has changed a lot.
North Barton, where I was born, has changed a lot.
A person who lives in Glasgow is called a Glaswegian.
My sister, who lives in Glasgow, prefers Scotland to England.
The room which I'm sitting in at the moment isn't very well lighted.
Our kitchen, which I'm sitting in at the moment, isn't very well lighted.

Using *that* instead of *who(m)* or *which* in identifying clauses

The politician **whom/that** I admire most is Ann Wesk, the leader of the opposition.
(BUT Ann Wesk, **whom** I greatly admire, is the leader of the opposition. NOT Ann Wesk, that I greatly admire, is ...)
The party **which/that** has been in power for the last five years is the Free Democratic Radical Conservative Party.
(BUT NOT The Free Democratic ... Party, that has been in power ...)

Identifying relative clauses without object pronouns

(This structure is more common in informal speech and writing.)

The eggs you're eating came from our farm. (= The eggs **that** you're eating ...)
That motorbike Jake built fell to pieces. (= That motorbike **that** Jake built ...)

Object pronouns can't be left out in non-identifying clauses

The party I support is called the New Democratic Movement.
(BUT The New Democratic Movement, **which** I support, is led by Arnold Kronsk. NOT The New Democratic Movement, I support, ...)
The party our MP belongs to is called the New Radical Alliance.
(BUT The New Radical Alliance, **which** our MP belongs to, ...)

Subject relative pronouns can't be left out

The people **who** live next door never get up before ten o'clock. (The people live next door never get up ...)
I'm going to do something **that** will really surprise you. (I'm going to do something will really surprise you.)

Reduced relative clauses

I know the man **sitting on the wall over there**.
  (= ... the man **who is sitting** ...)
Who is the woman **standing at the bus stop**?
Food **kept in a freezer** will stay good for several months.
  (= Food **that is kept** ...)
The forms **sent to the embassy** never arrived.
Three men **accused of organising an attack on an Irish police station** in which several officers were injured have been arrested.

Relative *what*

What I need is something to eat.
  (= **The thing that** I need is something to eat.)
You mustn't believe **what** is in the newspapers.
  (= You mustn't believe **the things that** are in the newspapers.)

Everything, all, nothing + *that*

I'll give you **everything (that)** you want.
  (... everything what you want.)
You believe me – that's **all that** matters.
  (... all what matters.)
Nothing (that) you say will make me change my mind.
  (Nothing what you say ...)

Which referring back to a whole sentence

He passed his exam, **which** surprised everybody.
  (... what surprised everybody.)
She cycles 50 miles every weekend, **which** is pretty good for a woman of 60. (... what is pretty good ...)

Relative clauses with *whose*

Jake Thong is an artist **whose** pictures sell for thousands of pounds.
An unsuccessful builder is one **whose** houses fall down.

Other structures

Tags, short answers and reply questions

You don't want to travel on Sunday, **do you**?
There isn't a seat free, **is there**?
You have got a ticket, **haven't you**?
These trains are dirty, **aren't they**?

'Don't forget your passport.' '**I won't**.'
'I wasn't travelling without a ticket.' 'Of course **you weren't**.'

'I'd love to go to America.' '**Would you**?'
'I'm trying to get a new job.' '**Are you**?' 'I certainly **am**.'

So is ..., so does ..., etc.

Sarah is interested in money, and **so is** Richard.
Oliver likes animals, and **so does** Celia.
Oliver used to like pop music, and **so did** Mark.
Sarah can't swim, and **neither/nor can** Mark.
Celia doesn't collect antiques, and **neither/nor does** Richard.

Emphasis with *it* and *what*

In my job, **it's** the travelling that I like.
In my job, **what** I like is the travelling.

It isn't cyclists that cause road accidents. **It's** bad roads.

What I like most about Mary is her sense of humour.
What I like least about Joe is his laugh.

Complex sentences with subject and verb separated

The year after I left school **was** a very happy time for me.
The worst solution when you have a problem and can't think of a good plan **is** to do nothing.
The tin behind the cookery books on the top shelf over the cooker **has got** some biscuits in.

Make + object + adjective

It **makes** me **cross**.
It **made** me **sick**.

I wish; *if only*

Talking about the present:

I wish it **was/were** cooler/warmer.
I wish I **could** sing.
I wish I **had** more money/time.
If only I **spoke** better English!
If only I **knew** more people!
If only people **were** more honest!

Talking about the future:

I wish the government **would do** something about unemployment.
If only somebody **would write** me a letter!

Talking about the past:

I wish I **had been** nicer to my parents when I was younger.
I wish I **had listened** to my mother's advice.
If only I **had taken** a different job!
If only I **had not got** married!

Different ways of using words

There's a lot of **snow** on the ground. (*noun*)
Do you think it will **snow**? (*verb*)

Shall I **warm** the milk? (*verb*)
The house isn't very **warm**. (*adjective*)

Connecting words

Although whales look like fish, they are mammals.
Bats are not birds, **although** they can fly.

I'm not sure **whether** I like this music or not.
I haven't decided **whether** I want to go to London or Scotland next weekend.
Can you tell me **whether** this is the right train for Belfast (or not)?

I'm going out, but I'm taking my umbrella **in case** it rains. (= ... because it might rain.)
I like to take a glass of water up to bed **in case** I get thirsty in the night. (= ... because I might get thirsty.)

A Frenchman went on holiday to California. He bought a bus pass **so that** he could travel cheaply. He took all his luggage in a backpack, **so that** he could get around easily.

He'll take the job **unless** the pay's too low.
(= ... **if** the pay's **not** too low.)
Unless I'm lucky, I'm going to fail my exams.
(= **If** I'm **not** lucky, ...)

He learned **that** it can be costly to attack one's own automobile.

A judge fined Jeffrey G. Janor $50 **after** hearing of **how** Janor beat upon his car with a tire iron.

Janor was on his way to a canoe outing **when** his Oldsmobile stalled.

He was picked up by friends, **who** transferred the canoe. **However**, his outburst was witnessed by a Mall security guard, **who** alerted police.

Prepositions and particles

Showing relative position

at the top (of)   at the bottom (of)   at the side (of)
at the front (of)   at the back (of)   in the middle (of)
on the right (of)   on the left (of)   inside   outside
near

Other expressions

stuck **in** the snow
He smashed its windows **with** a tire iron
He pulled **out** a pistol
six inches **of** snow
he pulled a tire iron **from / out of** the trunk
he smashed every window **in** the car
full **of** holes
he emptied half **of** a second clip of bullets **into** the car
he threw it **into** the snow
he returned **to** the tire iron
beating **on** the hood
jailed **for** discharging a firearm **in** the city

Irregular verbs

INFINITIVE	PAST	PAST PARTICIPLE	INFINITIVE	PAST	PAST PARTICIPLE
beat	beat	beaten	lie	lay	lain
become	became	become	make	made	made
bite	bit	bitten	mean	meant	meant
bleed	bled	bled	meet	met	met
break	broke	broken	put	put	put
bring	brought	brought	repay	repaid	repaid
build	built	built	ring	rang	rung
burn	burnt	burnt	rise	rose	risen
catch	caught	caught	run	ran	run
choose	chose	chosen	see	saw	seen
cut	cut	cut	send	sent	sent
deal	dealt	dealt	set	set	set
draw	drew	drawn	shine	shone	shone
drive	drove	driven	shoot	shot	shot
fall	fell	fallen	show	showed	shown
feel	felt	felt	sleep	slept	slept
fight	fought	fought	speak	spoke	spoken
find	found	found	spell	spelt	spelt
fly	flew	flown	spend	spent	spent
get	got	got	spit	spat	spat
go	went	gone	split	split	split
grow	grew	grown	steal	stole	stolen
hang	hung	hung	strike	struck	struck
hide	hid	hidden	take	took	taken
hold	held	held	teach	taught	taught
hurt	hurt	hurt	tear	tore	torn
keep	kept	kept	tell	told	told
lead	led	led	throw	threw	thrown
lean	leant	leant	upset	upset	upset
learn	learnt	learnt	wear	wore	worn
leave	left	left	win	won	won
lend	lent	lent			

Functions and notions

Asking about English

What's the English for …?
How do you say … in English?
What do you call a person who …?
How do you pronounce …?
How do you spell …?

Problems in understanding

Sorry, what did you say?
What do you mean?
Could you speak more slowly?

Ways of identifying people and things

the girl **in the corner**
the girl **sitting in the corner**
the girl **who is sitting in the corner**

the man **in a red T-shirt**
the man **wearing a red T-shirt**
the man **who is wearing a red T-shirt**

the picture **over the door**
the picture **hanging over the door**
the picture **which hangs over the door**

Physical descriptions

She has (she's got) blue eyes and brown hair.
a woman **with** blue eyes and brown hair
a blue-**eyed**, brown-**haired** woman

a man **with** a beard
a girl **with** glasses

a woman **in** a blue dress
a man **in** a grey jacket

Hair: long, medium-length, short; straight, curly, wavy; blond(e), fair, dark, brown, black, red, grey, going grey, white, thinning; a beard, a moustache, bushy eyebrows
He's (going) bald. He's got a bald patch.
Eyes: green, blue, brown, greenish-blue, grey
Nose: long, turned-up
Mouth: wide, generous; thin lips, full lips
Chin: pointed, firm, weak
Face: oval, round, long; high cheekbones; a scar
Forehead: high, low
Ears: big, small
Shoulders: broad, narrow
Build: thin, slender, slim, muscular, heavily-built, plump, overweight, fat
Height: tall, of medium height, short
Age: young, middle-aged, elderly, old; in his early thirties; in her mid-fifties; in their late forties
Expression: serious, cheerful, worried, friendly
General appearance: good-looking, pretty, beautiful, handsome, attractive, plain; well dressed, casually dressed
He looks old. She looks like a businesswoman.

Evaluating

I think the first one is very good.
I don't think much of the second.
What do you think of the fourth one?
There's nothing in it.
I think the fifth is better than the fourth.

Telephoning

Trying to connect you.
His/Her line's busy.
Can you hold?
Do you know his/her extension?
I'll see if I can transfer you.
I'm sorry. I've/You've got the wrong number.
His/Her number's ringing for you.
I'll put you through.
This is (*name*).
Who is that?
Speaking.
We got cut off.
This is a very bad line.
I'll ring you back.

Giving directions

across   along   down   in front of   opposite
past   through   towards

roundabout   traffic lights   T-junction   fork
bend

Go straight ahead for ... yards/metres.
Take the first/second/*etc.* on the right/left.
Turn right/left at ...
It's on your right/left.
You can't miss it.

Making dates and appointments

Are you free this evening?
Are you doing anything this evening?
I thought we might ...
unless you're too busy/tired.

I'm not sure.
It depends.
Maybe, maybe not.
I can't remember.

Just a minute.
Let me just look in my diary.

It looks as if I'm not free.
I'm not free after all.
I've just remembered.
No, I'm afraid I'm baby-sitting / washing my hair / going to the theatre / working / playing bridge / ...ing.
I really ought to wash my hair / write letters /...
I'm away tomorrow.
I've got a terrible headache.

What/How about tomorrow / the day after tomorrow?

I'm really a bit busy at the moment / for the next few weeks.
You know how it is.

It's ages since I ...
I haven't ... for ages.

I'll give you a ring one of these days / some time / when things get easier.

That would be lovely.
I'd love to.

Where shall we meet?
What time?
What time were you thinking of?

I'll come round to your place.
I might be a bit late.

That's difficult.
Could we make it a bit later?

See you then.

Contradictory, softened and emphatic answers

'My brother's just told me he's getting married next week.'
'Are you pleased?'
(−) 'Well, no, actually, I'm not.'
(±) 'Quite pleased, but he could have told me earlier.'
(++) 'I'm absolutely delighted.'

Suggestions

Why don't you …?
Why not …?
What/How about …ing?
I/We think you should …
You really ought to …
You could/might …
If I were you, I would …
A good way to … is to …
The best way to … is to …
I/We think it's a mistake to …
Stop …ing and start …ing

Discussion

Definitely.
Certainly.
Of course.
Do you think …?
Yes, I do.
I certainly do.
I agree.
Yes, I think so.
I'm not sure.
It depends.
What do you mean by …?
I suppose so.
I don't know.
Perhaps.
I don't think so.
I don't agree.
Definitely not.
Certainly not.
Of course not.

Some conversational expressions and their uses

Getting back to the main point: Well, anyway
Giving a reason for what one has said: I mean
Giving one's opinion directly: frankly
Expressing strong agreement: You can say that again.
Interrupting politely: Excuse me.
Criticising somebody's behaviour: Well, really!
Giving something: Here you are.
Trying to remember what one was saying: Where was I?
Softening what one has said: at least
Correcting oneself: or rather
Asking for something to be repeated: I beg your pardon?
Asking somebody to wait: Just a minute.
Giving an explanation: You see

Degrees

extremely   very   quite   not very   not at all

Proportions

(nearly) everybody   most people   some people
several people   a few people   hardly anybody
one person   nobody   the majority
two out of nine, three out of fourteen, *etc.*

Numbers, measurement and money

100   a/one hundred
121   a/one hundred and twenty-one
1,436   one thousand, four hundred and thirty-six
1,000,000   a/one million
1,000,000,000   a/one billion
$^1/_2$ a/one half
$^3/_4$ three quarters
$^2/_3$ two thirds
$^9/_{10}$ nine tenths
1.5   one point five
2.75   two point seven five
31 + 46   thirty-one plus forty-six
64 − 32   sixty-four minus thirty-two
17 x 81   seventeen multiplied by eighty-one
100 ÷ 10   a hundred divided by ten
5%   five per cent
30°C   thirty degrees Celsius (Centigrade)
90°F   ninety degrees Fahrenheit
£1.25   one pound twenty-five (pence)
$2.40   two dollars forty / two dollars and forty cents
40 km   forty kilometres
70 kg   seventy kilos/kilograms
15 lb   fifteen pounds
25 m   twenty-five miles/metres/minutes
60 ft   sixty feet
6 ft 3 in   six feet/foot three inches
4 gal   four gallons
30 kph   thirty kilometres an/per hour
75 mph   seventy-five miles an/per hour
a 40 km journey   a forty-kilometre journey
a £5 note   a five-pound note
a 500 gm packet   a five-hundred-gram packet
(the year) 1964   nineteen sixty-four
(the year) 1400   fourteen hundred
May 14, 1728   May the fourteenth / the fourteenth of May, seventeen twenty-eight

Words and expressions

Come and *go*

You must **come** and see us again one of these days.
I've found something very strange. **Come** and have a look.

I'd like to **go** away for a holiday soon.
Let's all **go** and see Harry this weekend.

Here and *there*

'Newport 361428.' 'Hello, is Helen **there**?' 'I'm sorry. She's not **here** just now.'

This and *that*

'Moreton 71438.' 'Hello, **this** is Judith. Is **that** Paul?'
This is a nice flat. And I like the way you've decorated it.
Listen to **this**. You'll enjoy it. It's a great piece of music.
I'll never forget **that** morning, nearly twenty years ago, when I first saw Mrs Newton.

Emphatic synonyms

angry – furious, enraged
break – smash
destroy – wreck
hit – beat
nervous – terrified
pleased – delighted
take – grab
unhappy – miserable
worried – frantic

'Was she **worried**?' 'She was **frantic**!'
'I suppose you were **angry**.' 'I was **furious**!'

British/US differences

British	US
boot	trunk
tyre	tire
bonnet	hood
car park	parking lot
learnt	learned
neighbouring	neighboring

Words for countries and regions: some examples

PLACE	PERSON	PEOPLE	ADJECTIVE
America	an American	the Americans	American
Australia	an Australian	the Australians	Australian
Belgium	a Belgian	the Belgians	Belgian
China	(a Chinese)	the Chinese	Chinese
Denmark	a Dane	the Danes	Danish
Egypt	an Egyptian	the Egyptians	Egyptian
England	an Englishman/woman	the English	English
France	a Frenchman/woman	the French	French
Ireland	an Irishman/woman	the Irish	Irish
Israel	an Israeli	the Israelis	Israeli
Italy	an Italian	the Italians	Italian
Japan	(a Japanese)	the Japanese	Japanese
Kenya	a Kenyan	the Kenyans	Kenyan
Scotland	a Scot	the Scots	Scottish/Scotch
Switzerland	(a Swiss)	the Swiss	Swiss
Wales	a Welshman/woman	the Welsh	Welsh

Informal and formal expressions

INFORMAL	FORMAL
We have thought about	We have considered
We are sorry	We regret
We can't	We are unable to
job	post
good enough	up to the level we require
	up to the standard required
	sufficiently good
need	require
you don't seem to have	you appear to lack

Word formation

Some common prefixes and suffixes

anti-	**anti**-American, **anti**clockwise	-ance	appear**ance**, insur**ance**
dis-	**dis**appear, **dis**honest	-en	wid**en**, strength**en**
mis-	**mis**understand, **miss**pell	-er	driv**er**, wait**er**
over-	**over**eat, **over**work	-ful	beauti**ful**, hope**ful**
re-	**re**write, **re**pay	-ise	computer**ise**, modern**ise**
un-	**un**happy, **un**able	-ish	redd**ish**, fatt**ish**
under-	**under**paid, **under**valued	-less	hope**less**, care**less**

Spelling and pronunciation

'Silent *e*'

mad made   win wine   hop hope   cut cute

Doubling

big bigger   run runner   mad madder
hot hotter   sit sitting   begin beginning

We don't double in unstressed syllables. Compare:

forgetting carpeting   regretted targeted
beginning opening   preferring offering

ck and *k*; *tch* and *ch*; *dge* and *ge*

After one short vowel: *ck*, *tch* and *dge*

back   neck   sick   rock   luck
catch   fetch   hitch   hutch
badge   edge   bridge lodge

After anything else: *k*, *ch* and *ge*

break   look   week   wake   joke   thank   walk
reach   coach   couch   search bench
cage   rage   charge arrange

Exceptions:

which   rich   much   such

Typical spellings of /ɜː/

hers   bird   turn   word

Typical spellings of /ɔː/

awful   caught corner walk   warm

Pronunciation of the letter *r*

Before a vowel sound: /r/

runs /rʌnz/   real /riːl/   hurry /ˈhʌri/   foreign /ˈfɒrən/
for ever /fəˈrevə/

In other cases: not pronounced in standard British English:

picture /ˈpɪktʃə/   first /fɜːst/   part /pɑːt/
tired /taɪəd/   modern /ˈmɒdən/

The commonest vowel in English: /ə/

America /əˈmerɪkə/   England /ˈɪŋglənd/
Europe /ˈjʊərəp/   Japan /dʒəˈpæn/
Belgium /ˈbeldʒəm/   Maria /məˈriːə/
Christopher Columbus /ˈkrɪstəfə kəˈlʌmbəs/

Intonation

'Cambridge 31453.' 'Mary?' 'No, this is Sally.'
'What's your name?' 'Mary.'

Contrastive stress

The American Democratic Party has quite similar policies to the American **Republican** Party.
The American Democratic Party has quite similar policies to the **Fantasian** Democratic Party.
The Fantasian Democratic Party has very different principles from the Fantasian Democratic **Union**.

Solutions to crosswords and problems

Lesson A8, Exercise 6

R	E	S	P	O	N	S	I	B	I	L	I	T	Y
E		U		W	O	N		O	N		N		N
T	I	P		N		O	R		T	Y	R	E	
U		P		O	W	N	E	R		O			A
R	U	L	E		W		D	O	T		N	O	R
N		I	N	D	E	E	D		S	U	R	E	B
	L	E	D		L	O	W	E	R		W	A	Y
Y	E	S		S		E	A	N			M		
	A		S	O		C	A	R		S	T	A	Y
U	S		C	A	T		A	R	T		Z		
S	T	O	C	K		G	O		A	R	M	E	D
U		P			O		O	N	E			R	
A	T	E		E	A	R	T	H		E	D	G	E
L		R		G	A	I	N		T	O		W	
	T	A	R	G	E	T		T	O	E	S		

Lesson B2, Exercise 6

Rule:
The letter doubles if it is a single consonant letter after a single vowel letter in a stressed syllable.

Lesson B8, Exercise 2

Say and *tell*
Tell is usually followed by a personal direct object; *say* is normally used without a personal object, or with *to* + a personal object. Compare:
I *told her* that it was important.
I *said* that it was important.
(OR I *said* to her that it was important.)

Lesson B8, Exercise 7

C	O	N	S	O	N	A	N	T		H	E	A	R	T
O	N		A		U		U	P		A	T			R
N	E	R	V	Y		T		R	A	S				U
C		E			H	O	N	E	S	T			A	S
R	U	N		A	O	H		H			C	U	T	
E		O	F	F	E	R		M	E	A	N		S	
T	O		O	R			A		M	O	U	T	H	
E		R	A	T	H	E	R		E			R		
	S	T	I	I		R	U	D	E			I	S	
	W	O	R	D		P	A	Y		M	E	A	T	
M	A	P		I			T	A	P				R	
I	N		S	P	L	I	T		O		T	O		I
N		H		L		E			Y				K	
E	A	S	Y		O	Y	E	S			M	E		
	N		N	U	R	S	E		O	V	E	R		

Lesson C2, Exercise 5

Rules:
a) When verbs of one syllable (or verbs stressed on the last syllable) end in one consonant after one vowel-letter, the consonant is doubled before adding '-ing'.
b) If the verb ends with 'e', this is left off before adding '-ing'.
c) Otherwise, '-ing' is simply added to the root verb.

Lesson C4, Exercise 7

1. The letters from South America had rare stamps worth thousands of pounds each.
2. Reilly gave himself away when he mentioned the name of his murdered brother-in-law before Montgomery did. From what Reilly told the colonel, he had at least three brothers-in-law.
3. In any book, page 123 and 124 fall on either side of the same page.

Lesson C8, Exercise 7

S	T	R	E	N	G	T	H	E	N		T	E	A	R
C		I		I		A		V	O	T	E		N	
R	E	D		C	U	E			R	A	I	N	Y	
E		E	M	E	R	G	E	N	C	Y		M		E
A	T		I		H		I			S	P	O	T	
M	O	O	D	Y		T	E	N		B	O	R	N	
	O		D	O	G		A	G	O		N	O		G
M		G	L	U	E		R		U	P		V		A
A	L	E	N	T		L	E	G		M	E	L	T	
C	A	G			I	H	E				E			
H	I	D	E		S	P	E	N	T		A	T		
I	N		A	T		A	R	E		A	L	O	N	E
N		C		O	R		V		N		N		X	
E	I	G	H	T		K	E	E	P		U			I
	N	O		O	N		R		U	P	S	E	T	

Lesson D1, Exercise 2

Rule 3 is correct.

Lesson D8, Exercise 7

A	T	M	O	S	P	H	E	R	E	■	O	■	M	E
C	■	A	■	L	■	L	■	M	O	V	E	■	■	L
C	■	N	■	B	A	L	D	■	O	■	E	■	W	E
O	V	A	L	■	N	■	E	N	T	E	R	■	■	C
U	■	G	■	W	E	A	R	■	I	■	■	N	U	T
N	E	E	D	■	T	■	L	O	O	K	■	O	■	I
T	■	■	E	■	■	Y	■	N	■	B	■	T	■	O
■	B	E	A	R	D	■	A	S	P	I	R	I	N	■
■	R	■	T	■	O	V	E	R	■	■	R	■	M	■
M	A	T	H	S	■	I	■	R	■	D	I	E	D	■
■	I	■	■	O	I	L	■	O	U	R	■	N	■	E
I	N	■	W	■	■	L	A	W	■	U	■	J	O	B
N	■	L	O	W	■	A	T	■	I	N	■	U	■	T
T	H	I	N	■	A	G	E	S	■	■	O	R	■	■
O	■	P	■	U	S	E	■	O	F	■	H	E	L	D

Lesson E8, Exercise 7

C	O	M	P	O	S	E	R	■	I	■	O	U	T	■
I	N	■	O	F	■	■	I	N	C	H	■	H	■	I
T	E	S	T	■	T	O	W	N	■	O	■	S	A	T
Y	■	O	T	H	E	R	■	S	C	U	L	P	T	■
■	M	■	E	N	■	D	I	■	L	■	I	■	■	■
O	P	E	R	A	T	E	■	D	■	D	A	T	E	■
B	■	X	■	M	■	L	I	E	S	■	C	■	A	S
J	■	I	T	■	■	S	■	■	A	C	T	■	T	O
E	■	S	■	T	H	E	O	R	Y	■	O	■	■	R
C	A	T	C	H	■	■	C	■	■	O	R	D	E	R
T	■	■	O	I	L	■	C	O	O	K	■	R	■	Y
■	■	H	A	S	■	B	U	R	N	■	A	I	M	■
F	U	E	L	■	N	O	R	■	L	■	■	V	E	T
I	■	L	■	O	■	O	■	B	Y	■	■	E	■	■
X	■	P	E	R	■	K	■	E	■	M	I	N	U	S

Key to Basic grammar revision exercises

Simple Present and Present Progressive

1 *Present Progressive*: B, C, E
Present Simple: A, D

2
1. is getting (*Rule E*)
2. repairs (*Rule A or D*)
3. turns (*Rule A or D*)
4. is increasing (*Rule B or E*)
5. always visits (*Rule A*)
6. is having (*Rule B*)
7. is playing (*Rule B*)
8. Do ... hurt (*Rule A*)
9. Are ... travelling (*Rule C*)

3 (Possible answers)

A woman is sitting at a desk. She is wearing a smart, dark business suit and a white blouse. She is explaining something to the man standing in front of her desk.

A man is wearing a white shirt with his sleeves rolled back. He's wearing a watch on his left wrist. He's wearing a striped tie and dark trousers and shoes. He is standing in front of a desk talking to the person at the desk in a friendly manner, discussing something in the letter he is holding.

A younger woman is standing up and reading a book. She is wearing glasses, a light-coloured blouse with a dark bow, a dark skirt and dark shoes.

A young man is trying to open a window at the back of the office. He is wearing a dark tie, a white shirt, a dark suit, and dark shoes.

4
2. a dentist who is cooking
3. an actor/actress who is swimming
4. a waiter who is singing (in a choir)

Simple Past and Past Progressive

2 *Simple Past*: A, C, E, F, G
Past Progressive: B, D

3
1. were waiting, came (*Rules B and G*)
2. washed, was putting (*Rules E and B*)
3. did ... leave (*Rule F*)
4. saw, felt (*Rule A*)
5. were watching, disappeared (*Rules B and G*)
6. did, studied (*Rules A and C*)
7. finished, was travelling (*Rules E and B*)
8. seemed, went (*Rule A*)
9. spent (*Rule C*)
10. was cutting, exploded (*Rules B and G*)
11. Was ... standing (*Rule D*)

7 The second caption ('I just shook his hand and he was sick.') is the correct one.

Present Perfect and Simple Past with time expressions

2 Only rule C is true. Note that the choice of tense depends on whether we are talking about a finished or unfinished *time period*, not a finished or unfinished action. (The Present Perfect often refers to finished *actions* – see examples 2, 4, and 10 in Exercise 1.)

3 *Finished time*: after I got home; in 1956; yesterday; ten years ago; until I was six; last week; when I was two
Unfinished time: since I was four; ever; for the last two days; always; since the war; never; recently/lately; since I had lunch; for the last year; this month; up to now; today
Either (depending on time of day): this afternoon
Note that *ever*, *never* and *always* can also refer to finished periods in certain contexts.
'When you lived in America, did you ever visit California?'
'No, I never did. I always preferred the east coast.'
Note also that *last year* refers to finished time but *the last year* refers to unfinished time.
He worked in Manchester last year (but now he works somewhere else).
She's worked for her father for the last year (and still works for him).

4 (Alternative answers with contracted or uncontracted forms are also possible in some cases.)
1. We *have just had* a terrible night – the baby *woke up* at three o'clock and *hasn't stopped* crying since!
2. She *forgot* to lock up last night.
3. He *hasn't talked* to her lately – have you?
4. I *spent* too much money last month.
5. Since he was six he *has always liked* Mozart.
6. I *worked* as a vet until I got cancer.
7. We *have lived* here for the last year.
8. We certainly *have had* a lot of rain this year!
9. They *got married* nearly ten years ago.
10. 'Has he *done* any work at all today?' 'He *rang* Angie Banks a few hours ago – otherwise not a thing.'
11. 'How's the weather?' 'Great. The sun *has shone* every day up to now.'
12. I *have been* lucky all my life.
13. *Have* you ever *wondered* what it's all about?
14. I *met* a lot of new people last year.

5
1. No. (The Past Simple indicates that the time has finished.)
2. Yes. (The Present Perfect indicates that the time hasn't finished.)
3. No. (The Past Simple indicates that the time has finished.)
4. When the visit will end. The other meaning might be expressed as 'How long have you been here (for)?'
5. Alex. (The Present Perfect in the Alex part of the sentence indicates that the time hasn't finished.)

7 Present Perfect

Present Perfect Progressive

2 (Contracted forms are also possible.)
1. How long *have* they *been playing* in the same orchestra?
2. I *have been sleeping* badly for the last month.
3. Your English *has been improving* a lot lately.
4. 'You look happy.' 'Yes, I *have been talking* to Alison.'
5. They *have been going out* together since April.
6. 'What *has* she *been doing* all day?' 'She *has been helping* me fix the car.'
7. He *has been working* on the computer for over six hours.

3 1. The Present Perfect Progressive is used to refer to *temporary* events or states which began in the *past* and are still continuing, especially when the focus is on the *length* of time involved.
2. It is also often used to refer to a recent continuing event or state which accounts for a *present* situation.

Rule 1: 1, 2, 3, 5, 6, 7
Rule 2: 4

5 The people have been
1. smoking a cigarette
2. having a drink
3. having a shower
4. repairing the car
5. doing the washing up
6. playing the violin
7. digging / working in the garden
8. riding
9. playing chess
10. reading

6 1. I have *loved* Spain since I first went there ten years ago.
2. How long has she *known* Jane?
3. We've *been trying* to talk to you since Wednesday.
4. How long has he *had* his dog?
5. How long have they *been learning* Chinese?

7 1. *They've been* in Nairobi since March.
2. How long *have you been using* a walking stick?
3. He *has been reading* the same book for the last two weeks.
4. How long *have you had* your cold?
5. She *is writing* a comic novel at the moment.
6. Hi! *I've been hoping* you would call.
7. What's so funny? Why *are you laughing* like that?
8. They *have known* about it for ages.

Note that in many languages other than English a present tense is used to talk about the duration of states and events which began in the past and are still continuing.

8 The first caption ('We've been living together for twenty-five years, Helen. You could at least give me a chance to run for it.') is the correct one.

Non-progressive verbs

1 1. dance; keep
2. don't remember
3. know; is … living; 's got; see
4. loves, don't believe; agree, says
5. don't like; think, tastes
6. Does … know, belong; Do … think; 's standing
7. are … talking; don't recognise
8. Do … want; tastes
9. remember; forget
10. smells; don't understand, know; doesn't matter
11. find; need
12. 's getting; Do … want
13. hate; don't mean

2 keep, remember, know, have (got), see, love, believe, agree, like, think, taste, belong, recognise, want, forget, smell, understand, matter, find, need, hate, mean

3 (Many possible answers.)

Since and for

1 *For* is followed by a reference to a period of time.
Since is followed by a reference to a 'starting point'.

3 1. for   5. since
2. since 6. for
3. since 7. since
4. for   8. for

4 (Alternative answers may be possible in some cases.)
1. Virginie has worked / been working here for two years / since … .
2. Pepe has lived / been living in Madrid since the end of last year / for … months.
3. Zara has been taking ballet lessons since she was five.
4. Pierre has had a car in Lyons for a year.
5. Joe has worked / been working for Bill since 1988 / for … years.
6. Theo has been visiting his family in Athens since last Tuesday / for the last … days.
7. Giulia has played / been playing chess since her last birthday.

Talking about the future

2 (Many variations in the wording are of course possible.)
TIM: Hi, Pat. This is Tim. How's it going?
PAT: Fine, thanks, Tim. You?
TIM: Oh, not too bad, I suppose. Look, are you free for a drink on Friday evening? About 8.30?
PAT: Let me just check my diary. (1) *Could we make it earlier? I'm meeting Tony at a quarter to eight.*
TIM: Sorry, I'm afraid I'm working until eight o'clock. Oh, dear. I really do need to see you. Could I call round on Saturday morning?
PAT: (2) *It depends. I'm having my hair done at ten to eleven, but I'm not doing anything until then.*
TIM: Mm. No, sorry, I'm not free till after eleven, I'm afraid. What about lunch?
PAT: (3) *Sorry, I'm not free. I'm having lunch with Sarah.*
TIM: Have you got any time in the afternoon?
PAT: (4) *Not really. I'm playing squash at five past three. Are you doing anything in the evening?*
TIM: Yes, I'm afraid so. I'm cooking dinner for Mark and Rose on Saturday evening.
PAT: (5) *Well, are you doing anything on Sunday morning?*
TIM: Yes, I'm going to church with Mum and Dad. What about the afternoon?
PAT: (6) *I'm looking after Ben and Tamsin all afternoon.*
TIM: And no doubt the evening's busy too?
PAT: (7) *I'm going to the cinema at twenty-five to seven. Would you like to call round afterwards – about nine o'clock?*
TIM: Well, OK – nine o'clock then. Better late than never. You see, I need to tell you about Jill. …

4 (Variations in the wording are of course possible.)
1. He's going to paint.
2. She's going to take a photograph.
3. They're going to play football.
4. They're going to have dinner.
5. He's going to switch on / watch the television.
6. She's going to write a letter.
7. He's going to open the window.
8. They're going to dance.
9. He's going to dive in / swim.
10. She's going to fill her car up.
11. He's going to phone someone / make a telephone call.
12. She's going to repair her bicycle.

7 (Other answers may also be possible.)
1. *going to* + infinitive
2. *going to* + infinitive
3. *will* + infinitive
4. Present Progressive

8
1. Watch out! That car *is going to pull out*!
2. There probably *won't be* another world war before the end of the century.
3. Great news! Rupert and Joy *are going to get* married.
4. *She's doing* her driving test on Thursday.
5. I hope *I'll find* somewhere to live in London.
6. My company *is going to move* to Liverpool at the end of the year.
7. *Are your parents doing* anything tomorrow evening?
8. Look at the sky. The sun *is going to come out* any minute now.

9
1. If I *hear* any news I *will call* you immediately.
2. We *will come* and see you when we *are* in Moscow.
3. If he *finishes* the job early I *will pay* him an extra £100.
4. Nothing *will happen* until the President *makes* a decision.
5. Perhaps you *will like* it if you *try* it.
6. She *will write* to us as soon as she *arrives*.
7. The situation *will be* worse before it *gets* better.

10 The third caption ('Open a window, will you? Mr Milliner is leaving.') is the correct one.

Infinitives with and without *to*

1 2. He *will come* later.
The exception is *ought*.

2 1. We *need to hurry*.
All of these verbs are followed by the infinitive with *to*.

3
1. 'Is that the phone?' 'Yes, I'll *get* it.'
2. She would like *to become* a lawyer.
3. Could you *tell* me your address, please?
4. We didn't expect *to see* them there.
5. Shall I *call* the doctor?
6. He hopes *to meet* her tomorrow.
7. You must *stop* doing that.
8. They might not *have* any left.
9. Would you prefer *to go* with him?
10. She managed *to fix* it herself.
11. Then it began *to snow*.
12. We don't *play* much tennis these days.
13. They really ought not *to take* so long.
14. He tried *to ring* her last week.
15. They shouldn't *say* things like that.

4
1. Her parents never let her *go* out.
2. I'm going to Paris *to learn* French.
3. Would you rather *stay* here?
4. We had better *take* the train.
5. 'I don't know where *to go* for my holidays.' 'Why not *visit* Kenya?'
6. Do you know how *to use* a computer?
7. Do they have *to shout* so much?
8. You can't make me *do* it!

Uses of *-ing* forms

1 Only rule 3 really corresponds to the facts (as exemplified in the six sentences).

2 Followed by an *-ing* form: *avoid, can't help, dislike, feel like, finish, imagine, (don't) mind, suggest.*
Followed by an infinitive with *to: agree, ask, begin, decide, forget, happen, learn, manage, seem.*

3 We normally use *-ing* forms as subjects of sentences.

4 We use *-ing* forms after all prepositions.

5
1. I stood there for an hour, *waiting* for the bus.
2. He read his essay again, *checking* for mistakes.
3. The earthquake struck at 2.35, *destroying* hundreds of houses.
4. They parked the car about a kilometre away, *going* the rest of the way on foot.
5. She looked around the room nervously, *hoping* he wouldn't be there.
6. I woke up very suddenly, *thinking* I'd heard a sound downstairs.
7. The river burst its banks, *flooding* the town.
8. She stared back at me, *saying* nothing.

6
1. doing
2. to study
3. wondering
4. Eating
5. to have
6. switching
7. to talk
8. working, living
9. to invite

7 The second caption ('Pembroke, have you been trying to make decisions again?') is the correct one.

Verbs with two objects

1
1. Indirect object: *her*. Direct object: *the truth*.
2. Indirect object: *me*. Direct object: *an orange juice*.
3. Indirect object: *John*. Direct object: *the butter*.
4. Indirect object: *you*. Direct object: *my stamp collection*.

2 (Many possible answers.)

3
3. I think you'd better write him a letter.
4. Can you get us some information about prices?
5. Would you mind giving Alex this package the next time you see her?
6. Could you do my brother a favour?
7. They keep sending us the wrong newspaper.
8. Let me show you the plans.
9. He's never bought me a present before.
10. Mrs Jones used to teach the children some lovely poems.
11. Would you pour me a glass of water, please?
12. It's OK; I'll pass him the salt.

4
1. Why didn't you give her a kiss?
2. Could you bring us the bill?
3. I'd like to buy you something for your birthday.
4. We haven't ordered the children anything yet.
5. May I offer you a lift?

5 (Many possible answers.)

6 The second caption ('He said they give him a headache when he takes them out.') is the correct one.

Reported speech

1 If the reporting verb is not past, the tenses in the reported speech generally remain the same as in the direct speech.
After past reporting verbs, we generally move the tense(s) in the reported speech 'one step backwards'.
Present → Past
Present Perfect → Past Perfect
Past → Past Perfect
will → *would*

2
1. He said (that) he was hungry.
2. She said (that) they had only just had lunch.
3. She thought (that) he was putting on weight.
4. She said (that) he needed to go on a diet.
5. He said (that) he wasn't fat.
6. She said (that) he didn't do any exercise any more.
7. He said (that) he didn't have / hadn't got time these days.
8. She said (that) he always used the same excuse.
9. He thought (that) they would have a row in a moment.
10. She thought (that) she had made a mistake getting involved with this man.
11. He said (that) he would start jogging again next week.
12. She thought (that) that wouldn't make much difference.
13. She said (that) she would believe that when she saw it.

3 The reported question uses statement word order (*subject + verb + object*, etc.) and not question word order (*verb + subject + object*, etc.) So:
He asked her who she was. (NOT ...who was she.)

If/whether is used when there is no question word in the direct question (in other words, when it is a *yes/no* question).

4
1. He asked (her) when she was going to tell him the truth.
2. She asked (him) what he meant.
3. He asked (her) where she had been all week.
4. She asked (him) why she should tell him.
5. He asked (her) why she hadn't phoned him.
6. She asked (him) why he couldn't mind his own business.
7. He asked (her) who he was.
8. She wondered how much he had found out.

5
1. He asked (her) if she took him for a fool.
2. She asked (him) if he could keep his voice down.
3. He asked (her) if she knew how he was feeling.
4. She asked (him) if he thought she cared.
5. He asked (her) if there was nothing more between them.
6. She asked (him) if there had ever really been anything at all.
7. He wondered if she could be serious.
8. She asked (him) if he had anything else to say.

6 Instructions and requests are reported using *infinitives*. *Say* is usually replaced by *ask* or *tell*.

Note the word order in negative infinitives:
He asked her **not to** be so cruel. (NOT ...to not be so cruel.)

7
1. He asked her not to go.
2. She told him to take his hands off her.
3. He asked her not to leave him.
4. She told him to leave her alone.
5. He asked her to give him another chance.
6. She told him to drop dead.
7. He asked her not to say that.
8. She told him to get out of her way.

8
1. *Say* (but not *tell*) is used when reporting direct speech.
2. Both verbs can be used in the 'reported speech' construction.
3. *Tell* is normally followed by an object (without *to*); while *say* can be followed by an object (with *to*), but doesn't have to be.
4. *Tell* (but not *say*) is used for reporting instructions and requests.

9 All the sentences should begin *He told her ...* and *She told him ...*

10 The first caption for the first cartoon ('Excuse me, can you settle an argument? My colleague here says we've scored nine goals so far but I say it's ten!') is the correct one.
The second caption for the second cartoon ('Your wife rang me to remind you to send me out for her birthday present from you!') is the correct one.

Articles

1 The nouns without *the* have a more general meaning, whereas the nouns with *the* refer to particular examples.

2
1. (–) men
2. *the* sun
3. (–) cigars
4. (–) dogs, (–) cats
5. *the* service
6. (–) time
7. (–) sugar
8. *the* dogs
9. (–) skiing
10. (–) rock, (–) jazz

3 None of the sentences is possible without an article. In English it is generally wrong to use a singular countable noun with no article.

5 The following words are either always uncountable or do not have singular countable uses, and therefore cannot normally be used with *a/an*: *advice, inflation, information, news, peace, rain, trouble, violence*. The other words are countable (*accent, chair, examination, wind*) or have countable uses (*ability, metal, noise, wood*) and can therefore be used with *a/an*.

If

1 *Rule*: In *if*-clauses, we use a *present* tense to talk about the *future*.

2 (Alternatives may be possible in some cases.)
If the weather is good tomorrow we'll go for a picnic.
If he passes his driving test I'll buy him a new car.
If she doesn't hurry up you'll miss your train.
If you eat all the biscuits now there won't be any left for later.
If he keeps on smoking his cough will get worse and worse.
If you're careful you won't have any difficulties.
If you don't stop shouting I'll call the police.

3 (Contracted forms are also possible in many cases.)
1. If you *want* to have a bath, I *will turn* the hot water on for you.
2. If she *hasn't got* enough money, I *will lend* her some.
3. If the weather *improves*, I think I *will walk* to the office tomorrow.
4. His mother *will be* very worried if he *doesn't get* home before midnight.
5. You *will find* it easier if you *try* to relax a little more.
6. If you *turn* that light on, you *will be able* to see everything a lot more clearly.
7. He *will give* you one if you *ask* him nicely.
8. If you *finish* your homework quickly, I *will let* you watch the television before you go to bed.
9. If we *notice* anything strange, we *will phone* the police immediately.
10. She *will kill* me if she *finds* me here!

4 (Various other answers are of course possible.)
1. sunstroke/ill/burnt
2. go without you
3. 'll need to work hard
4. do what I ask
5. you'll die
6. you'll get the sack
7. they won't like you
8. I'll stay at home

5 *Rule*: When we talk about an unreal or improbable situation, we use *a past tense* in the *if*-clause, and *would* in the rest of the sentence.

6 1. If we *had* more time, we *would visit* lots of other places.
2. Do you think they *would come* if we *invited* them?
3. What *would* you do if you *found* someone's wallet in the street?
4. If he *wasn't* so lazy he *would do* very well.
5. How *would* she react if you *told* her the truth?
6. If you *caught* the last train, what time *would* you arrive in Manchester?
7. Even if you *were* the only girl in the world, I still *wouldn't* marry you!
8. It *would help* us a lot if we *knew* what the thief looked like.

10 3. answer depends on students' views
4. answer depends on students' circumstances
5. b
6. answer depends on students' views
7. answer depends on local weather conditions
8. answer depends on students' circumstances
9. answer depends on students' state of health
10. b

11 The second caption ('If diseases were easier to pronounce, Mrs Jarvis, everyone would have them.') is the correct one.

12 *Rule*: When we talk about an unreal past situation, we use *a past perfect tense* in the *if*-clause, and *would have* in the rest of the sentence.

13 1. If you *had* listened more carefully, perhaps you *would* have understood the instructions.
2. They *would* have stayed in Egypt if they *had* been able to get different jobs.
3. If she *had* needed help, she *would* have asked for it.
4. We *would* have picked you up at the station if we *had* known when you were coming.
5. If I *had* been more confident I *would* have told her how I felt about her.

14 1. If he had been fit enough, perhaps he would have played in the cup final.
2. If she had slept better she probably wouldn't have felt so tired this morning.
3. He wouldn't have lost his job if the company hadn't gone out of business.
4. If her grandfather hadn't been a doctor she probably wouldn't have decided to study medicine.
5. He wouldn't have been feeling so sad if his girlfriend hadn't left him.
6. She probably wouldn't have become ill if she hadn't worked for two years without taking a holiday.
7. If her father hadn't left a box of matches on the kitchen table she wouldn't have lit a match and burnt herself.
8. She probably wouldn't have got lost on her way to her friend's house if she had had a map of the area.
9. If he hadn't forgotten to lock his car, perhaps it wouldn't have been stolen.

Passives

1 has been eaten; ate; was being eaten; had eaten

Rule for making passive verb forms:
1. Decide what tense you want to use.
2. Put the auxiliary verb *be* in that tense.
3. Add the *past participle* of the verb that you want to use.

2 1. Professor James will give the last lecture.
2. Thousands of tourists visit Paris each year.
3. My brother is driving us to the airport.
4. My husband usually does the ironing.
5. When she first met him the police were arresting him.
6. A German architect designed this building.

3 1. The house will be painted for us by Alan while we're away.
2. He was sure his papers had been moved.
3. This programme is watched by the whole family.
4. All the water has been drunk.
5. Your wallet has been found in the supermarket.
6. When she last worked with him, he was being trained to use a computer.

4 1. Over forty languages *are spoken* in Kenya.
2. The telephone *was invented* by a Scotsman.
3. Walk more quickly – I think we *are being followed*!
4. Windscreens *are made* from glass.
5. This novel *was written* by my grandmother.
6. My new car *is being delivered* tomorrow.
7. This church *was built* in 1365.
8. Your wedding dress *will be finished* in a couple of days.
9. Listen to this! A flying saucer *has been seen* over London.

6 1. Plastic is *used* in the manufacture of so many things these days.
2. We are *turning* the third bedroom into an office.
3. My car is *using* an awful lot of petrol at the moment.
4. These books are *sold* all over the world.
5. 'Where's John?' 'He's *doing* the washing-up.'
6. Where was your pullover *made*?
7. What are they *waiting* for?
8. The guitar has been *played* in Spain for many centuries.
9. He has been *playing* the guitar since he was a teenager.

7 The second caption ('I've been replaced by a doormat!') is the correct one.

Comparatives and superlatives

1 *Rule*: (The extension of the rule to cover superlatives is shown in brackets.)
– Adjectives with *three or more syllables* have *more* (and superlatives *most*).
– Adjectives with *one syllable* add *-er* (and superlatives *-est*); those ending in *-e* have *-r* (and superlatives *-st*).
– Adjectives with *two syllables* ending in *-y* have comparatives in *-ier* (and superlatives *-iest*). Others generally have *more* (and superlatives *most*).

2
	COMPARATIVE	SUPERLATIVE
bad	worse	*worst*
far	*farther/further*	*farthest/furthest*
good	*better*	best

3

big	bigger	biggest
crazy	crazier	craziest
deep	deeper	deepest
dirty	dirtier	dirtiest
easy	easier	easiest
expensive	more expensive	most expensive
fat	fatter	fattest
friendly	friendlier	friendliest
happy	happier	happiest
important	more important	most important
intelligent	more intelligent	most intelligent
long	longer	longest
nice	nicer	nicest
old	older	oldest
pleasant	more pleasant	most pleasant
possible	more possible	most possible
pure	purer	purest
serious	more serious	most serious
straight	straighter	straightest
tall	taller	tallest
young	younger	youngest

4 *Rule*: In general, we use *comparatives* when we simply compare one thing or group of things with another thing or group of things. We use *superlatives* to compare something with a group in which it is included.

5 1. Your cold seems a lot *worse* than mine.
2. He's the *most attractive* man in the world!
3. This is the *best* tea I've ever tasted.
4. I'm getting *sleepier* and *sleepier*.
5–12. Various possible answers.

7 1. Today's exam wasn't *as difficult as* yesterday's exam.
2. October wasn't *as cold/cool as* November.
3. Our children aren't *as noisy as* theirs.
4. Their house isn't *as cheap as* ours.
5. He isn't *as tall as* his father.

9 The second caption ('I don't want a rug that's more interesting than I am.') is the correct one.

Relative clauses

1 Bob is a man who has fair hair, who works as a chef, and who collects stamps.
Cathy is a woman who has a thin face, who works as a mechanic, and who likes going skiing.
Dan is a man who writes with his left hand, who works as a pilot and who speaks French.

2
1. a café
2. a compact disc
3. a composer
4. a bedroom
5. a diary
6. stairs
7. a greengrocer
8. sugar
9. a switch
10. a map
11. a journalist
12. a stapler
13. a rubber
14. a beard
15. a garage
16. toothpaste
17. a train
18. a plumber

3 1. *which* or *that* or nothing
2. *where*
3. *who* or *that*
4. *which* or *that*

4 Sentences 2, 3, 5, 7, 10 and 11 can be written without a relative pronoun.

Rule: You cannot leave out the relative pronoun when it is the subject of the relative clause. You cannot leave out *where*.

5 2. through 5. with
3. of 6. from
4. in

6 The first caption ('Of course I remember you're my ex-wife – it's your name that escapes me!') is the correct one.

Word order

1 These adverbs come *after am, are, is, was* and *were*. They come *before* other one-part verbs. They come *after* the first part of longer verb phrases.

2 (Many possible answers.)

3 (Possible answers. Various adverbs can go in the gaps. In some cases *sometimes* and *often* can go at the end of a sentence.)
1. I've … been out with Carol.
2. We … go to the theatre on Saturdays.
3. It might … take two hours.
4. I … do the cooking and the cleaning.
5. We have … spoken about it.
6. Everyone … starts work before eight o'clock here.
7. He could … remember everyone's faces.
8. They will … try to help you.
9. She's … been to South America.
10. I can … think creatively in the evening.
11. I … forget people's names.
12. We could … take the train.

5 *Rule*: Don't put adverbs immediately after the main verb.

6 1. He has *probably* forgotten the address.
2. Does she play chess *very well*?
3. They don't like coffee *very much*.
4. I heard she passed her exams *very easily*.
5. He did the work *rather carelessly*.

7 1. She doesn't *usually* come here on Thursdays.
2. They *probably* haven't got any left.
3. He *very often* leaves home before seven o'clock.
4. I'd like you to say these words *very slowly*.
5. We are *hardly ever* free during the week.

8 The second caption ('Go and see what's wrong with him. He doesn't usually bark for nothing.') is the correct one.

Acknowledgements

The authors and publishers are grateful to the following copyright owners for permission to reproduce photographs, illustrations, texts and music. Every endeavour has been made to contact copyright owners and apologies are expressed for any omissions.

page 5: *l* from *Parade* magazine and *Significa* by I. Wallace, D. Wallechinsky and A. Wallace (New York: E. P. Dutton, 1983). Reprinted with permission from *Parade* magazine. Copyright © 1983; *tr* from *The Evening Standard*, reprinted by permission of Express Newspapers; *br* from the 'Dear Abby' column, by Abigail Van Buren. Copyright 1985, Universal Press Syndicate. Reprinted with permission. All rights reserved.   page 7: article from *Poetry Review* Vol. 76 No. 3, reprinted by permission of Carol Rumens and the Poetry Society.   page 12: *t* from *The Book of Heroic Failures* by Stephen Pile, Futura Publications Ltd 1980, first published by Routledge & Kegan Paul 1979. Reprinted by permission of Rogers, Coleridge & White Ltd; *b* adapted from 'How I survived in Antarctica' by Helena Drysdale in *Marie Claire*, © European Magazines Ltd 1991 / Robert Harding Syndication.   page 19: *t* adapted from *You have been warned* by Fougasse and McCullough by permission of Methuen London; *br* from *The Book of Heroic Failures* by Stephen Pile, Futura Publications Ltd 1980, first published by Routledge & Kegan Paul 1979, by permission of Rogers, Coleridge & White Ltd; *cl* 'Car correspondence' from *Funny Ha Ha and Funny Peculiar*, and *bl* 'Last Monday...' from *The Best of SHRDLU*, both by Denys Parsons and published by Pan Books, by kind permission of Denys Parsons.   page 32: 'A woman ...', 'An elderly German ...' and 'The other morning ...' from *Funny Ha Ha and Funny Peculiar*, remaining items on page 32 from *Funny Ho Ho and Funny Fantastic*; both by Denys Parsons and published by Pan Books. Reprinted by kind permission of Denys Parsons.   page 34: 'What is he?' from *The Complete Poems of D.H. Lawrence*. Copyright © 1964, 1971 by Angelo Ravagli and C. M. Weekley, Executors of the Estate of Frieda Lawrence Ravagli. Used by permission of Viking Penguin, a division of Penguin Books USA Inc. and Lawrence Pollinger Ltd; 'Are you a work addict?' by Suzanne King, reprinted by permission of *Radio Times*.   page 36: *t* 'Revealing faces' reprinted by permission of *Bella*; *b* 'Reflecting upon love' by Charity Spain, first published in *The Guardian* ©.   page 39: *b* extract from *Eating and Allergy* by Robert Eagle. Reprinted by permission of A. P. Watt Ltd.   page 40: extract from *Fears and Phobias* by Dr Tony Whitehead. Reprinted by permission of Sheldon Press.   page 42: extract from *Darkness at Noon* by Arthur Koestler. Reprinted by permission of the Peters Fraser & Dunlop Group Ltd and Random House.   page 46: *l* poem by John Hegley reprinted by permission of the Peters Fraser & Dunlop Group Ltd; extracts from *The Explorer Book of Mysteries* by C. Fagg, D. Lambert, E. Maple, A. Wall and A. Williams, published by Kingfisher Books, copyright © Grisewood & Dempsey 1981.   page 52: 'Days' from *The Whitsun Weddings* by Philip Larkin. Reprinted by permission of Faber and Faber Ltd.   page 53: article by Brendan McWilliams. Reprinted by permission of *The Irish Times*.   page 55: 'The problems of policing...' from *The Bristol Evening Post*; 'In England ...' from *How to be an Alien* by George Mikes (Penguin Books, 1966), copyright © George Mikes, 1946; 'Have you ever noticed ...' by Russell Baker, first published in the *International Herald Tribune*, 23.9.79, New York Times Syndication and Sales Corporation.   page 56: detective stories from the 'Brain Bogglers' column of *Discover* magazine by Michael Stueben, later published in the *Reader's Digest*, March 1985. Reprinted by permission of the author and of the *Reader's Digest*.   page 60: 'The worst musical trio' from *The Book of Heroic Failures* by Stephen Pile, Futura Publications Ltd 1980, first published by Routledge & Kegan Paul 1979. Reprinted by permission of Rogers, Coleridge & White Ltd.   page 63: *bl* 'The commission' from *In the Glassroom* by Roger McGough, published by Jonathan Cape. Reprinted by permission of the Peters Fraser & Dunlop Group Ltd; *br* 'Good food dustbin guide' adapted from an article by Alex Finer in *The Sunday Times*, 16.11.75, © Times Newspapers 1975.   page 67: article by Peter Bradley in *Property Mover*. Reprinted by permission of *The Oxford Times*.   page 71: 'Lily Smalls' by Dylan Thomas from *Under Milk Wood*. Copyright 1954 by New Directions Publishing Corporation. Reprinted by permission of New Directions Publishing Corporation and by permission of David Higham Associates Ltd; 'Prehistoric woman' from *The Clan of the Cave Bear* by Jean M. Auel, published by Coronet. Reprinted by permission of Hodder & Stoughton Ltd / New English Library Ltd; 'The translator' from *Siege of Silence* by A. J. Quinnell, published by Coronet. Reprinted by permission of Christopher Little; 'On the river bank' from *Codeword Cromwell* by Ted Allbeury, published by Panther Books. Reprinted by permission of Blake Friedmann and HarperCollins Publishers.   page 77: *tl* 'First day at school' from *In the Glassroom* by Roger McGough, published by Jonathan Cape. Reprinted by permission of the Peters Fraser & Dunlop Group Ltd; *r* from *Black Boy* by Richard Wright. Copyright 1937, 1942, 1944, 1945 by Richard Wright. Reprinted by permission of HarperCollins Publishers and Random House UK Ltd.   page 78: extracts from *Lots of Love* and *The Facts of Love*, both by Nanette Newman and published by Collins, © Bryan Forbes Limited.   page 80: *t* extract from *How to be an Alien* by George Mikes (Penguin Books, 1966), copyright © George Mikes, 1946. page 83: 'Curaçao' from *Bear on the Delhi Road* by Earle Birney, by permission of Earle Birney; 'I dreamed I was walking alone' by Leon Rosselson (words only) © 1966 Harmony Music Ltd, 1a Farm Place, London W8 7SX; 'Stopping by woods on a snowy evening' from *The Poetry of Robert Frost* edited by Edward Connery Lathem. Copyright 1923, © 1969 by Holt, Rinehart and Winston. Copyright 1951 by Robert Frost. Reprinted by permission of Henry Holt and Co, Inc and by permission of Random House UK. page 85: extract from an article by Clive Ponting, first published in the *New Statesman*, 1986. page 88: 'I know what love is ...', 'You must take care of love ...' and 'My cat falls in love ...' from *God Bless Love* by Nanette Newman by permission of I CAN (Invalid Children's Aid Nationwide); 'If you don't want ...' from *Vote for Love* by Nanette Newman, © Bryan Forbes Limited. page 92: extract from *The Joy of Knowledge Encylopaedia* by Dr Alex Comfort. Reprinted by permission of Mitchell Beazley Publishers. page 94: extract from *The Unsafe Sky* © William Norris. page 98: extract from an article by Dr Vernon Coleman, first published in *The Daily Mirror* 12.5.79. Reprinted by permission of the author. page 99: 'Drowned people could recover safely' adapted from an article in *The Guardian*; 'ZZZZZZ ...' adapted from an article by Gyles Brandreth. Reprinted by permission of Victorama Ltd; 'Bedrest is bad for you' from *Living* magazine. page 101: 'Fire and ice' from *The Poetry of Robert Frost* edited by Edward Connery Lathem. Copyright 1923, © 1969 by Holt, Rinehart and Winston. Copyright 1951 by Robert Frost. Reprinted by permission of Henry Holt and Co, Inc and by permission of Random House UK. page 103: *t* and *bl* by Paul Sieveking © *Fortean Times*; *br* from *Coincidence* by Brian Inglis, reproduced with permission of Curtis Bown Ltd, London. Copyright © Brian Inglis 1990. page 104: extracts from *Coincidence* by Brian Inglis reproduced with permission of Curtis Bown Ltd, London. Copyright © Brian Inglis 1990. page 106: *tl* from *The Guinness Book of Records* by permission of Guinness Publishing; *tr* from an article by Tana de Zulueta in *The Sunday Times* © Times Newspapers Ltd 1975; *r* from an article in the *International Herald Tribune*, © International Herald Tribune. Reprinted with permission. page 108: *tl* from the *Daily Mirror* by permission of Syndication International; *tr* article by Stephen Ward and *b* reprinted by permission of *The Independent*. page 111: *tl* and *c* both adapted from articles in *The Guardian* ©; *r* by permission of *The Oxford Times*.

The authors and publishers are grateful to the following copyright holders for permission to reproduce the following cartoons:

pages 5*l* and *r*, 8, 9*l*, 11, 15, 21, 22, 24, 27, 30, 31, 33, 38, 41, 43, 45, 47, 49, 53, 55, 64*tl* and *tr*, 66, 68, 70, 74, 75, 76, 82, 88, 99, 100, 104, 106, 111, 116, 119, 122, 123, 124, 126*b*, 129, 130, 131, 132, 133: all reproduced by kind permission of *Punch*. pages 6, 9, 105*t* : *The Spectator*. page 14: cartoon by Sempé copyright C. Charillon – Paris. pages 23, 110: copyright Harmsworth Magazines Ltd. page 64*b*: by Raúl Hernán Ampuero, reproduced by kind permission of the cartoonist. page 71: *Private Eye*. page 78*l* Hector Breeze; *r*: Ronald Searle / Tessa Sayle Agency. page 105*b*: *Daily Mirror*. page 112: © 1993 by Norm Rockwell. Distributed by Kings Features Inc. page 126*t*: *Weekly News* / D. C. Thomson & Co Ltd.

The authors and publishers are grateful to the following illustrators and photographic sources:

Kathy Baxendale, pages 13*t*, 16*b*, 17, 35, 51, 76. Peter Byatt, pages 16*t*, 18, 48, 73, 81, 96*t*, 97. Celia Chester, pages 37, 54, 66, 96*b*. Anthony Colbert, pages 26, 42. Tony Coles (*John Hodgson*), pages 65, 93, 115, 118, 121. David Downton, pages 11, 69, 89. Edward McLachlan, page 13*c*.

page 12: Rick Price / Survival Anglia. page 36 *heart*: Ace Photo Agency / Mike Shirley; *oval* and *square*: The Image Bank; *broad*: Picturebank Photo Library Ltd; *round* and *small*: Picturepoint Ltd; *thin*: Tony Stone Worldwide / Dale Durfee.

(*t* = top   *b* = bottom   *c* = centre   *l* = left   *r* = right)